E-Governance in India

E-Governance has been one of the strategic sectors of reform in India since the late 1990s under the rubric of 'good governance' agenda promoted by International Organizations. As India's policy focus changed towards economic liberalization, deregulation and privatization proliferating domestic and foreign investment, ICT (Information Communication Technology) has been one of the leading areas for such heightened investment. Consequently, there has been a burgeoning interest in deploying ICT, in revamping the public service delivery and eventually the overall system of governance.

This book analyses e-Governance in India and argues that such initiatives did not take place in isolation but followed in the footsteps of a broader governance reform agenda that has already made considerable impact on the discourses and practices of governance in India. Employing interdisciplinary methodology by combining approaches from the Political Sciences, Sociology and Postcolonial/Transcultural Studies, this book presents a qualitative account of the policies and practices of e-Governance reform in India along with a detailed case study of the Common Services Centres (CSCs) Scheme under the National e-Governance Plan of the Government of India and its resultant impact on the overall system of governance. It unfolds general theoretical issues in terms of the relationship between technology and governance and the entanglement of politics, technology and culture in the complex whole of governance. This furthers our understanding of the impact of the transnational governance reform agenda on postcolonial and post-communist societies of the developing world.

Making an important and original contribution to the emerging field of e-Governance and to the existing body of research on governance in general, this book will be of interest to students and scholars of Political Science, Political Sociology, South Asian Politics and Governance.

Bidisha Chaudhuri completed her PhD at the South Asia Institute, Heidelberg University, Germany. She is currently a consulting faculty member at the Centre for Information Technology and Public Policy (CITAPP) at the International Institute of Information Technology, Bangalore, India. Her research interests include governance, gender and development, ICT for development, policy reform and South Asian politics.

Routledge advances in South Asian studies
Edited by Subrata K. Mitra
South Asia Institute, University of Heidelberg, Germany

South Asia, with its burgeoning, ethnically diverse population, soaring economies and nuclear weapons, is an increasingly important region in the global context. The series, which builds on this complex, dynamic and volatile area, features innovative and original research on the region as a whole or on the countries. Its scope extends to scholarly works drawing on history, politics, development studies, sociology and economics of individual countries from the region as well those that take an interdisciplinary and comparative approach to the area as a whole or to a comparison of two or more countries from this region. In terms of theory and method, rather than basing itself on any one orthodoxy, the series draws broadly on the insights germane to area studies, as well as the tool kit of the social sciences in general, emphasizing comparison, the analysis of the structure and processes, and the application of qualitative and quantitative methods. The series welcomes submissions from established authors in the field as well as from young authors who have recently completed their doctoral dissertations.

1. **Perception, Politics and Security in South Asia**
   The compound crisis of 1990
   P. R. Chari, Pervaiz Iqbal Cheema and Stephen Philip Cohen

2. **Coalition Politics and Hindu Nationalism**
   Edited by Katharine Adeney and Lawrence Saez

3. **The Puzzle of India's Governance**
   Culture, context and comparative theory
   Subrata K. Mitra

4. **India's Nuclear Bomb and National Security**
   Karsten Frey

5. **Starvation and India's Democracy**
   Dan Banik

6. **Parliamentary Control and Government Accountability in South Asia**
   A comparative analysis of Bangladesh, India and Sri Lanka
   Taiabur Rahman

7. **Political Mobilisation and Democracy in India**
   States of emergency
   Vernon Hewitt

8. **Military Control in Pakistan**
   The parallel state
   Mazhar Aziz

9. **Sikh Nationalism and Identity in a Global Age**
   Giorgio Shani

10. **The Tibetan Government-in-Exile**
    Politics at large
    Stephanie Roemer

11. **Trade Policy, Inequality and Performance in Indian Manufacturing**
    Kunal Sen

12. **Democracy and Party Systems in Developing Countries**
    A comparative study
    Clemens Spiess

13. **War and Nationalism in South Asia**
    The Indian state and the Nagas
    Marcus Franke

14. **The Politics of Social Exclusion in India**
    Democracy at the crossroads
    Edited by Harihar Bhattacharyya, Partha Sarka and Angshuman Kar

15. **Party System Change in South India**
    Political entrepreneurs, patterns and processes
    Andrew Wyatt

16. **Dispossession and Resistance in India**
    The river and the rage
    Alf Gunvald Nilsen

17. **The Construction of History and Nationalism in India**
    Textbooks, controversies and politics
    Sylvie Guichard

18. **Political Survival in Pakistan**
    Beyond ideology
    Anas Malik

19. **New Cultural Identitarian Political Movements in Developing Societies**
    The Bharatiya Janata Party
    Sebastian Schwecke

20. **Sufism and Saint Veneration in Contemporary Bangladesh**
    The Maijbhandaris of Chittagong
    Hans Harder

21. **New Dimensions of Politics in India**
    The United Progressive Alliance in power
    Lawrence Saez and Gurhapal Singh

22. **Vision and Strategy in Indian Politics**
    Jawaharlal Nehru's policy choices and the designing of political institutions
    Jivanta Schoettli

23. **Decentralization, Local Governance and Social Wellbeing in India**
    Do local governments matter?
    Rani D. Mullen

24. **The Politics of Refugees in South Asia**
    Identity, resistance, manipulation
    Navine Murshid

25. **The Political Philosophies of Antonio Gramsci and B. R. Ambedkar**
    Itineraries of Dalits and subalterns
    Edited by Cosimo Zene

26. **Suicide Protest in South Asia**
    Consumed by commitment
    Simanti Lahiri

27. **E-Governance in India**
    Interlocking politics, technology and culture
    Bidisha Chaudhuri

E-Governance in India
Interlocking politics, technology and culture

Bidisha Chaudhuri

LONDON AND NEW YORK

First published 2014
by Routledge

2 Park Square, Milton Park, Abingdon, Oxfordshire OX14 4RN
711 Third Avenue, New York, NY 10017

Routledge is an imprint of the Taylor & Francis Group, an informa business

First issued in paperback 2017

Copyright © 2014 Bidisha Chaudhuri

The right of Bidisha Chaudhuri to be identified as author of this work has been asserted in accordance with sections 77 and 78 of the Copyright, Designs and Patents Act 1988.

All rights reserved. No part of this book may be reprinted or reproduced or utilised in any form or by any electronic, mechanical, or other means, now known or hereafter invented, including photocopying and recording, or in any information storage or retrieval system, without permission in writing from the publishers.

Notice:
Product or corporate names may be trademarks or registered trademarks, and are used only for identification and explanation without intent to infringe.

British Library Cataloguing in Publication Data
A catalogue record for this book is available from the British Library

Library of Congress Cataloging in Publication Data
Chaudhuri, Bidisha.
E-governance in india: interlocking politics, technology and culture / Bidisha Chaudhuri.
    pages cm. – (Routledge advances in South Asian studies)
  Includes bibliographical references and index..
  1. Internet in public administration–India. 2. Information technology–India. 3. Communication–Technological innovations–India. 4. India–Politics and government. I. Title.
  JF1525.A8C45 2014
  352.3′802854678–dc23
                                                                2013045144

ISBN: 978-0-415-73790-6 (hbk)
ISBN: 978-0-8153-7474-9 (pbk)

Typeset in Times New Roman
by RefineCatch Limited, Bungay, Suffolk

I dedicate this book to my mother, Mrs Anjana Chaudhuri, for teaching me the meaning of strength and vulnerability at the same time.

Contents

List of figures and tables xii
Preface xiii
Acknowledgements xiv
List of abbreviations xv

1 Introduction 1

E-Governance in India: an overview 1
*Governance and strategic reform: posing the research
   questions 5*
*From government to governance: tracing the North–South
   trajectory of governance discourse 10*
*'Good governance': the global agenda of governance reform and
   changing societies 13*
*The politics of governance reform: changing patterns of
   governance in India 16*
*Politics, technology and culture: an analytical puzzle of
   e-Governance 19*
Conclusion: structure and scope of the book 24

2 Methodology 28

*Introduction: a conceptual dilemma of governance and 'good
   governance' 28*
*Theorizing e-Governance reform in India: an inter-disciplinary
   approach 30*
*Evaluating e-Governance reform in India: the framework of
   analysis 36*
*Conclusion: methodological challenges of a context-specific analysis
   of governance 46*

3 E-Governance in India: an overview 50

Introduction: e-Governance as a strategic reform and the Indian State 50
E-Governance policies: the pre-liberalization policy regime (1970–1990) 51
Shifting policy framework in post-liberalization India 54
From policy to an action plan: NeGP 2006 63
E-Governance practices from the pre-NeGP era to NeGP experiences: a paradigmatic shift? 64
The 11th Report of the Second Administrative Reform Commission (ARC), 2008: a snapshot of practices and recommendations in the post-NeGP policy regime 72
E-Service Delivery Bill, 2011: the future of e-Governance in India 75
Conclusion: the hiatus between policies and practices 76

4 E-Governance in context: a case study 78

Introduction: CSCs and context-specific understanding of e-Governance 78
What are CSCs?: a comprehensive account of CSCs roll out in India 78
Regional narratives of CSCs: an account of four sample states 82
E-Governance reform and regional contexts: a comparative perspective 94
Conclusion: questioning technological determinism 101

5 Negotiating politics, technology and culture 102

Introduction: ramifications of e-Governance on the quality of governance in India 102
Politics of governance reform and e-Governance in India 106
Connecting technology and governance: a means to an end or an end in itself? 107
Hybridizing e-Governance reform in India: contradiction or consolidation? 110
Manoeuvring legitimacy with strategic reforms: a democratic dilemma 113
Conclusion: researching governance through the prism of e-Governance 115

6 Conclusion 120

Transcending the Indian context: from area studies to theory of governance 120

Shifting discourses of governance 122
Politics of governance reform and changing societies 125
E-Governance reforms in changing societies: mapping the trends 126
Emerging models of governance: innovations or subversion? 127
An interdisciplinary approach to e-Governance: methodological implications 128
Further research 129

Methodological appendix	131
Glossary	136
Notes	137
Bibliography	140
Index	149

Figures and tables

Figures

1.1	State, society and governance in a modern state	8
1.2	The complex of governance: the emerging paradigm	11
2.1	A stylized model of governance: realms and actors	36
2.2	A dynamic neo-institutional model of governance based on elite strategies	37
2.3	Policy network of e-Governance in India	39
2.4	The research design	47
4.1	Matrix of rural development through e-Governance reform	79
4.2	Three-tier implementing structure of the CSCs Scheme	80

Tables

2.1	Defining indicators of improved quality of governance	40
4.1	Service status of CSCs	81
4.2	Comparative status of the CSCs in the four sample states	93
Appendix table 1	Sources of data	132

Preface

This book is an adaptation from my doctoral thesis titled 'Hybridizing E-Governance in India: The Interplay of Politics, Technology and Culture' which I completed in December 2012 at the Faculty of Economics and Social Sciences at Ruprecht-Karls-Universität Heidelberg, Germany.

This book is driven by a simple endeavour to unravel the technological determinism that existed in the development regime of the Indian State and which still continues to determine the policy paradigm. Given the recent popularity of ICT tools in governance and other development practices in India, it was thought to be an appropriate time to publish this book. The Indian experience of e-Governance reform that appears to be an endless negotiation between politics, technology and culture will hopefully resonate with the experiences in other developing countries that are also confronted with a surge of such wide-scale reform.

The field research which is a crucial pillar of this book was conducted between November 2010 and July 2011. Hence some of the facts about the Common Services Centres (CSCs) Scheme might have been changed. However, since the case study was based on a narrative style qualitative analysis, a few changes in information will not affect the overall argument of the book.

Acknowledgements

I would like to express my deepest gratitude to a few people without whom this book would not have been possible.

First of all I am sincerely grateful to my supervisor Professor Subrata K. Mitra for his constant support, encouragement and above all absolute patience throughout this academic journey. He has been a guide in the true sense of the term as his involvement with this book has surpassed mere professional advice. It was his faith in my abilities more than my own conviction which encouraged me to write this book.

I would like to thank my friends and colleagues and senior scholars at the Cluster of Excellence: 'Asia and Europe in a Global Context' at the Karl Jasper Centre for Transcultural Studies, Heidelberg University for providing a vibrant and ever-stimulating research environment through my doctoral research. The financial and academic assistance of the Cluster has rendered the process of this work rather smooth and enriching.

I would also like to extend my thanks Mr Abhishek Singh (former Director of e-Governance, Department of Electronics and Information Technology, Ministry of Communication and Information Technology, Government of India) and his entire team for supporting my research and for providing all the possible assistance throughout my fieldwork in India.

I would like to thank the editorial team, especially Dorothea, Jillian and Rebecca at Routledge, UK for their patience and support. I would specially mention Dorothea here as she really thought that I could write this book when I had serious doubts about finishing my dissertation in the first place.

I am also obliged to my present employer, the Centre for IT & Public Policy at the International Institute for Information Technology (IIIT)-Bangalore, India and particularly my colleague Dr Amit Prakash for their unconditional support and mostly for bearing with me throughout the process of preparing this manuscript.

Last but not the least, I would like to thank my parents, parents-in-law and specially my husband, Sumit for their love, care and constructive criticism that has provided me with the much needed strength and sanity during the entire period of research that finally led to this book.

Abbreviations

AP	Andhra Pradesh
ARC	Administrative Reform Commission
B2C	Business to Citizen
BCP	Business Continuity Planning
BDO	Block Development Officer
BJP	Bharatiya Janata Party
BPR	Business Process Re-engineering
BSNL	Bharat Sanchar Nigam Limited
BSP	Bahujan Samaj Party
CAP	Central Agri Portal
CBOs	Community-Based Organizations
CCC	Course on Computer Concept
CIN	Corporate Identity Number
CMC	Computer Maintenance Company
CSC	Common Services Centre
CSS	Central Sector Schemes
CSSs	Centrally Sponsored Schemes
DAC	Department of Agriculture and Cooperation
DAR&PG	Department of Administrative Reforms and Public Grievances
DfID	Department for International Development
DISNIC	District Information System of the National Informatics Centre
DIT	Department of Information Technology
DOE	Department of Electronics
DOEACC	Department of Electronics and Accreditation of Computer Courses
DOT	Department of Telecommunications
DR	Disaster Recovery
DRDA	District Rural Development Agency
DTH	Direct-To-Home
DTP	Desktop Publishing
EC	Electronic Commission
ECIL	Electronic Computers of India Limited
FGD	Focused Group Discussion

G2B	Government to Business
G2C	Government to Citizen
G2G	Government to Government
GAPs	Good Agricultural Practices
GIDC	Gujarat Industrial Development Corporation
GOI	Government of India
GPRS	General Packet Radio Service
GVMC	Greater Visakhapatnam Municipal Corporation
ICTD	Information Communications Technology for Development
ICTs	Information Communication Technologies
IGPVSY	Indira Gandhi Vivah Shagun Yojna
IMF	International Monetary Fund
IMSC	Inter-Ministerial-Standing Committee
IPSS	International-Package-Switching-Services
IT	Information Technology
LIC	Life Insurance Corporation of India
MGNREGA/S	Mahatma Gandhi National Rural Employment Guarantee Act/Scheme
MIS	Management Information System
MMPs	Mission Mode Projects
MRTP	Monopolies and Restrictive Trade Practices
NASSCOM	National Association of Software and Service Companies
NDC	National Development Council
NeGP	National e-Governance Plan
NGO	Non-Governmental Organization
NIC	National Informatics Centre
NICNET	Nationwide Communication Network
NPM	New Public Management
NREGA/S	National Rural Employment Guarantee Act/Scheme
NRHM	National Rural Health Mission
PAN	Personal Account Number
PDC	Primary Data Centre
PMGSY	Pradhan Mantri Gram Sadak Yojana/Prime Minister Rural Road Scheme
PPP	Public–Private Partnership
PRIs	Panchayati Raj Institutions
RAR	Rapid Assessment Round
RIV	Rajiv Internet Village
RoR	Land Record Certificates (Record of Rights)
RSDPs	Rural Service Delivery Points
RTI	Right to Information
SAPs	Structural Adjustment Programmes
SCA	Service Centre Agency
SCs	Scheduled Castes
SDA	State Designated Agency

SDCs	State Data Centres
SKD	Simple Knock Down
STD	Subscribers Trunk Dialing
STPs	Software Technology Parks
STs	Scheduled Tribes
STS	Science and Technology Studies
SWANs	State-Wide Area Networks
TAN	Tax Account Number
TAXNET	All India Income Tax Network
TNCCs	Transnational Computer Companies
TSTSP	Technical Support and Training Service Provider
UID	Unique ID
UIDAI	Unique Identification Authority of India
UNDP	United Nations Development Programme
UNESCAP	United Nations Economic and Social Commission for Asia and the Pacific
UNESCO	United Nations Educational, Scientific and Cultural Organization
UPS	Uninterruptible Power Supply
USOF	Universal Service Obligation Fund
UT	Union Territories
VCE	Village Computer Entrepreneur
VLEs	Village Level Entrepreneurs
VLWE	Village Level Women Entrepreneurs
VOs	Voluntary Organizations
VSAT	Very Small Aperture Terminal
WTO	World Trade Organization
ZBB	Zero Based Budgeting*Appendix table 1* Sources of data

1 Introduction

E-Governance in India: an overview

The relationship between technology and governance is a pertinent yet relatively under researched field of study. In the last two decades there has been an unprecedented upsurge in the use of Information Communication Technologies (ICTs) geared towards 'good governance' goals, both across developed and developing countries. For developing countries it has also been popularized by International Organizations under the banner of 'E-Governance for Development' or 'E-Governance for Good Governance' and eventually has taken an important position in the governance reform agenda of the national governments.

On 15 August 2002, on the occasion of India's Independence Day, the Prime Minister announced 15 important initiatives to be endorsed by the Government of India (GOI). E-Governance was placed under this list of initiatives which stated that the GOI will formulate a comprehensive programme in order to promote and expedite e-Governance at all levels of the government. The overall aim of this programme will be to improve efficiency, transparency and accountability in government–citizen interface (Mathur *et al.* 2009). In the same year, the Prime Minister's statement at the National Development Council (NDC) in December 2002 asserted that e-Governance geared towards better governance, is a priority area for the GOI and this is prominently reflected in the Tenth Plan (ibid.).

The thrust on e-Governance is emblematic of a major shift of discourse from government to governance in the rhetoric of the Indian State. This shift reflects across a range of policy documents and government reports. The National Human Development Report (2001), published by the GOI dedicated a whole chapter on 'Governance for Human Development' which reinforced the importance of governance and 'good governance' for sustainable development and promoted subsequent adaptation in the current governance practices by changing the scope and role of the state in relation to the market and the civil society (Choudhary 2007). Similarly, in the Tenth Five Years Plan (2002–2007) and the Eleventh Five Years Plan (2007–2012), governance received special attention of the policy-makers and thereby was allotted a separate chapter unlike previous planning documents. A close look at these chapters brings out two important dimensions of this shift of focus from government to governance. Firstly, there is a growing importance of the market and the civil society and secondly, this burgeoning state-orientation towards governance is mandated by the transnational paradigm of 'good governance'. The Tenth Plan defines governance as the management of processes within a society that raise individuals' choices for realizing their capabilities in an effective environment. It reiterates that,

> [Governance] covers the State, civil society and the market, each of which is critical for sustaining human development. The State is responsible for creating a conducive political, legal and economic environment for building individual capabilities and encouraging private initiative. The market is expected to create opportunities for people. Civil society facilitates the mobilisation of public opinion and people's participation in economic, social and political activities. . . . With the acceptance of market liberalism and globalisation, it is expected that the State yields to the market and the civil society in many areas where it, so far, had a direct but distortionary and inefficient presence. . . . It means extension of the market and the civil society domain at the expense of the State in some areas. It also implies an increase in the area of their respective overlaps.
>
> (GOI 2002, pp. 177, 181)

As the Tenth Plan acknowledges the influence of market liberalism and globalization on the framework of governance, similarly the Eleventh Five Years Plan talks about improving the quality of governance within the broader framework of 'good governance' which is argued to be covering 'all aspects of interface between individuals and business on the one hand and government on the other' (GOI 2007, p. 223). Elaborating on some distinctive features of 'good governance' the Eleventh Plan document stresses factors such as accountability, transparency, efficiency of service delivery, decentralization, rule of law or sound legal framework and inclusiveness and so on. The issues and strategies of reform discussed in these Plans range from narrow administrative reform to broader political reform and include right to information, civil service reform, procedural reform, judicial reform, using information technology, people's participation, decentralization, partnership approach with extra-state spheres and so on (Choudhary 2007). There is another side of this governance reform trajectory which directly relates to issues of economic reform such as privatization, deregulation, disinvestment, corporatization and social sector reforms (ibid.). The underlying agenda of all the discussions concerning reform in India is 'institutional reform' which is further illustrated through themes such as decentralization, simplification, transparency, accountability and e-Governance (ibid.). These common themes have gradually made their way into the checklists of all government ministries and departments under the broader framework of governance reform. Consequently, both the Tenth and Eleventh Plan talk about 'e-Governance for good governance' and better service delivery (GOI 2002, 2007).

As it emerged from the above discussion, e-Governance has taken up an important position in the state initiatives for overall governance reform in India in recent times. There are many conceptualizations of e-Governance. Most of these conceptualizations are formulated either by International Organizations or developed countries which have made considerable progress in the field. The term e-Governance is often interchangeably used with the term e-government. The 11th Report of the Second Administrative Reform Commission (ARC), 2008 on e-Governance attempts to summarize some of the basic definitions of the term. The World Bank's definition of the term says, 'E-Government refers to the use by government agencies of information technologies (such as Wide Area Networks, the Internet and mobile computing) that have the ability to transform relations with citizens, businesses and other arms of government' (GOI 2008, p. 8). These technologies not only improve the delivery of government services to citizens but also empower citizens through access to information. It further improves interactions of the public sector with business and industry, reduce corruption, increase transparency as well as revenue growth, and also reduce cost for service delivery (ibid.). The United Nations Educational, Scientific and Cultural Organization (UNESCO) defines the concept in relation to the broader concept of governance as it argues, 'Governance refers to the exercise of political, economic and administrative authority in the management of a country's affairs, including citizens' articulation of their interests and exercise of their legal rights and obligations. E-Governance may be understood as the performance of this governance via the electronic medium in order to facilitate an efficient, speedy and transparent process of disseminating information to the public and other agencies, and for performing government administration activities' (ibid., pp. 8–9). The Council of Europe refers to e-Governance as 'the use of electronic technologies in three areas of public action: relations between the public authorities and civil society, functioning of the public authorities at all stages of the democratic process (electronic democracy) [and] the provision of public services (electronic public services)' (ibid., p. 9). The United States E-Government Act 2002 defines it as the 'the use by the Government of web-based Internet applications and other information technologies, combined with processes that implement these technologies, to (A) enhance the access to and delivery of Government information and services to the public, other agencies and other Government entities; or (B) bring about improvements in Government operations that may include effectiveness, efficiency, service quality, or transformation' (ibid., p. 9). In an attempt to adapt the concept to the Indian context, former President of India, Dr A. P .J. Abdul Kalam promoted the idea of 'A transparent smart e-Governance with seamless access, secure and authentic flow of information crossing the interdepartmental barrier and providing a fair and unbiased service to the citizen' (ibid., p. 10).

By conjuring up all these diverse formulation of the term e-Governance can be defined as deployment of ICT for improving information and service delivery, encouraging citizen participation in the decision-making process and making government more accountable, transparent and effective through greater coordination among private sector and civil society organizations (Deva 2005). It is also important to distinguish between the concepts of e-government and e-Governance. E-Governance is a broader idea which encompasses a political as well as a technical dimension. The political dimension relates to the state's institutional arrangements, decision-making processes, implementation capacity and the relationship between, the government with citizen, businesses and the civil society. The technical dimension refers to the issues of service delivery and public management. E-government, though sharing some goals with e-Governance, is better understood as a subset of e-Governance concentrated on increasing administrative efficiency and reducing corruption (Bhatnagar 2009). The other two terms that need some elucidation here are 'change-management' and 'business-process re-engineering'. These two terms appear quite extensively in most of the literature and they are crucial in understanding both e-government and e-Governance. 'Change Management is a structured approach to transitioning individuals, teams and organizations from a current state to a desired future state. It involves a series of changes beginning with vision, introduction of skills, adding incentives and resources and designing an action plan bringing positive results' (Sachdeva 2009, p. 109). Business Process Re-engineering (BPR):

> [I]s the redesign of business processes and the associated systems and organizational structures to achieve a dramatic improvement in performance . . . [It] requires . . . an agency to implement substantive reform in organizational structure, initiate a change in culture and mind-set, train and improve skills of its people and put in place an appropriate supporting ICT infrastructure to enable online processes that are timely and efficient to both the user and the government agency.
>
> (Bhatnagar 2009, p. 78)

E-Governance has been one of the strategic sectors of reform in India since the late 1990s under the rubric of the 'good governance' agenda promoted by International Organizations. Since 1991, India's policy focus changed towards economic liberalization, deregulation and privatization proliferating domestic and foreign investment. Information Technology (IT) has been one of the leading areas for such heightened investment. Though the Indian government has been taking interest in IT infrastructure development and computerization of public administration already since the 1980s, until the late 1990s, the use of ICTs in public service delivery has been pretty low. It is around 1997–1998 that using ICT tools oriented towards development goals became more and more popular within the public sector. However, the majority of these reform initiatives were initially aimed at urban middle-class citizens for improving their experience of public service delivery. This picture slowly changed as the potential of ICTs for rural development caught the fancy of policy-makers. Hence, since the beginning of the twenty-first century, comprehensive policy frameworks have been formulated at the national level to implement e-Governance across India reaching out to even remote rural areas. The policy goals of such initiatives are two folds: to widen the outreach of public services and to improve the quality of public services (Sreekumar 2008; Madon, 2009). This policy-orientation towards e-Governance reached its crest with the approval of the National e-Governance Plan (NeGP) in May 2006 which envisages:

[To] Make all Government services accessible to the common man in his locality, through common service delivery outlets, and ensure efficiency, transparency, and reliability of such services at affordable costs to realise the basic needs of the common man.

(GOI 2006b)

The NeGP along with 27 Mission Mode Projects and eight components adopts a holistic approach to streamline all e-Governance initiatives across the country. This marks a shift in the governmental approach towards e-Governance as most of the initiatives before NeGP were tackled in an isolated manner with individual impetus. There was a severe problem of sustainability even for successful initiatives and there was hardly any scope for sharing the experiences. Evidently, NeGP addresses these gaps by bringing in an integrated approach to all e-Governance initiatives. Besides engaging in the administrative reform by improving public service delivery model, NeGP also deals with broader issues of governance reform espoused by the GOI. One such example is the public–private partnership model and thereby the active role of private sectors in the implementation of most of the initiatives undertaken under the NeGP.

It is in this context of recent policy shifts towards e-Governance as a strategic sector of reform by the Indian State that this book sets out to analyse how such reform initiatives are shaped up by the continuous interplay of politics, technology and culture. In addressing this analytical puzzle, we need to first cast our glance at the concept of governance, reform and its relevance for the research questions that this study aims to address.

Governance and strategic reform: posing the research questions

The statement – '[G]overnance, more than the innate cohesion of Indian society and culture, or the specific context of colonial rule and transfer of power, is the key to India's resilience' (Mitra 2006, p. 2) – unequivocally hints at the instrumentality of the concept of governance in explaining the strength and sustainability of a postcolonial nation such as India. However, undoubtedly it is not just an Indian problem. The significance of governance as a political and social problematic has caught the fancy of policy-makers, academicians, development practitioners and social activists with similar rigor and severity. Consequently, in recent times one can witness an increasing focus on governance across developed as well as developing countries, albeit varying in terms of their origin and contexts.

The international political scenario has essentially changed since 1989 as the bipolarity of the Cold War period gave way to a multipolar locus of power in world politics. This was soon reflected in the shift in the international development discourse. The focus was now on democracy, participation, efficiency, accountability and so on. Unlike the previous decade, the 1990s brought the limelight back on state and institutions and consequently 'governance' moved into the agenda across a wide range of discussion involving academicians, development practitioners, politicians, bureaucrats, private sector entrepreneurs and civil society activists. This swing became more prominent in most of the changing societies of postcolonial and post-communist nation-states where governance reform became a priority for governments and a prerequisite for economic development.

However, this new agenda setting around governance (or governance reform) in the international political and development discourse and the issues emerging from these debates were already confronted in most of the Western democracies already in 1970s. Three main concerns of these debates were focused on three main functions of the state, namely regulation, welfare and development which in turn addresses the issues of ungovernability related to distrust and disagreement with the state, crisis of welfare state in the face of increasing demand related to public sector deficit and lastly the incapability of the state to perform unilaterally to solve social and economic and other developmental problems (Kooiman 1993). These concerns led to different measures by different states, which found its expressions in terms like privatization, deregulation, agencification, decentralization, development of policy networks, public administration reform and so on (Kjaer 2004). Parallel to these reshuffling in the role of the state was a growing citizen demand for better and more responsive public service delivery which also resonated in the mounting power of the media and the influence of the civil society (Fritzen 2009). In post-Cold War times, these issues became relevant in most developing and changing societies[1] which were further fortified by a renewed interest in democracy and sustainable development. Evidently, while the recent focus on governance in Western developed nations rose more or less from the internal issue of governability, in developing nations the impetus came mostly from external forces such as the international donor agencies.

Amidst myriad attempts at governance reform, the concept of governance went through considerable reconfiguration. On one hand international development paradigm and policy-makers take predominantly a techno-managerial position in addressing the issues of governance, while on the other hand social science research maintains to view governance as a function of orderly rule and a synchronized relationship between state and society. Although these spectrums by no means suggest an exhaustive account of all the possible perspectives on the concept, they nonetheless demonstrate the contentious nature of the concept. However, before delving further into the specific dimensions of governance and governance reform that this book undertakes to investigate, it is worthwhile to dwell a little deeper into the concept of governance itself at the outset.

The basic dictionary meaning of governance describes it as an act or manner of governing of a state or an organization (Oxford Dictionaries Online 2011). The term has often been used synonymously with government which changed during 1980s when political scientists included civil society actors into its definitions. Even within political science, different subfields treat the concept rather differently. Scholars in public administration and public policy while talking about public sector reform refers to governance as a self-organizing network involving a plurality of actors and organizations which further blurs the traditional boundaries of public and the private (Kjaer 2004). For the theorists of international relations, the focus is more on global governance which refers to a system of rule at all levels of human activity aimed at decision-making of transnational nature (Rosenau 1995). Of course, the definition of global governance is conceived differently by its proponents, even though the spotlight remains on the creation of global organizations such as the World Trade Organization (WTO) and growth of non-governmental movements and institutions outside the purview of the nation-state. In the subfield of comparative politics, which largely engages in the systematic comparison of the political system, during the 1980s state institutions and their effects became a common theme. This was different from its previous preoccupation with political culture, parties, electoral behaviour and so forth. While bringing back state institutions into focus comparative politics, in recent times, became seriously engaged with the state–society interactions. Governance, in this sense, is about managing the political rules of the game both at the formal and informal level (Kjaer 2004).

Needless to say that, despite its different usage in different approaches, governance as a concept frequently transcends these analytical boundaries. Therefore, 'governance can be conceptualized in terms of how authority, resources and power are distributed among the public, private and people sectors and various levels of government (from a supranational to community level)' (Fritzen 2009, p. 1). This definition of governance implicates all the three approaches discussed above at the same time. Governance can also be referred to as the 'development of governing "styles" in which boundaries between and within public and private sectors become blurred. The focus in this case is on governing mechanisms that do not rest on recourse to authority and sanctions, but draw their legitimacy from popular consent' (Mitra 2006). This public policy meets comparative politics definition of governance definitely hints at the democratizations process which is more pertinent in the context of changing societies. Moreover, since public policy is affected by both domestic and international politics and affairs, international relations notions of governance also stands relevant. Here, governance also becomes a relevant topic for other disciplines such as development economics, development studies, organizational studies and political sociology and so on.

Besides having overlapping zones of understanding, all the approaches conceive of governance as something broader than government which is concerned about the rules of the game. Their preoccupation with rule-making also grows out of their common orientation towards institutions and institutional change. There are many versions of institutionalisms which are albeit based on two basic assumptions about human behaviour. The first is rational-choice approach where preferences are exogenous to individuals and an individual chooses from a list of alternative actions to maximize utility. The second is sociological where preferences are endogenous and the individual behaviour is determined by certain values and norms he or she is socialized into. Both these assumptions are crucial to explain two basic questions that institutionalism set out to address: (i) how institutions affect political behaviour; and (ii) how institutions emerge and change.

8 Introduction

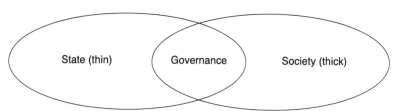

Figure 1.1 State, society and governance in a modern state
Source: Mitra 2006, p. 21

This latter concern of institutionalism has caught much fancy of the governance theorists (Kjaer 2004).

Institutionalism conceives governance as setting, application and enforcement of rules which not only determines the framework in which citizens, government and politics interact but also shapes the spheres of civil society (Kjaer 2004). This way of defining governance combines the structure of rules with agency of change. Therefore, governance as a process lies in the interplay of structure and agency in which the state interacts with society. In precise terms, 'governance, conceptualized as the overlap of the thin norms of the state and the thick perceptions of social groups is the interface of societies and institutions' (Mitra 2006, p. 21). This is further elaborated in Figure 1.1.

Until now it becomes clear that recent developments in governance theory has opened up alternative ways of looking at political institutions, domestic–global linkages, transnational cooperation and different forms of public–private exchange (Pierre 2000). However, one fundamental point which needs to be addressed here is the contradiction inbuilt into the very concept of governance. Governance is always perceived differently by those who govern and those who are governed as they belong to the opposite ends of social distribution of power. The immediate question that one tends to ask is how orderly rule is achieved in spite of this inevitable hiatus between perceptions. The answer lies in conceptualizing power as productive, technical and positive. Power needs to be visualized as a productive network which runs through the entire social body surpassing its mere negative function of repression (Foucault 1980). In Foucault's own words,

> [F]rom the seventeenth and eighteenth centuries onwards, there was a veritable technological take-off in the productivity of power. Not only did the monarchies of the Classical period develop great state apparatuses (the army, the police and fiscal administration), but above all there was established at this period what one might call a new 'economy' of power, that is to say procedures which allowed the effects of power to circulate in a manner at once continuous, uninterrupted, adapted and 'individualized' throughout the entire social body. These new techniques are both much more efficient and much less wasteful (less costly economically, less risky in their results, less open to loopholes and resistances) than the techniques previously

employed which were based on a mixture of more or less forced tolerances (from recognized privileges to endemic criminality) and costly ostentation (spectacular and discontinuous interventions of power, the most violent form of which was the 'exemplary', because exceptional, punishment).

(Foucault 1980, p. 119)

Foucault maintains this same notion of 'economy of power' within the context of the modern state. While acknowledging the significance of the state and its apparatus (army, police, judiciary and so on) he reiterated the fact that one must look much beyond the juridical-legal aspect of the state and focuses more on the relations of power already existent in the society. He cites two reasons for this: firstly, the state cannot entirely occupy the field of actual power relations despite its omnipotence and secondly, the state being a superstructure operates only on the basis of an already existing network of power relations. Therefore, the 'metapower' of the state which draws on a number of prohibitions and sanctions, 'can only take hold and secure its footing where it is rooted in a whole series of multiple and indefinite power relations that supply the necessary basis for the great negative forms of power' (Foucault 1980, p. 122).

This Foucauldian notion of power both in terms of 'economy of power' and 'networks of power relations' beyond repressive state apparatus serves two purpose for our understanding of governance in the modern state. Firstly, for a system of governance to accomplish orderly rule, it is important for the state institutions to take root into the existing system of social relations which are characterized by different power positions and a distinct hiatus between the governed and those who govern. Secondly, this hiatus needs to be bridged not only by repressive state apparatus but also by manoeuvring the network of power relations. It is this effective manoeuvring of the hiatus between two different power positions that elicit interest in the concept of legitimacy of rule, particularly within a democratic set-up.

Legitimacy can be derived through democratic procedures as a common agreement or acceptance of the governing authority or it could also be derived through effective policy implementation geared towards common good. It is the latter aspect of the term that renders institutional and strategic reform an integral part of the political elites' strategy to enhance the legitimacy of the rule. However, it is also important to keep in mind that the concept of legitimacy becomes rather complicated while analysed in connection with two other related concepts: efficiency and accountability. On one hand, legitimacy is contingent upon efficiency on the part of the governing elites involving both the public and private realm of governance. On the other hand, too much emphasis on efficiency within the context of democratic governance might lead to lesser accountability. The issue of accountability gets further complicated when private sector and civil society actors get involved in decision-making and public service delivery processes, as has happened in recent times through the emergence of multiple-stakeholders' policy networks.

This study places itself in the intersection of different conceptualizations of governance. That is to say, it explains how governance reforms of a techno-managerial variety (as propagate by international donor agencies) can improve the level of governance which hinges upon the state–society dynamics. In illustrating this broader argument, the study draws on the case of India and the e-Governance as a specific field of strategic reform[2] in the Indian context. The basic research question that drives this study is: Does strategic reform matter in improving the quality of governance? This broader question is followed by two corollaries: (i) Why are some strategic reforms successful in enhancing governance while others fail?; and (ii) Does the gap between policies and practices of reform necessarily denote a legitimacy deficit in governance? In probing these questions, the study deploys a novel interdisciplinary methodology by combining a neo-institutional model of analysing governance (political science) with a social constructivist approach of analysing the relationship between technology and governance (sociology) and the conceptual tool of hybridity to critically comprehend the emerging patterns of governance in India (Postcolonial/transcultural studies). While the neo-institutional model of governance explains the role of strategic reform in determining the level governance, social constructivism demonstrates how social and cultural factors embedded in the local contexts influence the effectiveness of reform initiatives. This implies a probable hiatus between the intentions and outcomes of reform which could be symptomatic of a legitimacy deficit. Here, Postcolonial/transcultural perspective enabled with a conceptual tool of hybridity leverages the analysis of governance by mending the hiatus between policies and practices of reform. In short, state-centric as well society-centric approaches are coalesced to understand the dynamism of the concept of governance and this dynamism is further explicated within an interdisciplinary methodological framework.

From government to governance: tracing the North–South trajectory of governance discourse

The context in which governance came to the fore in much of academic and development discourse has already been touched upon in the previous section. It is nonetheless imperative to invest a little more attention on this aspect as this context is particularly instrumental for the shift that has taken place in the lexicon of governance. Moreover, mapping the different trajectory of the governance discourse in developed and developing parts of the world is also crucial for comprehending the politics of governance.

The most fundamental paradigm shift in this regard has been the moving focus from government to governance. This does not mean that the conceptual difference between government and governance is a new theoretical development. What it actually means is that this difference has been highlighted in recent times and the focus is now more on the governance than on the government. Moving from a purely abstract level of analysis, one feels compelled to ask what this shift actually implies in real terms.

In discussing the government, the focus remains primarily on the sphere of state and its institutions and a structural-functional approach is mostly deployed in analysing the realm of state. This structure-based understanding of the state was

Introduction 11

slowly replaced by a process-based conceptualization of governance where two other spheres got considerable importance, namely the market and the civil society. The growth of market and civil society has sometimes coincided with the shrinkage of state or at least ineffectuality of state. Thus, governance forms a complex whole (see Figure 1.2) of interconnected spheres of public (which includes the state), private (which includes market) and citizens (which includes the civil society) in which the relationship between these spheres vary according to the distribution of power, resources and authority among them (Fritzen 2009).

It can be conferred that until the power, authority and resources were monopolized by the public sector, government was the focus of all analysis either in the welfare state model of most democracies or the centralized planning model of erstwhile communist states and its followers. However, since the 1980s even the public sector started changing considerably with the introduction of differentiated levels of governance ranging from village (local) to supranational (global) governing bodies. This development coincided with the popularity of the neo-liberal philosophy which propelled the free rein of market and shrinkage of the state. This of course, changed the way different spheres of governance were related and also their respective roles in the system.

Since the early 1990s, with the collapse of the Soviet bloc, centralized planning and its close followers who relied on a mixed economic model in a democratic set-up opened up more to the liberal economic policy. This created different repercussions in different set-ups which were in turn shaped by the specific historical and contextual trajectories of those regions. The common development that was experienced across region was the emergence of identity politics and social movements involving civil society and peoples' participation (Jayal and Pai

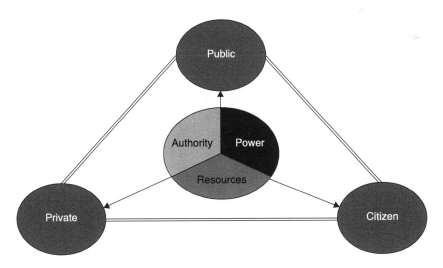

Figure 1.2 The complex of governance: the emerging paradigm
Source: Author (adapted from Fritzen 2009)

2001). Furthermore, by this time, the free market policy was slowly being replaced by 'retreat back to state' approach which again changed the balance of relationship between public, private and citizen. Hence the discourse shifted its focus from government to governance dealing more with the changing patterns of relationships between multiple spheres of governance.

After scrutinizing the generalized context in which this broader and heterogeneous concept of governance has emerged, it is time to map the North–South divide in the entire trajectory. This is important in order to understand the factor of path dependency of certain events and concepts which would later help building right perspectives to merge area studies in general theorization. In most Western democracies, privatizations, deregulations and cut down on public expenditure were direct effects of fiscal crisis which pushed most of the governments in these countries to search for new public management systems. They wanted to employ new strategies of management to reform public administration which in turn meant reorganizing the state along the line of the private sector. These developments were not so much about reducing the role of the state but including private actors (in delivering public services) who were supervized and monitored by state bureaucracies according to the financial and performance criteria. Another major development in reorganization of a state's role was the creation of European Union and other even wider institutions which tried to introduce a global regime in trade and environmental regulations. These national and transnational events questioned the role of state as regulator of economic and other policies, as a sole provider of basic services, but not so much as a broker of social consensus (Jayal and Pai 2001). This definitely points towards the importance of state–society relations in governance analysis.

In most of the non-Western nations (some of which were actually very new), on the other hand, the governance discourse did not grow out of an existential reality of those nation-states. Like many other conceptual realties it flew from the Western debate on governance in a manner which closely resemble modernization theory of development. Focusing strictly on the last two decades of the twentieth century, it becomes fairly evident that most of the shifts in governance debate and practices in the developing world have been prescriptive in nature, as imposed by the aid conditionality of donor agencies, mainly the World Bank. A World Bank document in 1989, on sub-Saharan Africa, suggested that most of the bank's programmes and policies are failing due to the crisis of governance in that region. Hence heavy governance reform packages were recommended as a development management mechanism, which later became popular under the umbrella term of 'good governance' (Jayal and Pai 2001).

Following the East Asian crisis in the latter half of the 1990s, the excessive dependence on market-oriented development was questioned and the role of the state again came under much discussion, and the relationship between state and plurality of actors outside the state became more significant for broadening the governance paradigm. Newer notions of the processes of governance started addressing the core of the governance. The thrust was not only on including multiple actors but also to attend to the qualitative aspect of governance.

Therefore, it was not enough to have civil service reform, new public administration management strategies and privatization of services, but it was now impending to take account of factor such as participation, decentralization, responsiveness and more broadly social justice and equality (Jayal and Pai 2001). It seems clear here that new parameters of measuring governance in changing societies have emerged. However, these parameters are also not completely divorced of prescriptive flows of reform agenda closely associated with democracy and sustainable economic development.

The above trajectories indicate that for developing countries recent shifts in the governance discourse comes in a package of 'good governance', however problematic that may appear. In order to deepen one's understanding of governance especially in the context of changing societies, it is important to debunk the notion of 'good governance' and unravel the politics of its language and outcome. Before doing so, a brief overview of the concept is imminent.

'Good governance': the global agenda of governance reform and changing societies

Following the aftermath of the Cold War, the last decade of the twentieth century witnessed renewed interest in democracy, participation, transparency and efficiency (Woods 1999). This wider context of political transition coincided with the massive failure of Structural Adjustment Programmes (SAPs) in most of the developing countries. Henceforth, the international development community especially the World Bank woke up to a new realization that governance reform is the key to all developmental problems in underdeveloped and developing nations. Unlike SAPs which emphasized the role of market as opposed to the state, this new approach towards reform brought the role and capacity of the state and institutions under serious consideration (Joseph 2001). Interestingly enough the governance reform agenda became quietly complementary with two related themes of democracy and economic development. Together they formed a triad of a magical solution to all the anguish and distress associated with underdevelopment. This triad focused together on political system, institutional structures and governance processes within a framework of public–private partnership (Santiso 2001). All these new developments became popular under the umbrella term of 'good governance'. In the last two decades 'good governance' has become the buzzword in the international development community. The term is packaged in such codes of morality that it seems to be devoid of any politics at all. However, quite contrarily in marrying the free market with a strong civil society, 'good governance' promises to provide new standards of rule which protect the citizens from the political societies and undemocratic governments (Corbridge *et al.* 2005).

As has already been mentioned, 'good governance' emerged alongside (or as a result of) a set of other agendas which challenged the prevailing ideas on the state size, locus of authority relationships and the way government authority is organized. Privatization, decentralization, global governance, participatory democracy (democratization), deregulation, public administration reform – all these agendas play out simultaneously in the current debate on governance and culminates into the popular approach of 'good governance'. There is as such no definition of 'good governance'. It is rather an ideal-typical construct (somewhat in a Weberian sense[3]) which delineates the parameters of governance through certain indicators. The qualifier 'good' clearly denotes the better standards of such a formulation and hence the imperative to achieve them. The World Bank has identified three discrete aspects of governance which needs to be emphasized for reform:

> i) the form of political regime; ii) the process by which authority is exercised in the management of a country's economic and social resources for development; and iii) the capacity of government to design, formulate and implement policies and discharge functions.
>
> (Bandyopadhaya 1996)

Four key dimensions of this reform are as follows: (i) public sector management (capacity and efficiency) which involves civil service reform and privatization initiatives; (ii) accountability which would enable institutions to hold the government accountable, for example an ombudsman; (iii) the legal framework for development which implies making and enforcing rules to control the market, for example enforcing private property rights; and (iv) information and transparency which hints towards free media, publicizing public expenditure, for example the right to information (Jayal and Pai 2001; Kjaer 2004). This implies significant changes in the ways power, authority and resources would be allocated and aligned with close links between democracy, economic development and 'good governance'. As far as the criteria of 'good governance' are concerned, the United Nations Economic and Social Commission for Asia and the Pacific (UNESCAP) sets out eight major characteristics. It is participatory, consensus oriented, accountable, transparent, responsive, effective and efficient, equitable and inclusive and follows the rule of law.

The United Nations Development Programme (UNDP) elaborates on five basic principles of 'good governance'. They are as follows: (i) Legitimacy and Voice as characterized by participation based on freedom of association and speech, capacities and consensus-oriented policies and procedures; (ii) Strategic vision and direction by leaders based on a sense of common good rooted in history, culture and social complexities; (iii) Performance based on responsiveness, efficiency and effectiveness to serve all stakeholders; (iv) Accountability of public, private as well as civil society sector based transparency of processes and free flow of information; (v) Fairness based on equity and rule of law (Graham *et al.* 2003).

Now the question arises as to how can we understand these broad and general norms in specific political and cultural contexts? Or how to transform such a normative concept into an operational concept of governance? This new agenda of 'good governance', though based on the premise of early liberal theories puts emphasis on a market concept of equality which strives for empowerment of citizens by making them economically self-sustaining and enabling them to enter into market transactions. The cooperation of private agencies and non-governmental organizations (NGOs) are crucial for this purpose. Under this new-found concept of equality and active participation of different actors citizens are often viewed as end users or customers whereas the government acts as the service providers. Improving the quality of these services and reaching out to a wider base of customers with the help of the private and non-governmental stakeholders are the central objectives of the governance reform projects and calls for complete overhaul of public administration (Joseph 2001).Therefore, as an issue of public policy 'good governance' has moved not only into the agenda of the World Bank but has also become a common parlance of national governments and local political actors. In short, 'good governance' provides a universal recipe with a gradually growing mix of deregulation, privatization, civil service reform and decentralization (the associated agendas of reform) which are deemed to produce better governability across societies (Corbridge *et al.* 2005).

However, the international development community soon realized that supporting institutional reform was more difficult than implementation of a particular project. The domestic politics in developing countries started becoming explicitly dependent on external influences of the international development agencies. For example, the World Bank's demand for economic austerity could trigger off social protest which would then bring changes in the regime structure. On a more subtle note, some donor-supported programmes could strengthen one ministry over the other thereby influencing the internal institutional structure of the government. In this way, 'good governance' programme and its implementation across societies raised serious debate about the role of external actors in processes of state-building (Kjaer 2004). 'Good governance' agenda touched upon the sensitive aspects such as distribution of power and resources in developing societies which were anyway fraught with internal issues of growing ungovernability. This agenda was much more political in nature than earlier interventionist approaches of the international development community and hence created much more resistance in the local community and institutional set-up. As a result, they changed their agenda in certain ways. The movement was from demanding 'good governance' *ex ante*, i.e. governance reform being a conditionality of aid, towards *ex post* selectivity, i.e. taking 'good governance' as a qualifier to receive assistance. The usage of 'good governance' has changed from being something to be promoted in developing countries to rather being a requirement before which loans could be disbursed. In short, these practices of international institutions as far as governance is concerned raised two very important issues in the debates within comparative politics: (i) how external forces influence domestic politics; and (ii) whether it is at all possible to transfer the models of 'good governance' built on Western ideas to non-Western setting (ibid.).

These are pertinent questions which turn our focus to developing societies where model 'good governance' has made its foray into public policies and developmental initiatives of the state. In most of the postcolonial and post-communist countries the 'good governance' or governance reform agenda has significantly impacted not only the state policies but also the overall governance structure and practices which manifest in changing contours of state–society relationships. In order to understand how a transnational agenda of governance reform influence the national rhetoric of governance, we bring a context-specific understanding of governance into the forefront of analysis. Here, India serves as a case of those changing societies where transnational governance reform strategies have shifted the national discourse on governance. The motivation behind choosing India is neither to establish an Indian exceptionalism in governance analysis, nor to ignore cultural idiosyncrasies embedded in the Indian context. In fact the aim is to re-emphasize the context-specific understanding of governance. Keeping the basic research questions in mind, the Indian case elucidates how far reform initiatives inspired by transnational paradigm can take root in the local contexts of governance. Taking a critical stand against the 'good governance' paradigm, this research nonetheless seeks to trace the impact of reform strategies promoted by the same paradigm.

The politics of governance reform: changing patterns of governance in India

The fall of the Soviet Union in 1989, put a serious question mark on the feasibility of centralized planning which was coincided with a cynicism against the mixed economy as India continued to struggle with problems of poverty, unemployment, lower rates of growth. This led the Indian state to adopt International Monetary Fund (IMF) driven SAPs, which inaugurated economic liberalization in India in 1991. These transformations of India's political economy manifest not only in liberal economic reforms but also in the political realm such as the increasing influence of Hindu cultural nationalism and mobilization of identical politics through empowerment of historically subordinate sections of the populations, decentralization of governance through constitutional amendments (73rd and 74th) and strengthening of *Panchayati Raj* Institutions (PRIs) (Ruparelia *et al.* 2011; Farrington *et al.* 2009; Jayal and Pai 2001). The impact of such wide-ranging economic and political reform is still unfolding and is fraught with much ambivalence. However, all these trends have serious implications for the issues of governance. Identity politics and subsequent political mobilization do claim recognition of the state while challenging the particular regime and its legitimacy. Though they do not question the role of the state as such, nevertheless they do call for some reform of the state institutions. The processes of economic reform on the other hand, challenge the role of the state especially in the productive and redistributive aspects of the social order and stress the sphere of market. At the same time, a series of social movements and institutional experiments have taken up some of the responsibilities traditionally bore by the state, such as sustainable development, alleviating poverty and other such social causes. This definitely shifts the balance between state, market and civil society and also their sphere of influence in the society (Jayal and Pai 2001). While pointing out the need to look beyond the mere economic aspect of the reform, Jean Dreze and Amartya Sen, aptly argue:

While much energy has been spent on sorting out these issues, too little attention has been paid to what is lacking in the current orientation of economic policy in India. The removal of counter-productive regulations on domestic production and international trade can form a helpful part of a programme of participation and widely-shared growth, but it may achieve relatively little in the absence of more active public policy aimed at reducing the other social handicaps that shackle the Indian economy and reduce the well-being of the population.

(Dreze and Sen 1996, pp. 187–8)

One obvious change of all these interconnected events was weakening of the omnipresent status of the state and rise of extra-state spheres. The impetus for change, although, were both exogenous and endogenous. The exogenous factor was definitely the intervention of the international development community and the consequent adoption of economic liberalization policy that primarily benefited the market in general and transnational corporations in particular, evidently at the expense of the national bourgeoisie. Endogenous factors of change were manifold. Firstly, it was the weakening of the central power followed by the rise of regional political parties, regionalization of the political system, increasing demands for separatism and political mobilization along caste/ethnicity axis. Secondly, with the state's inability to tackle issues of poverty and development, there was a boom of civil society organization taking up the social and developmental causes. Thirdly, the tendency towards deinstitutionalization has increased through unparalleled cases of corruption and failure in law enforcement (Jayal and Pai 2001). However, the decline in state authority and rise of private and people sectors should not be seen as state versus extra-state spheres. In fact, changing parameters of governance have led to more cooperation between all these sectors, even though neither the process of partnership nor the outcomes of such partnership have been smooth and devoid of controversy.

Jayal (2001) captured these diverse changes in six models of governance that emerged in the political discourses of India post-economic liberalization in 1991. She described these models of governance as being alternative to the 'pre-existing centralized (albeit formally federal) structure of governance, and its twin, the command economy with centralized planning' (ibid., p. 133). The first model of governance is described as rolling back the state which was part of the economic reform agenda. This model manifested in a mixed form in India. There has been a significant cut-down on the public expenditure in the social sector, albeit without much downsizing or disinvestment of the state. However, exogenous factors of globalization posed serious challenge to state capacity to intervene within society and beyond. The second model is purported by practices of social movements challenging the state discourse on development. Often debated as the 'new social movements' of India these movements, on one hand delegitimize the modernizing elitist tendencies of the developmental state and on the other hand, promote the idea of a citizen-centric participatory democratic polity. The third model of governance is characterized by capturing of the state power by *dalit* parties such as *Bahujan Samaj* Party (BSP) which views economic inequalities as functions of political inequalities. Hence, the state as the main agent of redistributive system needs to be controlled by the disadvantageous *dalits*. The fourth model of governance is built on the notion of franchising the state where increasing number of national or international NGOs take over the developmental functions of the state either as a substitute of the state or as a franchise or as a public service contractor. The fifth model is based on the growing incidence of partnership between the state and the Community-Based Organizations (CBOs). These partnerships can be both top-down state initiatives and bottom-up approach where the state follows up on the path charted by the CBOs. Both the fourth and the fifth model hint at the emergence of a significant sphere of civil society and their changing relationship with the state. The sixth and the last model is that of a state-driven decentralized model based on 73rd and 74th constitutional amendments in 1992.

This major reform policy in the governance and administrative sector is one of the crucial yet usually sidelined in the general discussion on reform (Mooij 2005). The 73rd and 74th amendments made way for a two-three tier *panchayat* system in every state with provision for direct elections in village, block and district levels thereby strengthening institutions of local self-government. The principal features of such a decentralizing measure were: representatives to all the three levels were to be elected for a five-year term; one-third of the seats were reserved for women; mandatory reservations for scheduled castes (SCs) and scheduled tribes (STs) proportional to their population were introduced; the *gram sabha* or the voting public attained the constitutional status as the formal deliberative body at the village level; provisions were made for individual states to enact further reservations for other backward groups (Farrington *et al.* 2009). Another important aspect of the village *panchayats* is that they act as local mechanisms to increase transparency and accountability in government functioning. For example, distribution of governmental schemes is often fraught with stories of corruption, nepotism and misallocation. Through the decentralized model, village *panchayat* are expected to play a positive role to salvage such misappropriation as they enjoy considerable authority in identifying beneficiaries for most governmental schemes (ibid.). However, in an interesting observation Jayal pointed out:

> [T]hough these Amendments were intended to bring about both the democratization and the decentralization of governance, democratization – through the provisions for reservations for women as well as for members of the scheduled castes and tribes – clearly appears to have outpaced decentralization.
>
> (Jayal 2001, p. 149)

The above-mentioned models of governance quite painstakingly summarize the changing patterns of the state–society relationships that emerged in the political landscape of India following the economic liberalization in early 1990s. Another important aspect of the reform process that some of these models suggest that there has been a conscious effort on the part of the state to initiate significant strategic reforms, be it in specific sector or in reforming governance networks (e.g. by including extra-state spheres) or in changing orientation of state institutions (e.g. by adopting citizen-centric delivery models). In short, governance reform has occupied a significant place in state planning and programmes. It is in this planning mode that there has been considerable attention on ICTs for revamping the operations and functioning of the entire system of governance by contriving the technical as well as developmental role of the state. This strategic reform orientation of the Indian state towards electronic governance can be captured under the label of 'e-Governance for good governance' or 'e-Governance for development' (Sreekumar 2008; Madon 2009). The following section illustrates the general state and importance of e-Governance reform in India as a broader part of the governance reform agenda.

Politics, technology and culture: an analytical puzzle of e-Governance

Governance as a social and political concept traverses state and society, those who govern and the governed. Hence, governance can be manipulated by both the ruler and the ruled depending on the context of the rule. This implies a continuous interaction between the structure and agency, between the state-institutions and the stakeholders[1] which transform the system of governance and thereby renders it a dynamic concept. The basic question that this research sets out to investigate is how strategic reform affects the level of governance, or in other words, how can the state–society interface be influenced by strategic reform policies and practices. Policy-making and its implementation by the state institutions lie on one hand of this spectrum. The other side involves the reception and adaptation of such policies among the stakeholders. Both sides of reform, that is policies and practices involves a set of actors who are embedded in a particular cultural context. As this research focus on reforms initiated in the sphere of ICTs, understanding the impact of technology also adds to the broader research question. In order to analyse the impact of e-Governance reform on the level of governance it is important to establish the link between politics, culture and technology. Thus, the analytical puzzle of e-Governance in this research links politics, culture and technology in a complex and overlapping relationship. In resolving this puzzle three theoretical and methodological perspectives have provided the significant heuristic devices. They are neo-institutionalism, social constructivism and transcultural perspectives. Although these academic dispositions are discussed in much detail in the chapter on theories and methodology, it is absolutely necessary to pronounce the relevance of these scholastic principles for the current research endeavour.

Neo-institutionalism engages with both formal rule-bound state institutions and the informal matrix of values and norms embedded in society in order to understand the impact of institutions on political behaviour and also institutional change. Therefore, it provides a theoretical model to investigate on one hand how rules are made and applied, and on the other hand how rules are simultaneously manipulated by different actors (Kjaer 2004). In other words, it explains how the structure of rules originates and gradually shifts through the agency of the actors.

These actors include not only the elites who can directly influence the institutional set-up but also average citizens who usually reside on the receiving end of the institutional rules. Applying these basic principles in our specific research problem neo-institutionalism explains how reform policies are initiated and implemented through elite strategies and how they are perceived and received by the stakeholders. While exploring e-Governance reforms, neo-institutionalism also probes why and how it became a part of the elite strategy in the post-economic liberalization years in India. Neo-institutionalism becomes even more relevant in the context of postcolonial states like India where elite strategies serves as significant tools to leverage the gap between imported categories of colonial institutional structure and embedded inheritance of cultural norms (Mitra 2006). In short, neo-institutional paradigm explains the politics of strategic reform in e-Governance and how the dynamic interplay of structure-agency within a specific cultural context shift the contours of governance.

By now it has been reiterated that cultural norms and values embedded in a societal context influence the behaviour of the actors engaged in the system of governance irrespective of their power position. When technology is added to this complex relationship between politics and culture, it is not enough to understand the politics of strategic reform. In this case, the explanatory rigor comes from analysing how use of technology figures into these reform strategies and how the impact of technology is in turn determined by the interactions between institutional structures and societal contexts. For this purpose, e-Governance reforms lie at the intersection of politics, technology and culture and hence needs to be analysed through the critical lens of social constructivism. Social constructivism serves a two-level analytical purpose. At the first level, it explicates how both institutions and actors being socially constructed are entangled within the historically produced and culturally bound web of meaning, rules and preferences (Barnett 2005). At the second level social constructivism, as opposed to technological determinism expounds how actors and contexts determine the impact of technology. Social constructivism therefore shows how ICTs policies are formulated and received in India depending on the different subject positions of the actors and their respective contexts (Sreekumar 2008). While measuring e-Governance, the 'e' part which denotes the technological contribution to the 'governance' needs to be disaggregated. This implies taking up a social constructivist orientation towards technology instead of relying on technological determinism. In simple terms, the basic assumption in this analytical frame is that technology does not automatically improve public service delivery or enhance governance.

Needless to say, both neo-institutionalism and social constructivism aid in the context-specific understanding of e-Governance albeit from a different theoretical lens. However, both theories, having their roots in Western/ European history and context bear the risk of misrepresenting a non-Western, postcolonial system of governance. Such Eurocentric grand theories often explain India either as an ever catching up deficient state or as a society of exotic aberrations. Instead of absolutely rejecting these theoretical models, this research strives to minimize this risk by introducing a postcolonial and/or transcultural perspective[5] which strive to counter the hegemonic claims of Eurocentric knowledge system. A transcultural perspective as a transdisciplinary methodology analyses social, political, cultural and historical phenomena as a product of a multidirectional transcultural flow of concepts and categories which acquire different meaning in different local contexts through active agency of the actors (Mitra 2012). In comprehending such entangled trajectories, transcultural perspective presents an analytical and methodological toolbox comprised of concepts such as 'flows', 'asymmetry', 'hybridity' and so on (ibid.). While analysing e-Governance in the postcolonial context of the Indian state and society, hybridity plays the most instrumental part as it brings out the role of agency of multiple actors irrespective of their power position in the most prominent way. Hybridity, though originating in biological sciences, has taken up an important position in cultural studies, humanities and social sciences. Postcolonial studies, particularly the writings of Homi Bhabha have made hybridity a popular concept by perceiving it as a political strategy in the hands of the governed (Bhabha 1994) or simply the 'weapon of the weak'.[6] It is this notion of hybridity which is directly linked to the notion of political agency that strikes a chord with context-specific analysis of governance and also links it to the basic framework of neo-institutional and social constructivist approaches. However, hybridity in this study is meant to serve a broader purpose. Firstly as a political strategy, it shows how in a postcolonial context, the gap between imported institutional set-up and inherited categories of social norms are mended through a continuous yet non-linear process of hybridization and how they culminate into different hybrid institutions and practices in order to achieve a state of equilibrium within the system of governance. Secondly as an analytical category, it explains how the state–society relationships being entangled in multidirectional transcultural flows are manoeuvred by different actors in different contexts. In terms of understanding the impact of e-Governance reform on the level of India's governance, hybridity helps explaining the gaps that we often encounter between the policies at the macro level and their (diverse) implementation at the micro level. In doing so, it effectively points out how both e-Governance policies and practices in India go through the process of hybridization and create hybrid institutions which in turn help the reform initiatives (often promoted by a transnational/transcultural agenda of governance reform) to take root in the Indian context. Hence hybridity aids the analysis of both processes and outcomes of e-Governance reforms in India.

These three analytical perspectives combined together create a compact base for addressing three basic research questions which are closely related to each other: (a) does strategic reform help improving the level of governance; (b) why some reforms initiatives are more effective while others fail; and (c) how the gap between state and society, between policies and practices can be understood not merely in terms of legitimacy deficit but as contributing to the resilience of governance. In order to resolve these questions, e-Governance policies and practices and their impact on India's governance is analysed here. Importantly, it is crucial to mention here that though e-Governance policies form a substantial category in the analysis; this research does not intend to focus exclusively on policy outcomes of e-Governance in India. Instead it strives to analyse e-Governance as a strategic reform sector in its entirety, that is, why and how e-Governance reform came into the policy discourse, how these reform initiatives gradually changed the policy networks, how introduction of e-Governance impacted the governing styles and how practices of e-Governance are slowly taking root into the contextual realities of India. Therefore, this study does not merely evaluate the impact of a particular e-Governance policy, but rather e-Governance serves here as case in point to reflect how certain strategic reform agenda (propagated by transnational and national institutions) take shape in the material and cultural contexts of a society and impacts its overall governance mechanism. For this overarching understanding of e-Governance reform and its impact on governance, it was only importunate to move beyond the policy-outcome approach and to devise a rather complex analytical frame combining different theoretical and methodological perspectives.

In order to evaluate if the strategic e-Governance reform can enhance the level of governance four main theoretically informed conjectures[7] are formulated within the context of ICT policy and e-Governance initiatives in India. They are as follows:

C1: E-Governance reforms that make public service more easily and regularly accessible for citizens will improve the quality of governance

According to this conjecture, accessibility of public services is crucial for improving the system of governance as it makes the system more inclusive and effective. In a densely populated country like India, where accessibility of public services poses serious administrative and infrastructural challenge, ICTs bear the potential of taking these services to the doorsteps of the citizens even in the remotest corner. Availing of public services by more and more citizens renders state institutions and machinery more efficient; it makes the distributive function of the state more adept and thereby ensures enhanced legitimacy of state institutions. All these factors hint towards improved interaction between state and society and hence improved level of governance. To denote that e-Governance reform leads to better accessibility of public services and hence to improved level of governance three indicators are deployed: increased citizen participation, predictability of services and transparency of processes.

C2: E-Governance reform initiatives that aid in improving the coordination between all the stakeholders in turn improve the quality of governance

As described earlier governance as a concept is consisted of both ruler and the ruled which represents different power positions. Being at the core of differential power distribution, it often embodies conflicting interest groups. Given the inherent inequality of the concept, lack of transparency and absence of clear accountability structure might lead to miscommunication and resulting animosity among different stakeholders involved in the complex of governance. As e-Governance reform has the potential to make service delivery process more transparent, the interaction between state, market, civil society and citizens can resultantly become more transparent. Similarly transparency of processes also helps create a clearer structure of accountability among stakeholders through introduction of ICT tools, change-management and BPR. Thus, better transparency and accountability serve as the indicators of improved coordinators among stakeholders which in turn will have a positive impact on the overall system of governance by making it more efficient, effective and inclusive.

C3: E-Governance initiatives that take social and cultural factors embedded in the specific contexts into consideration improve the level of governance

As governance lies at the intersection of state and society, it is not enough to render the public service delivery accessible and efficient through intervention of ICT tools. At the same time it is important for e-Governance reform to take root into societal structure. In other words, such reform initiatives need to take local social and cultural factors into consideration in order to be effective. Without such considerations, even reform initiatives with the best of intentions can fail at the grass roots levels of implementation. Hence, it can be inferred that e-Governance reform that are better adaptable to the local context will ensure greater participation by all stakeholders. These will increase the acceptability and legitimacy of such reform initiatives and consequently the level of governance.

C4: E-Governance reforms that improve the delivery mechanism of public service will improve the level of governance

The first conjecture reflects on how citizens can access public services in a better way. However, public service also requires improvement in delivery model which implies internal improvement within the state machinery. E-Governance reform holds the capacity to revamp the delivery mechanism of the public services through the use of ICT tools and related public administration reform tools such as change-management, BPR, training modules and so on. The impact of such reform on the state machinery that delivers public services can be indicated through higher predictability of services and better accountability within the delivery chain.

It is pertinent to mention that most of the indicators described here are also present in the 'good governance' paradigm as espoused by the World Bank and the United Nations organizations. Nonetheless the difference remains in the approach while collecting and analysing the relevant data. 'Good governance' is a top-down approach that outlines a prescriptive list of indicators as universal normative standards of governance without much regard for context-specificities (except in the rhetoric). Given this universal normative approach to governance, it often labels governing systems of developing nations as inadequate whenever there is a gap between policy prescription and actual practices. This book on the contrary, counters such ideological bias by constructively analysing the context-specific implications of these gaps rather than simply labelling them as legitimacy deficits. Furthermore, the introduction of adaptability as an indicator strengthens the claim of context-specific inquiry of e-Governance. Consequently, unlike the 'good governance' approach, this governance analysis focuses on the legitimacy of the rule by converging the rulers' category with the perceptions of the ruled.

These four main conjectures that drive this research infer that introducing ICTs would lead to better predictability of service delivery, higher transparency in the rules and processes of public administration, greater accountability of the service provider and enhanced reach of public services or inclusion of wider mass into service delivery mechanism. However, they also stress the importance of adapting to embedded social conditions and cultural values in fully realizing the potential of these technologies and the counter-productive forces of technologies. The vital challenge here is to incorporate these social and cultural factors into a comprehensive frame of analysis in a systematic manner.

E-Governance initiatives in India are comprised of both policies and practices. Hence, besides exploring the major policies, a case study of one of the major e-Governance projects in India called the Common Services Centres (CSCs) Scheme was incorporated into the framework of analysis to demonstrate how politics, technology and culture get entangled in the implementation of e-Governance initiatives. An extensive four-state fieldwork was conducted based on qualitative interviews involving all the stakeholders, both at the state level and at the national level. As the CSCs Scheme is formulated as a structured project, the stakeholders were predefined. In addition, a group of experts specializing in e-Governance in different capacities have been interviewed.

Conclusion: structure and scope of the book

There are two major areas of e-Governance which this book studies in order to evaluate the four main conjectures, namely policies and practices of e-Governance in India. The following chapter (Chapter 2) outlines some of the major conceptual categories and methodological design with a note on the methods adopted for this study. One important section of this chapter spells out the methodological challenges associated with the context-specific analysis of governance and also present some of the probable resorts attempted in this study. The next chapter (Chapter 3) engages in describing the state of e-Governance in India through policies and practices. In the first step, the policy documents related to such strategic reform are analysed which include the Information Technology (IT) Act 2000; Amendment to the IT Act 2008; NeGP (2006); 11th Report of the 2nd Administrative Reform Commission (ARC) 2008; selected chapters of the Tenth and Eleventh Five Year Plan (2002–2007 and 2007–2012). A qualitative research method has been adopted to derive at an in-depth understanding of the policy directions and guidelines and their potential impact on the framework of governance stretching across almost a decade. These policy documents are analysed mainly within the theoretical framework of neo-institutional model of governance and help to discern the policy framework for e-Governance reforms in India. The next segment of the chapter elaborates on the practice of e-Governance in India with a particular focus on the NeGP. Chapter 4 puts the experiences of e-Governance within the Indian context by presenting the case study of the CSCs Scheme. The field narratives of the case study are elaborated here as regional experiences of the four sample states which are generated out of the same pan-national initiative. At the end, these narratives are compared and interwoven into a cohesive account of India's experiences of e-Governance reform. The objective of this chapter is to demonstrate how regional contexts play a catalytic role in coping with e-Governance reforms which in turn facilitate a context-specific understanding of e-Governance.

Following the lead from the regional comparisons, Chapter 5 evaluates the ways in which e-Governance reforms influence the existing system of governance, i.e., to what extent the initial conjectures about the relationship between e-Governance reform and overall governance can be supported by the policies and practices elaborated in the previous chapters. As such, reform processes are often fraught with contradicting realities; the analytical narratives take up the conceptual tool of hybridity to explain the myriad levels of negotiations and subversions that undergo the entire trajectory of e-Governance reforms in India. The aim of this chapter is to establish how e-Governance reforms are deployed as a techno-managerial fix to manipulate the legitimacy deficit in a postcolonial system of governance and how they could gradually transform that very system of governance in a steady yet non-linear fashion. The concluding chapter also explains how e-Governance research can enrich governance research and how the Indian context holds wider implications for overall understanding of governance issues, governance in terms of its interface with technology, with politics of reform or with culture.

Governance being the interface of state and society can be analysed from different academic approaches and from different perspectives even within the same disciplinarian boundary. For example, social anthropology and political science would approach the problematic of governance quite differently. Similarly within the purview of political science, public policy and international relations theorists would focus on different aspects of governance. Though this study of governance often transcends these scholastic boundaries, nonetheless it strives to combine the public policy approach with comparative politics approach within the broader framework of political sociology. This implies that it examines how particular public policy reforms harness the state–society relationship in an effective manner. In doing so, we start at the level of policy formulations and then unravel how they take the form of concrete schemes and finally the processes and outcomes of their implementation at the micro level. Such multi-faceted focus renders the analysis of governance both state-centric and society-centric as it not only explores how political elites initiate policies, but also how bureaucrats implement these policies (sometimes with the help of private actors) and how finally these policies are received by the citizens. All these processes take place in a particular political, social and cultural context which shapes the behaviour of all the actors and ultimately their interactions with each other. The interlocking of these political, social and cultural factors makes the reform process a complex, yet crucial, node in the analytical puzzle of governance.

Following the economic liberalization in India in 1991, there were several major policy reforms which went much beyond the economic sphere. One such reform was in the field of ICTs and its subsequent impact on the public service delivery model and the system of governance, in other words e-Governance reform. Given its significant impact on governance e-Governance reform has been critically scrutinized starting from e-Governance policy formulation, implementation and its reception by the stakeholders. Hence both governance and e-Governance are treated as conceptual variables where the latter's impact on the former are considered to be of considerable significance. Having clearly set the scope of this study, it would be only imminent to draw the circumference of the enquiry as well.

Governance as a conceptual variable lies at the crossroad of politics, culture, economy and society. Consequently, there are myriad categories that can contribute to the quality of the governance. In other words, indicators of 'good' or 'bad governance' can range from law and order management to the state of justice, from public service delivery mechanism to social discrimination, from developmental schemes to economic inequality and so on. This research by no means claims to present an exhaustive account of all the factors which either enhance or reduce the quality of governance. Instead it confines its attention to one particular strategic reform which is considered to have a positive impact on the level of governance. Even while examining the effects of e-Governance, this study does not claim to explore all the dimensions of such reforms. For example, one of the most desirable and projected outcomes of using ICTs in public service delivery is reduced corruption. Though some evidences in the same direction could be drawn from the field experiences, this book does not involve in a deeper understanding of the same. The reason behind this exclusion is not to undermine corruption as a significant indicator of governance. The answer lies within the research design. Drawing any significant generalizations on the relationship between e-Governance reforms and corruption demands an impact assessment study over a longer period of time which could assess the status before and after reforms interventions. This is clearly beyond the scope of this research. The other limiting element of this research is its heavy reliance on qualitative data. Though treating governance as a conceptual variable, the analytical frame deployed here is based on purely qualitative data. Therefore, while evaluating the quality of governance in terms of the outreach and effectiveness of the strategic reform, an attempt has been made to look for gaps in the policy documents and its subsequent implementations. However, all the gaps are not interpreted automatically as a failure of the policies but weighed carefully to see how sometimes these gaps in fact help a policy to be absorbed in the local context. In other words, instead of finding simple explanations for policy effectiveness or policy failure, the focus is more on the conflicting zones of policy processes instigated by a certain reform agenda and the way apparent policy deficits can be actually turned into policy resolve. The final point of contestation is the India-centric analysis of governance. Rather than denying the specificities of the Indian context the study attempts to counter this bias in three ways: firstly, by adding the four federal states as additional layers of regional complexities which make the Indian case study more dynamic; secondly, by presenting India as only a case in point (not the case) to showcase a context-specific understanding of governance; and thirdly, India represents a case of many other postcolonial and post-communist societies, where the domestic as well as international impetus to governance reform played a crucial role in influencing the context of governance.

E-Governance and its impact on overall quality of governance is an emerging field of study within academia. Hence, despite its limited scope this study intends to make an important and original contribution to the existing body of research on e-Governance and governance in general. In addition, by connecting the Indian case study to the general theories of governance this piece of work attempts to demonstrate how area studies can contribute to the process of theory-building.

2 Methodology

Introduction: a conceptual dilemma of governance and 'good governance'

E-Governance reform initiatives in India are set in the wider backdrop of 'good governance' or governance reform agenda. We already took a look at what implications the 'good governance' agenda has had on the discourse of governance in recent times. However, before developing a methodological design for examining e-Governance reforms in India, understanding the conceptual overlapping between e-Governance, governance reforms and the 'good governance' paradigm becomes extremely crucial. Good governance as a paradigm rose in prominence in the last two decades since the end of the Cold War. It is formulated as a developmental jargon tailored in accordance with neo-liberal economic policies by International Organizations such as the World Bank, UNDP and so on to promote wide-ranging programmes of governance reform across all developing nations. The World Bank recommends governance reform involving three major areas namely:

> i) the form of political regime; ii) the process by which authority is exercised in the management of a country's economic and social resources for development; and iii) the capacity of government to design, formulate and implement policies and discharge functions.
>
> (Bandyopadhyay 1996)

Four key dimensions of this reform are as follows: public sector management (capacity and efficiency) which involves civil service reform and privatization initiatives; accountability which would enable institutions to hold the government accountable, for example an ombudsman; the legal framework for development which implies making and enforcing rules to control the market, for example enforcing private property rights; and information and transparency which hints towards free media, publicizing public expenditure, for example the right to information (Jayal and Pai 2001; Kjaer 2004). UNESCAP sets out eight major characteristics. It is participatory, consensus oriented, accountable, transparent, responsive, effective and efficient, equitable and inclusive, and follows the rule of law. 'Good governance', which is also interchangeably used with 'democratic governance', 'governance for sustainable development', 'human governance' and so on has been developed as one of the major criteria for aid conditionality and also a significant field of development intervention.

A few characteristic features of 'good governance' paradigm which have serious implications for the current debate on governance can be outlined here. Firstly, this paradigm is a customized recipe to tackle the problems of governability in postcolonial and post-communist nation-states. Secondly, given its target recipients, 'good governance' comes in a full package of democracy promotion and market-led economic growth and development. Thirdly, while criticizing the regulatory role of the state it nevertheless recognizes the role of the state in providing a stable institutional arrangements and rule of law in changing societies. Fourthly, it conceives of governance as a matrix of interdependent stakeholders such as state/public sector, market, civil society and citizens where the state will function as one of the service providers. Fifthly, it espouses a market concept of equality and empowerment which views citizens more as customers or clients and enables them to enter market transactions in a more non-restricted environment. Lastly, it stresses the importance of public private partnership in improving service delivery to the citizens. Evaluated on the basis of these tenets, 'good governance' presents a mix of moral and technical fix for shifting the state-centric governance agenda to a multi-centred governance reform agenda where politics takes a back seat.

It is in this shifting discourse of governance that e-Governance reforms needs to be analysed as they determine the policies, parameters, actors of such emerging patterns of reforms in governance. As e-Governance reforms are primarily driven towards achieving principles of 'good governance', even the criteria for their evaluation are more often than not influenced by the same paradigm. Hence the notions of e-Governance and 'good governance' has grown so intertwined, it becomes almost impossible to talk about one without the other. However, this conceptual proximity poses serious methodological dilemma given the inherent ideological bias innate to the concept of 'good governance'. Moreover, its one-size-fits-all modernizing approach renders it unachievable in most of the societies it is originally aimed at and puts a question mark on the legitimacy of the paradigm itself. Nonetheless, despite these critical aspects in mind, the influence of 'good governance' agenda as endorsed by international donor agencies on e-Governance reform measures and in turn on the existing systems and practices of governance in developing societies cannot be completely overlooked. Therefore, the methodological design of understanding e-Governance reforms in India needs to confer the inevitable presence of the 'good governance' paradigm albeit the value-loaded nature of the concept and take sufficient measures to critically examine its implications rather than giving it a blind eye. For instance, one of the interesting aspects of such governance reform agenda is that, despite promoting private sector growth, it once again brings the focus back on the state institutions and their importance as a steering authority and paves the way for a neo-institutional model of analysing governance. Thus, as we move forward to establishing the links between governance reform, politics, technology and culture, the theories that dominate the analytical framework need to be etched out in some details.

Theorizing e-Governance reform in India: an inter-disciplinary approach

Does strategic reform improve governance?: a neo-institutional model of governance

Institutionalism focused on formal rules, procedures, organizational set-up including constitutions, electoral system and political parties, and also on the behaviours of the actors within these institutions. Institutionalism dominated the field of politics and public administration up until 1940s before it was heavily criticized for its reliance on specific institutional settings by some universal theories such as the behaviouralist school, rational choice theorists and so on. Neo-institutionalism emerged as a response to these criticisms and in addition to its earlier preoccupation with formal rules, procedures and organizations it broadened its concept of institutions by including norms, habits and cultural customs. There are many varieties of neo-institutionalism such as rational choice institutionalism, historical institutionalism, sociological institutionalism and many more. Rational choice institutionalists study how institutions shape the behaviour of the rational actors whereas the historical institutionalists explore how past institutional arrangements influence subsequent political processes which can also be referred to as 'path dependency'. Sociological institutionalism on the other hand, looks at how informal ideas, values and norms shape policy frameworks and in turn the political process (Bevir 2009). Notwithstanding their many differences, neo-institutionalism as a whole identifies two basic factors in human behaviour which are either exogenous (as in rational choice school) or endogenous (as in sociological school). March and Olsen (1989) describe them as 'logic of consequentiality' and 'logic of appropriateness' though they reiterate the fact that in most cases it is the latter that guides human behaviour (Kjaer 2004). Instead of posing these two categories as binary oppositions, it would probably be more discreet to see human behaviour as both rational and normative at the same time while keeping in mind the Weberian concept of 'value rationality'.[1]

In governance research neo-institutionalism becomes extremely crucial as governance is comprised of formal rules, procedures and organizations of state institutions vis-à-vis informal norms, values and customs of the society locked in a complex and dynamic relationship with each other. There are two most important areas of investigation within institutionalism; firstly, the impact of institutions on political behaviour and second the origin and transformation of institutions (Kjaer 2004). Governance covers both these areas of study as it starts from the setting of the rules (origin of institutions) and follows it though the application and enforcement of these rules which affect political behaviour and political process and finally how institutions themselves evolve in the process.

Neo-institutionalism as a theoretical paradigm becomes even more imperative in the contexts of governing developing countries in the non-Western world.

As Mitra (2006) explains, 'crucial to the neo-institutional model is the "room to manoeuvre" that the constitution permits the political elite (a democratic regime, as opposed to military rule, offers more scope for negotiation and bargaining) and the political accountability of the elites, which makes it necessary for them to engage in purposeful social intervention' (Mitra 2006, p. 16). On the basis of this perspective he develops a neo-institutional model of governance to explain how institutional change can indeed add to the stability and resilience of the system of governance in a changing society where there is a considerable hiatus between the imported categories of state institutions and the inherited values of the culture. In addition to elucidating the inevitable and positive link between institutional change and buoyancy of a governance system, this model also points out the importance of policy responsiveness, reform programmes in bridging the gap between the macro and micro level, between national and local contexts, between imported and inherited categories, between rational and sociological and most importantly between governed and those who govern. Hence, this model serves as the underlying analytical axis while issues of e-Governance reform are selected for evaluating governance in India.

Does technology improve governance?: a social constructivist approach

Social constructivism bears a strong resemblance with sociological institutionalism as discussed above. Social construction denaturalizes what is taken for granted, questions the origin of what is now seen as a fact of life and considers the alternative ways that could have produced a different condition. Therefore, at the core of social constructivism lie the socially constructed nature of actors and their identities and interests. Instead of assuming that actors are born outside and prior to society, as individualism does, constructivists claim that individuals are produced by their social and cultural environment; and historically produced and culturally bound knowledge comprised of symbols, rules, concepts, categories and meanings shapes how individual actors in the social setting would construct and interpret their world. While perceiving ideas as structurally rooted, constructivism views actors' interpretation of the material reality directly impacting the dynamic relationship between ideas and material forces. There are a few basic tenets of this paradigm. Firstly, it takes the concept of power beyond material facades and explores an ideational notion of power, which allocates differential rewards and capacities through knowledge, fixing of meaning and construction of identities. Secondly, the meanings that are constructed and shaped by the underlying cultures are the central features of politics as they determine the actions and interests of the actors. Thirdly, it places a great importance on institutions albeit as embodied in norm, practices and formal organizational structures (Barnett 2005).[2] Social constructivists view actors as bound through a web of meanings which are inscribed in beliefs, signs, languages, conscious and intuitive knowledge within a cultural context. This web of meanings forms the core of politics and hence the core of governance. There are two ways of analysing these meanings that constructivists engage themselves in. On one hand, there is synchronic analysis of meanings abstracted from the realm of history. On the other hand, the diachronic studies explore the development of meanings over time. This latter analytical model explicates how agents could alter and structurally shift the web of meanings while deploying them in a particular context. According to social constructivist paradigm, both institutions and actors are embedded in the conditional system of meanings. Hence governance being an interface between the two also need be understood how these meanings are constructed, deployed and transformed. Therefore, it can be said that constructivists take a keen interest in demonstrating how agents produce structures and vice versa.

As this research not only focuses on the system of governance but also how this system is shifting through the use of ICT tools, social constructivism as a theoretical framework becomes even more relevant. It presents a view of technology which runs against technological determinism. Technological determinism not only conceives of technology to be autonomous and neutral but also presupposes its quintessential role in economic and social development (Bijker 2009). Taking a critical stand against this essentialist conception of technology, social constructivists tend to explore how actors and contexts influence technology. They further disaggregate the perception of technology from different subject positions of the actors involved. For example, in disbursing e-Governance projects, decision-making elites rationalize to build an efficient system. However, citizens, who are at receiving end of these projects experience and appropriate these technologies varies according to their life world. Hence, the value of information generated by such new information communication technology does not automatically follow from their inherent virtue but is contingent upon the context of their application and the web of meanings that they construe (Sreekumar 2008).

Social construction of technology is a distinct field of study which emerged from three different areas of research, namely, the science-technology-society (STS) movement, the sociology of scientific knowledge and the history of technology (Bijker 2009). Without going further into the history and development of social construction of technology, it is important here to establish the crucial links between this theoretical framework and this study which touches upon a cross-cutting theme of technology and governance. Firstly, social construction of technology point out the social and political intervention in the course of technology. Secondly, it raises a few concepts such as 'interpretive flexibility' and 'relevant social groups' which could shape the analytical frame for understanding the linkages between technology and governance. Interpretive flexibility stresses the fact that technology is socially and culturally constructed which makes it open to different interpretation and meaning. The act of interpreting technology within a specific context hinges upon the subject positions of the actors, such as users or producers of technology (ibid.). It is important to mention here that this study should not be viewed as an analysis of e-Governance founded within the frame of social construction of technology albeit a few heuristic tools have been adopted to understand the constructivist nature of technology. Since both technical subjects and objects are organized in terms of socially and culturally contingent variables, technologies (both in its design and social incorporation) cannot be fully comprehended without scrutinizing its context (Feenberg 1999).

How to tackle legitimacy deficit in a postcolonial context while deploying ICTs for governance reform: hybridity and a transcultural perspective on politics

The problem of balancing the state–society continuum in governance analysis can be accomplished through a skilful combination of a neo-institutional and social constructivist approaches. Social constructivist model of governance aids in analysing how institutional change occurs through political behaviours of actors ensconced in particular cultural and social contexts. In other words, it explains how society affects state and its institutions. The neo-institutional model on the other hand helps explain how elites work as brokers between state and society and how they devise strategies (either of sanction or welfare) to accommodate embedded values in imported institutions. An elite strategy in developing societies recognizes this asymmetrical relationship between the state and society and strives to leverage through institutional innovation, in public administration, in legal framework, in social policies. There are many such examples in India which ranges from the provision of personal laws for different religious groups to the provision of constitutional amendment, from introducing *panchayati raj* as a method of decentralization to positive discrimination or reservation policies for socially marginalized groups. These institutional reforms emerge out of the contextual realties of a society where culture, history and politics are all entangled in the same whole. Moreover, these new institutional set-ups often take quite a leap from their imported counterparts. In simple terms, the above-mentioned institutional innovations are meant to promote democratic consolidation in India, yet they are produced keeping the Indian context in mind.

However, most of the analysis of governance in developing societies irrespective of their approach tends to explain shifts and variations in the institutional set-up in terms of grand theories of politics which have their historical roots in the Western European contexts. This often leads to misrepresentation of other societies either in terms of a deficiency syndrome with a perpetual imperative to catch up or as an exotic deviant. An evident case of the former perspective is reflected in the 'good governance' paradigm which not only sets out universal standards of governance across societies but furthermore, by adding the prefix 'good' labels all other forms of governance inadequate. In the latter perspective, the stability (or the absence of it) of a system of governance is explained in terms of the innate cultural qualities (or lack of it) of a particular society. To avoid such epistemological shortcomings, a combination of neo-institutional and social constructivism is deployed in this research. However, as both of these school of thought also cater to some grand narratives of theory-building, a distinct methodological perspective is required which would address the epistemic ruptures in classical theoretical framework and approach the same realities in a different way.

An emerging perspective of transculturality aims to fulfil this search for a noble methodological approach. Even though it can be deployed across all societies, transcultural methodology becomes even more relevant while studying non-Western societies.

Being an emerging perspective, the scope and limits of transculturality is still evolving and hence makes it difficult to delineate its salient features in an exhaustive fashion. Transculturality 'help(s) us look at our material differently than before, it may be useful to develop new research questions and perspectives, even finding new, hitherto neglected material (because some of it used to be considered "just an Asian copy" of a "European original", for example). This approach may also open the possibility for letting the hitherto silent speak and hitherto unheard voices be heard' (Cluster of Excellence: Asia Europe in a Global Context 2012).[3] Thus, instead of arriving at an all-encompassing definition of transculturality, it would be more prudent to explore how transcultural methodology can enrich analysis of governance.

The underlying assumptions of transculturality are that 'even the seemingly most local phenomena are part of transcultural flows of concept and things. Cultures are not "social groups or geographies, but social imaginaries that express or create distinction and asymmetrical flows" and "rather than passive consumer of alien concepts, local societies imbue them with meaning in the process of using them" ' (Mitra 2012, p. 111). Following these basic postulations transcultural methodology presents a distinct analytical toolbox consisting of 'flow', 'asymmetry', 'hybridity' which transcends disciplinary boundaries both in terms of its origin as well as applicability. All these concepts are deployed as heuristic devices to add explanatory value to the existing framework of analysing social, cultural, political and historical phenomena. In case of political analysis of governance in postcolonial India, hybridity appears to be one of the most relevant analytical categories.

As transcultural methodology postulates that there are continuous multidirectional cultural flows and that alien concepts acquire new meaning in the local context, it questions the possibility of authenticity in any ideas, institutions and practices. This is where the notion of hybridity becomes pertinent that can be viewed as 'the natural consequence of the real world process of institution making, and the adaptation of alien institutions into the native medium' (ibid., p. 112). Hence, hybridity not only underlines the agency of the local context but also becomes an analytical category to explain the complexity of governance in India rather than its deficiency or uniqueness.

Hybridity became a popular concept in Postcolonial studies especially in the writings of Homi Bhabha since the 1980s. The term originates in biological sciences to describe mixing of species. But while making an inroad into cultural studies and humanities and social sciences it conjures up a different connotation. Hybridity, in these disciplines implies a 'third space' (Bhabha 1994) which is emblematic of an entanglement that defies the notion of authenticity. While keeping some elements of the original duality, it nonetheless represents a new entity (ibid.; Mitra 2012; Prabhu 2007). In the context of Postcolonial studies, hybridity is viewed as a political strategy in the hands of the governed to exert their agency (Bhabha 1994). It is this particular conceptualization of hybridity that renders it an important explanatory tool to analyse governance in India. As depicted in the dynamic neo-institutional model of governance (Mitra 2006, p. 16), elites in postcolonial India need to devise noble strategies (through manipulating policy, initiating reform and constitutional amendment and so on) to mend the legitimacy deficit generated between alien institutions and local contexts. As Mitra (2012) argues, hybrid institutions emerge out of a larger political project where elites and counter-elites bargain and manoeuvre strategies to achieve a political goal or to seek legitimacy of rule. Moreover, he does not confine hybridity only to a postcolonial context; rather arrest the concept in colonial rule, in anti-colonial movement, in democratic transition, in postcolonial nation-building and governance. This application of hybridity as a political strategy is entirely different from the use of the same notion in comparative politics where it is often used to differentiate between authoritarian regimes from the liberal democracies.

Hybridity both as a political strategy and as analytical category assists in the understanding of e-Governance as a strategic reform and its implications for overall governance in India in some specific ways:

- To understand the application of e-Governance as a political strategy of reform initiated by the policy-making elites in India. Here hybridity takes us beyond the conventional framework of neo-institutional model of governance.
- To understand the political agency of the different actors through tracing the process of hybridization of e-Governance institutions and practices at the local contexts. Here hybridization enriches the explanatory framework that unravels the process of social construction of technological development.
- To understand the complex nature of the institutions and their implications for the system of governance in India.
- To add explanatory rigor to the structure-agency dynamics within the matrix of governance.

In elucidating these particular aspects of governance as political problematic, there are two aspects of the notion of hybridity that need to be understood, firstly, hybridization as a process and secondly, hybrid institutions and practices as a product of that process. However, at the same time one needs to keep in mind that this is a continuous yet non-linear and discursive process of transforming governance. For example, before consolidation of the colonial state of British India, the East India Company as a private corporation served many state functions such as revenue collections, state-wide accountancy, production of statistical records, etc., which were later transferred to the colonial state authority (Kaviraj 2010, p. 143). A similar trend could be found in the recent concept of 'franchising the state' to private corporations and non-governmental organizations, which has risen as one of the alternative models of governance in the recent political discourse of post-liberalized India (Jayal and Pai 2001, p. 143). One could find more such instances. Keeping these past references in mind, e-Governance policy networks involving different stakeholders can be seen as a continuous yet non-linear process of hybridization to adapt colonial administrative structure better in the postcolonial local contexts in India. In another example, the concept of 'political society' as espoused by Partha Chatterjee (2004) can well represent a hybrid institution which is equivalent to the notion of civil society, yet somewhat different due to its different historical and political trajectories embedded in the contexts of a postcolonial society. In the case of e-Governance initiatives in India, rural internet kiosks or tele-centres operated by local operators can be projected as hybrid institution geared to mend the digital divide as well as literacy gaps inherent in the local context. There are many such examples that can be cited here. Thus, by adopting a transcultural methodology to critically scrutinize the impact of e-Governance reform on the level of governance, this book seeks to acquire an analytical edge that can establish novel ways of understanding the resilience of democratic governance in India.

Evaluating e-Governance reform in India: the framework of analysis

Actors/stakeholders

It is clear by now that governance as a concept does evoke neither a distinct definition nor a single frame of analysis. Therefore, any comprehensive research on governance needs to clearly delineate its conceptual and theoretical/analytical frame of reference at the very onset. This study focuses on governance in relation to institutional arrangements and political processes of formulating and implementing policy reforms involving a diverse set of actors. Needless to say, although the state still lies at the centre of policy-making and policy reform, a host of non-state actors are linked through formal and informal institutional networks. These networks of national and domestic actors together lay the foundation of the system of governance. This network of actors has been captured quite effectively by Ahrens and Mengeringhaus (2006) in Figure 2.1.

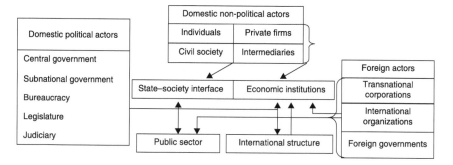

Figure 2.1 A stylized model of governance: realms and actors
Source: Ahrens and Mengeringhaus 2006, p. 78

Methodology 37

This model of governance maps all the actors and demonstrates how policy goals are devised and achieved through coordination among these actors. One of the most important aspects of this model of governance is that it emphasizes the role of public policy in economic performance and development. The aim of this investigation, however, is limited to introspect how public policy formulation and implementation, particularly in terms of reform strategies, bring structural changes in the system of governance. E-Governance initiatives or in other words reform programmes facilitated through information communication technology serve as a focal point for analysing the same. While the ultimate aim of analysing governance differs, the above model nevertheless, quite aptly places the actors in the matrix of governance. Hence, by simply replacing 'economic institutions' with 'e-Governance institutions', the same model could be deployed within the purview of the current study. There are two aspects of policy reform and e-Governance initiatives which can be traced through this network of actors. Firstly, the foreign actors depicted on the right-hand side of the figure represent the wider international policy environment and explain the origin of certain policy agendas and reform strategies. For example, the emergence of e-Governance as one of the reform areas in India emanates from recent insurgence of 'good governance' agenda across developing nations under the influence of International Organizations such as the World Bank. Secondly, domestic political and non-political actors described in this figure narrate how certain policy reforms are rolled out in a particular context. For example, the formulation and implementation of the NeGP in India is based on a public–private partnership model and evidently involved state, private firms, civil society and citizens.

Moving to the issue of governance reform and its impact on the overall system of governance a neo-institutional model of governance developed by Mitra (2006) needs to be discussed here in further details. This neo-institutional model relates governance as a variable concept which depends on political institutions, state–society interface, role of elites and some other variables (as described in Figure 2.2).

There are a few overlapping aspects of this model which become crucial in conducting research on governance particularly in the context of developing

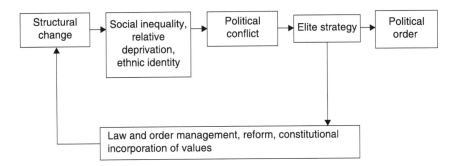

Figure 2.2 A dynamic neo-institutional model of governance based on elite strategies
Source: Mitra 2006, p. 16

countries. Firstly, the key to governance, according to this model, is the 'room to manoeuvre' (Mitra 1991) that the institutional arrangements provide the political elites with. In a democratic set-up this provision for institutional change resolves both the issues of accountability and legitimacy. It explains how political elites being accountable to their local and regional context initiate reform and hence in turn enhance legitimacy leading to the resilience of the system. Secondly, this model suggests an exceedingly significant role of the political elites in the system of governance. As Mitra argues, '[T]he response of the decision-making elites to crises through law and order management, strategic reform and redistributive policy and constitutional change in order to give legitimacy to contested, embedded values, acts as a feedback loop that affects the perceptions of crucial variables ... by people at the local and regional level' (Mitra 2006, p. 16). The political elites act as nodal points of political actions connecting national to the regional and local institutions. Thirdly, this model brings out the relevance of policy responsiveness and reform strategies in bridging 'the hiatus between the locally embedded values and those espoused by the macro-arena' (ibid., p. 16).

However, the question remains why certain policy reform is favoured over the others. At this point, both the above models need to be looked at in conjunction with each other. In Figure 2.1, a policy network of domestic and international, political and non-political actors are hold responsible for policy reform. Whereas in Figure 2.2, domestic political institutions, state–society interface and political elites, are described as harbingers of policy reform and institutional change. Combining these two models it can be said that policy reforms are simultaneously influenced by the international political trends and domestic political realities. The domestic politics gets further complicated by continuous political exchange between national, regional and local political elites and non-political actors. Therefore, any process of policy formulation and implementation needs to navigate through these complex nodes of a governance system. Again while reiterating the role of elite strategy in policy responsiveness, Mitra (2006) pertinently points out, 'In a case of successful transaction, competing elites choose their options in a manner that maximizes benefits and minimizes transaction costs, and negotiate on the basis of a complex repertoire that combines instruments of rational protests with elements of participation such as contacts with high-level decision-makers, lobbying, voting and sending petitions' (ibid., p. 16).

While choosing e-Governance reform in India as the specific research focus, the broader parameters and operational concept need to be adapted to the context of ICT policies and practices and India's governance. One such concept is of policy networks. As we discussed in the previous chapter, governance in recent times does not confine itself to the sphere of government. It involves multiple actors and how these actors together influence the policy regime. The actors and their relationships in such policy networks, of course, varies from sector to sector. For this purpose, before proceeding with the policies and practices of e-Governance in India, it is essential to take a close look at the policy network of e-Governance initiatives in India to better understand how e-Governance reforms are formulated, implemented and appropriated. Across all the policy documents and literature on e-Governance in India five major actors can be identified. They are as follows: (i) state/public sector, (ii) market/private sector (both domestic and foreign), (iii) civil society, (iv) citizens and (v) International Organizations. All these actors together form the policy network for e-Governance reforms in India; albeit the state still remains at the centre of such network as the main steering authority, coordinating body and as the facilitator.

Since this study approaches governance from a public policy perspective, it thereby focuses on governance as an interactive process between different actors. The basic assumption behind such an approach is that no single actor has either the capacity or the resources to resolve policy implementation. Yet this interactive process depends on the forms of partnership it adopts (Mitra 2006). For example, there are three basic forms of partnership: principal–agent, inter-organizational negotiation and systemic coordination (ibid., p. 26). In the principal–agent model one actor (principal) hires or contracts the other actor (agent) to deliver a particular task. In the second model different organizations undertake a joint project by coalescing their capacities and resources through negotiation. The systemic coordination is one step ahead of the first two as it involves a self-governing network where a mutual understanding and shared vision acts as the driving force of the partnership. These different models of partnerships also significantly influence the process of governing. Hence, while mapping the actors and their relationship within the policy network of e-Governance in India, it is also pertinent to shed some light on the notion of public–private partnership. This is a model of cooperation between public sector institutions with private organizations in implementing policy goals and is popularly known as the Public–Private Partnership (PPP) model. The PPP model as it is practiced in India within the confines of e-Governance follows more or less the first form of partnership, i.e. principal–agent relationship.

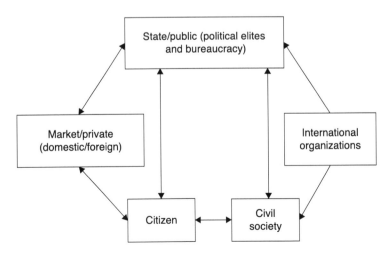

Figure 2.3 Policy network of e-Governance in India
Source: Author

Methodology

Usually a state department or a public sector institution either at the national or regional level hires or outsources a particular task (often service delivery) to a private firm on the basis of a formal contract. Though there are other actors and other variety of relationships within the policy network, the PPP model dominates the majority of e-Governance literature and practices.

The actors and the policy networks that they develop guide the process of policy formulation and its subsequent implementation in terms of e-Governance reform in India. However, evaluating the actual impact of such reforms becomes a daunting task given the complex relationship between politics, technology and culture and also the dynamics of regional contexts within India. Firstly, it becomes difficult to directly associate a policy change with institutional change as politics, technology and culture renders the process of change complex and sometimes contradictory. Moreover, the Indian context adds to the complexities with its regional and local variation and presents an ever more interesting case for analysis. Taking these challenges into account, a framework of qualitative analysis is developed in the following section.

Indicators

In order to evaluate how e-Governance policies and practices are influencing the governing system in India ranging from the macro level of state to the micro levels of the society, a case study of the CSCs Scheme (which is one of the pivotal National e-Governance projects in India) has been adopted. Four general conjectures about e-Governance reform interventions (as mentioned in the Introduction) is evaluated in terms of the indicators which link them to a certain quality of

Table 2.1 Defining indicators of improved quality of governance

Indicators: Increased citizen **Participation** (C1, C3), Increased **Predictability** in Service Delivery (C1, C4), Increased **Transparency** in the system (C1, C2), Increased **Accountability** in the system (C2, C4), **Adaptability** to suit local contexts (C3)

Attributes

Participation: Numbers of footfall per CSC, preference of CSC over other delivery outlets, integration of VLEs as rural entrepreneurs	**Predictability**: Speed of delivery of services, compliance to committed time frame, standardization of the quality of services
Accountability: Availability of public grievance redressal mechanism, the quality of public–private partnership, attitudes of public servants, eliminations of intermediaries, responsible engagement of VLES	**Transparency**: Availability of information of services, options for accessing information, quality of information, simplification of procedures
Adaptability: use of local languages, catering to specific social groups, integrating social and community goals, use of innovation by stakeholders	

Source: Author

governance, namely accountability, adaptability, participation, predictability and transparency. Each of these indicators is further defined according to certain attributes (see Table 2.1). The careful combination of these indicators with the four basic conjectures would formulate the main analytical grid for evaluating governance within the framework of this research.

Methods: case study of the CSCs Scheme under NeGP

A case study method is particularly appropriate when one needs to focus more on the processes rather than the outcome. In this book we are concerned more with the processes of e-Governance implementation and not whether an e-Governance initiative is a failure or a success. The purpose of this case study is to capture the practices of e-Governance in India with a pervasive approach and intricate details so that it can lead to better understanding of its implications for India's governing system in general. Under NeGP, there were many e-Governance projects which could have been adopted for a case study. Any of the MMPs involving considerable citizen interface could have served the purpose of this research. Notwithstanding this understanding, however, the CSCs Scheme was deliberately selected for the case study. The motivation for this selection was influenced by a few cogent factors. Firstly, being the most important front-end physical delivery point for NeGP, the CSCs not only serve as one of the most pervasive Integrated MMPs but also build the common support infrastructure for e-Governance along with the State-Wide Area Networks (SWANs) and the State Data Centres (SDCs) under the NeGP. Secondly, the CSCs are not only extensive in terms of its geographic spread but also intensive in terms of its penetrative potential down to the villages of India. Thirdly, the scheme has become a flagship project of the NeGP as it is designed with a bottom-up approach to provide services to citizens within proximity of their households which is the main vision enshrined in the Plan. Fourthly, the project is conceived as a potential agent of social change where the spillover effects of ICTs could be manifested in active community participation in the process of governance. Fifthly, a PPP model, combination of rural entrepreneurship with market mechanisms and the physical and technology infrastructure are considered to be the three most important catalysts of change under the CSCs Scheme. Sixthly, as CSCs have been actively engaged in absorbing other similar initiatives already operating in some states and in collaborating with other MMPs, it also reflects the state of e-Governance across states in general. Finally, this scheme conjures up all the crucial characteristics of e-Governance reforms in India in terms of actors, parameters, contextual complexities, challenges and so on (as discussed in previous sections) and hence presents a complex yet inclusive case of e-Governance initiatives in India. Hence, CSCs presents a holistic view of the e-Governance initiatives involving all the possible nodes of reform. Keeping these factors in mind, therefore, CSCs serves a perfect case for assessing the wider impact of e-Governance reforms beyond mere technological upgradation.

Four sample states, namely, Andhra Pradesh, Gujarat, Rajasthan and West Bengal were selected keeping in mind their different roll-out status as well as their geographical attributes. For each state a minimum of two CSCs were visited while the selection criteria was based on the days of operations. The basic idea was to reach out to CSCs which are considered to be operating quite effectively. However, depending on time and other opportunities, some CSCs were visited without any prior selection or plan. Hence the number of CSCs visited varied from one state to the other. For example, while only three CSCs per state were visited in Rajasthan and Gujarat, in West Bengal and Andhra Pradesh a total of eight and five CSCs were visited respectively. The four states were chosen as they all represent certain unique aspect as far as general governance situation and e-Governance status is concerned. Rajasthan is a fairly underdeveloped state which is known for its strong traditional roots. The general perception of governance situation is not very high. In terms of e-Governance, Rajasthan had recently tested success with its *e-Mitra* project in urban centres for public service delivery. As far as the CSCs Scheme was concerned, the Rajasthan government tried to extend their urban success story into the rural areas. However, the problems they faced were manifold. Though a lot of enthusiasm was surrounding the project, the rate of roll-out was fairly low. Gujarat is one of the most successful states in India both in terms of economic as well as e-Governance reform with a relatively high level of growth rate. Despite its success story, the state often finds itself embroiled into controversy because of its government led by democratically elected Hindu nationalist party *Bharatiya Janata* Party (BJP) and its charismatic chief minister, Narendra Modi. Even though the Modi government has been able to attract both domestic and foreign private investment into the state, this highly developed image of Gujarat is often marred by his allegedly authoritarian style of leadership and also by the poor track record of the state in human development index especially in the case of minorities and women. However, if we strictly keep our focus on public service delivery through e-Governance initiatives, Gujarat is one of the few states in India where CSCs roll-out status has been a hundred per cent. West Bengal lies on the other spectrum in terms of governance as it was governed by the democratically elected Left Front for the longest time in history (34 years). It represents a unique form of democracy where the state machinery is often allegedly controlled by a highly organized party bureaucracy. However, during the field trip the political environment was quite volatile as the state assembly election was impending in two months and there was a general trend of anti-incumbency. This resulted in much political violence along with increasing Maoist influence in some districts of the state. Within months after the fieldwork the Left Front lost in the elections and was replaced by a regional party *Trinamool* Congress (in alliance with Congress). Status of e-Governance in the state can be said to have medium success with a slow pace of progress for CSCs. Andhra Pradesh is the pioneering state of India as far as e-Governance is concerned. The IT sector has been the major growth engine for the state's economy. However, since the defeat of ex-Chief Minister Chandra Babu Naidu, e-Governance reform had taken a back seat as being politically unpopular. Though most of the state departments were fairly advanced in rolling out public services through e-channels, CSCs were caught in the middle of myriad political and administrative bottlenecks. Beside these unique trajectories, all the four states represent the wider geographical expanse of India and at the time of the fieldwork they represented different stages of implementation for CSCs. These variations further strengthen the context-specific understanding of e-Governance reform processes.

Methods of data collection and analysis[4]

The methods of data collection were mainly qualitative interviews along all three levels of implementing structures, i.e. with village level entrepreneurs (VLEs), representatives of SCAs and representatives of state designated agencies (SDAs). In addition villagers, especially those who visited the centre, were also interviewed. A minimum of two CSCs have been visited/studied in each state. Per centre, one focused group discussion (FGD) was conducted with the villagers, including village leaders. Qualitative interviews with VLEs, field coordinators of SCA and other officials at both SCA and SDA levels were conducted. While choosing the interview partners the attempt was to keep a balance between implementing partners (project team) and receiving partners (villagers/citizens) and also within the project team a balance between public and private partners was sought. The number of representatives from each of these groups differed from one state to the other. This depended on the availability of such representatives during the field visits. For example, numbers of VLEs interviewed in Rajasthan were more than the actual centres visited. The reason behind this was that the field visit in the state coincided with the VLE workshops held in the state capital which gave access to a large number of representatives associated with the project. In another instance, in West Bengal, the numbers of VLEs interviewed were highest (eight in total) as the project team in Delhi insisted on some interactions with CSCs that were not functioning quite successfully and hence equal number of fully operational (four) and not operational (four) CSCs were visited.

A group of experts were interviewed mainly in Delhi. These experts ranged from university teachers to independent consultants, from researchers to civil society activists, from retired bureaucrats to state ministers, from technocrats in the central ministry to the World Bank professionals specializing in the field of e-Governance. The interviews with these experts were not confined to the CSCs Scheme. Rather, the discussion during these interviews revolved around the general issues of e-Governance, implications of e-Governance on the overall level of governance, the current scenario and the future of e-Governance in India.

All the interviews were conducted face to face. Since most of the interviews were purely qualitative, the course of one interview varied considerably from the others. However, the overall attempt was to focus on certain issues depending on the subject position of the interviewee. Some of the interviews were tape recorded and some were not, depending on the situation in which the interview was conducted (e.g. in a crowded place) or according to the comfort of the interviewee (e.g. some of the government officials did not feel comfortable being recorded) or during the focused group interviews with the villagers (as it involved multiple number of respondents at the same time) or sometimes purely depending on technical reasons. In some interviews with VLEs and villagers, additional assistance for translation in local language was required, especially in Andhra Pradesh. In such cases, field coordinators served as the translators and interpreters. All the interviews were loosely structured, that is, though certain core issues were addressed, questions did not follow a strict sequence or pattern. The questions were asked in a more open-ended fashion where the interviewee could give their opinion more freely and elaborately on any of the relevant issues.

The qualitative interview data collected were further supported by several policy documents and other primary sources including different project documents and photographs taken during the fieldwork. Besides these qualitative materials some quantitative studies done by independent market research groups and submitted to ministries were also accessible. These quantitative studies on the CSCs Scheme were conducted mostly as interim assessment or as rapid assessment surveys across the country. Access to these studies was crucial in developing the preliminary conjectures (mentioned in the Introduction) that form the basis of this research endeavour.

Qualitative interviews were selected as the main method of data collection for three specific reasons. Firstly, the entire fieldwork was conducted as an individual endeavour with active support from the project teams. In such circumstances, conducting a survey would imply strong involvement of project members in collecting the survey data. This could have led to serious concerns about the reliability of data collected as such. Secondly, given the time and individual effort it was practically impossible to collect an extensive amount of data. Therefore, the focus was on the limited yet intensive and in-depth information about the field and the project. Qualitative interviews with all the stakeholders representing different set of interests were best suited for the purpose of the case study. Thirdly, as already mentioned, some of the quantitative survey data conducted by independent research groups was accessible before commencing the fieldwork. The facts and figures available through these studies provided the necessary points of departure for framing the case study of the CSCs Scheme and sieving out the major issues to be covered by the qualitative interviews.

Those interviews which could be taped were transcribed. For interviews which could not be taped, field notes were deployed for documentation. These transcripts and field notes were analysed to elicit certain patterns of responses, behaviour and issues across groups of respondents. Such analyses often expanded beyond mere verbal communication. As most of the interviews were conducted face to face, many audio-visual observations of the space and social interactions were also documented through field notes. For example, most of the VLEs were interviewed within their workspace. Hence, in addition to direct interview their everyday practices in dealing with citizens, private partners (field coordinators), *panchayat* officials, their ability to handle the technology, the infrastructural capacity of the kiosks – all these could be documented through close observation. Moreover, photographic evidences also served as an important material of analysis.

The next step was to categorize these patterns in relation to different pre-defined indicators of improved level of governance (see Table 2.1). As these indicators were well defined in accordance to certain attributes, developing links between the data and the categories of indicators were a rather adept process. For example, speed of delivery of services which denoted predictability of services could be realized by observing the first-hand service delivery processes within the kiosk and the number of footfalls per kiosk, which was an attribute of increased participation by citizens, could be verified by interviews across different sections of villagers, VLEs and SCAs. Similarly transparency of information could be assessed by availability of information of services as displayed by the individual VLEs and the adaptability could be denoted by the use of local languages in such displays. The photographic materials were crucial evidences in establishing these specific attributes of certain indicators. These are only a few instances to demonstrate the process of analysing the available data. While analysing policy documents the overall approach can be summarized as an interpretive policy analysis approach which differs from an economic approach of cost-benefit analysis. In the interpretive approach, the focus was on the language and rhetoric of policy documents and the interpretation of their meaning by different actors in different contexts. It is important to mention here that these intensive qualitative data with a rather small database could pose some problems of generalizability of the findings. However, by acknowledging this issue the research findings should be taken more as indicative of certain trends in e-Governance practices rather than conclusive of any larger claims on the same.

Limitations of the case study

The CSCs Scheme is a pan Indian project with a much wider scope and a great many stakeholders. The scale and depth of such a project render it to be complex in terms of the structure, organization and process. Doing a case study of such a project is, therefore, trifled with many complexities as it requires both extensive and intensive methods of analysis. As this case study was conducted by a single individual, only four states within the project could be covered over a nine months period. However, this lack of a larger frame was somewhat balanced by an attempt to gain an in-depth overview of the project. A serious attempt of intensive scrutiny of the CSCs was taken up through qualitative interviews with representatives of all the stakeholders that include private sector (SCA), public sector (SDA), consumers/ citizens and intermediaries (VLEs). Despite sincere efforts, this study nonetheless is impaired with a few limitations and they ought to be laid out in clear terms. Firstly, the scope of the study is limited to only four states where CSC is being implemented and even within these four state only two districts per state was covered under this study and a limited number of CSCs were visited per state as a representative sample of all the centres. Secondly, the timeline of the study is rather wide which might lead to discrepancies in findings as different states were at different levels of implementation during the fieldwork. Since this was an on-going scheme, findings could have been different in different times. Thirdly, the focus was more on the qualitative aspects of the project, such as awareness among villagers about the services, rather than on the quantitative aspect, such as the number of transactions. Fourthly, the number of representatives of stakeholders differed from one state to another which might have led to disparities in the findings. All these limitations were already accounted for while planning this case study and therefore have also been addressed carefully while analysing the findings. For example, while choosing the four states, it has been tried to make them as representative as possible in terms of their geographical span (North–South and East–West span of the country), and also in terms of the roll-out status of CSC. All the states represented in the study covered almost all broad geographical areas of the nation and each of them had a different roll-out status ranging from very high to very low. The limited number of CSCs per state was balanced by the insights gathered from SDA and SCA representatives about the general status of CSC implementation in the state. Therefore, the specific narrative of each CSC visited was further supplemented by a general overview of the state-level realities. On the basis of these complementary set of views, a comparative understanding of the states could be established. The qualitative nature of the interview helped understanding of the complexities of the situation in different states. For example, every state adopted a PPP model. However, the exact nature of such a partnership model is difficult to evaluate through mere quantitative analysis.

This case study has been put forward as an individual effort and hence is purely based on the researcher's observation and interpretation albeit backed by much secondary research on the subject. Given the awareness of its limitations, this study has been careful to present its findings and formulate its analysis. There might still be some significant aspects of CSC project which have been overlooked at the expense of others. Therefore, by no means does this case study claim to be an exhaustive study of the CSCs Scheme. The sole aim of this case study is to assess the overall impact of the scheme on service delivery mechanism and thereby on the influence of e-Governance reform on the quality of governance in general.

Now to summarize the overall framework of this study it can be said that on the basis of three wider theoretical perspectives, it examines the processes of e-Governance reform in India through a qualitative case study method involving all stakeholders within such reform measures, ranging from policy-makers to bureaucrats, from private-sector actors to ordinary citizens. The overall research design which was illustrated in detail above is captured in Figure 2.4.

Conclusion: methodological challenges of a context-specific analysis of governance

Following Foucault's notion of governmentality, it can be established that the point of departure for any governance analysis should be the underlying power relations between the ruler and the ruled (Foucault 1980). Within any system of governance, this hiatus between the ruling class and its citizens need to be continuously manipulated in order to sustain legitimacy and to maintain the status quo. Within a democratic system of governance, the methods of manipulation have to be bound by rules (e.g. the constitution) and hence are often conjured up

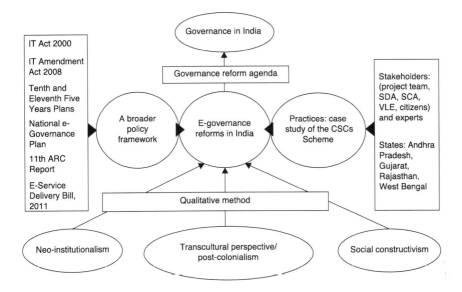

Figure 2.4 The research design
Source: Author

in two-track strategies of the elites, such as punishment and welfare (Mitra 2006). Foucault also talks about socialization, education, administrative tools of computing, accounting and the entire system of knowledge as key factors in the techniques of governmentality (Foucault 1980). However, looking at governance purely from the perspective of elite strategy or focusing only on the techniques of governmentality presents only a partial picture. They present a state-centric approach of governance which renders the citizens as powerless receiving agents of institutional rules and structures. Whereas 'the complex genealogy of governance explains why its state-dominated understanding, and the panoply of institutions that sustain it, are so often contested by political actors locked in combat against one other, or against the state itself' (Mitra 2006, p. 21). This hints at the duality of the concept of governance which poses similar challenges to the study of both the state and the society. For that reason, it becomes imperative to explore the 'weapon of the weak' (Scott 1985), the agency of the governed to alter the structural forces of governance. The previous analysis of structure-agency dynamics becomes crucial here as well. This research attempts to analyse governance both from state-centric and society-centric perspectives. This means the focus is neither purely on structure nor on agency, but on how these two intersect. The duality of governance as a concept is well captured in Figure 1.1 (Mitra 2006).

Applying this dual conceptualization of governance in the context of developing societies poses serious analytical as well as methodological challenge. The primary hiatus inherent in a system of governance is further widened by the gap between alien institutional set-up and embedded socio-cultural make-up in most of postcolonial and post-communist societies. In the case of India, its colonial past reflects strongly in its state institutions, starting from administration to legal framework, from judiciary to bureaucracy. Most of these institutions originated in Western Europe at a particular historical juncture. The history and contexts were both different when they were applied on the Indian soil. Consequently, the process of their adaptation and evolution also took different courses which were definitely fraught with conflict, violence and ruptures. To elaborate a little more on this rupture, a simple comparison between the European and Indian context could be illuminating. In Europe, the nation-states were built upon a collective identification with and sense of belonging to a nation. Hence, the modern state followed nation-building. In India, the situation was just the reverse. India inherited a modern state at the time of Independence (in 1947) and its ruling elites were left with the daunting task of nation-building afterwards (Scott 1985, p. 208). Evidently, the state and society were not immediately at sync and this made the act of governing further complex. This historical dimension for state–society hiatus acquires a whole new meaning under the cultural logic. The regional and local variations coupled with major cultural rifts based on religion, language, gender and so on renders governance in India an overwhelming experience. With a continuous conflict between modern categories and primordial identities politics becomes a relentless process of negotiation and accommodation. Moreover, interestingly enough, the very institution of modern democracy ushered in new networks of shared interests and pressure groups which has injected power into pre-modern identities (ibid., p. 207). This implies a parallel battle between old elites and new elites which might lead to elite fragmentation (ibid., p. 19) and further engendering governance.

All these historical and cultural dimensions do not only make the task of governing difficult but also cause enough bewilderment for the observers and analysts of governance. The first methodological dilemma that arises in analysing governance in India and for that matter any developing societies is the issue of methodological individualism. On this issue Mitra (2006) raises a few pertinent questions which need to be dealt with seriously in our analysis of governance in India. Firstly, 'how appropriate is a model based on methodological individualism to the analysis of changing societies where moral bonds are based on primordial identities?' (ibid., p. 13). Secondly, 'can rules based on individual calculations of benefits gain acceptance in societies based on caste, class, tribe, race, language, partisanship and religion?' (ibid., p. 13). A rational choice neo-institutional model of governance exhibits certain liberal bias such as putting individual choice at the core of political institutions which eventually find expressions in a state-centric view of governance. This bias, of course, needs to be balanced by a society-centric view where citizens' perception of rules and institutions affect governance as much. In this research a social constructivist approach provides a heuristic balance to the neo-institutional model. Furthermore, in the case of measurement the governance indicators are adopted in a way so that they can capture the dual aspects of governance. For example, while assessing accountability of the public service delivery system, it is not sufficient to explore the structural aspects of it within the public institutions. It is also crucial to evaluate to what extent citizens can exert their rights to hold a public officer responsible for delivery of certain services. Similarly, it is not enough to make information available through a government website under the transparency clause, whether this information is actually empowering citizens is also equally relevant.

The study of e-Governance reform in India is guided by the neo-institutional model of governance. The social constructivist approach is added to this model to explicate how the relationship between technology and governance is mediated through social practices embedded in a particular context. This context-specific understanding of governance faces a serious methodological challenge while Eurocentric grand theories are applied in the non-Western postcolonial context such as India. However, the solution does not lie in rejecting these theories altogether but in addressing the gaps in the existing models to render the context-specific analysis of governance possible. In an attempt to counter this analytical problem, the concept of hybridity under the transcultural perspective on politics has been deployed. The analytical category of hybridity explicate how the policies and practices go through a process of hybridization in order to bridge the hiatus between 'imported' institutional set-up and the 'inherited' social set-up. In analysing this process of negotiation, hybridity also emerges as a political strategy dispensed with the agency of the actors involved. Such a theoretical and methodological combination serves to address the basic research questions that this book sets out to address. The next step is to apply them in the specific context of e-Governance reform in India. For this purpose, the policies and practices of e-Governance in India will be studied in much depth and detail within the broader political, social and cultural contexts. The following chapter takes up to exhibit and explain the policy framework and its concomitant implementation.

3 E-Governance in India

An overview

Introduction: e-Governance as a strategic reform and the Indian State

The majority of literature on governance reform in India establishes e-Governance as a major area of reform since the late 1990s (Sreekumar 2008; Madon 2009; Gupta 2010). One of the major reasons cited for this gradual growth in e-Governance is the IT boom in India in the post-liberalized years. The recent policy drive towards e-Governance reform in India has been part of a major developmental goal of taking IT to the masses. This clearly marks a shift from the earlier policy paradigm. Madon (2009) aptly summarizes the Indian experience of e-Governance in two phases; the first phase spanned from the late 1960s/early 1970s to the late 1990s; the second phase started from the late 1990s and is still in progress. She further drew the characteristic features of both the phases. In her own words:

> In the first phase, efforts to develop e-government were concentrated on the use of IT for in-house government applications with a principal focus on Central Government requirements such as defence, research, economic monitoring and planning, and certain data-intensive functions related to elections, conducting of national census and tax administration ... the introduction of IT in the public sector did not result in automation of many key departmental activities. In the second phase, the implementation of the [N]ational IT Task Force and State Government IT policies symbolized a paradigm shift in e-Governance policies towards using IT for a wider range of sectoral applications reaching out to a large number of people in rural as well as urban areas. Moreover, there has been a movement towards a greater input of non-governmental organizations (NGOs) and private sector organisations in providing services to public. These projects have been influenced by the increasing focus of international agencies such as DfID, G-8, the UNDP and the World Bank under the banner of 'E-Governance for Development'.
> (Madon 2009, p. 269)

Even though, it is widely accepted that the State had played a minimalist role as far as the IT sector is concerned in India, a close and careful reading of the pre-liberalization policies reveals quite the opposite (Saraswati 2008). State intervention in the IT sector took off in 1970 with the foundation of the Department of Electronics (DOE) to oversee IT policy-making. Since then there have been contrasting yet considerable interventions by the State in devising an IT policy regime which has had significant impact on the way the industry has shaped up (ibid.). For the purpose of this research, the focus is more on the current policy framework commencing from the year 2000. However, to acknowledge the role of the State in IT sector growth it is important to shed some light on the history of IT policy-making in India.

E-Governance policies: the pre-liberalization policy regime (1970–1990)

Under the rule of J. L. Nehru (India's first Prime Minister), the Electronic Committee or Bhabha Committee was set up under the chairmanship of Homi Bhabha (who was also the head of the Atomic Energy Commission) in the aftermath of the India–China war, in order to develop an indigenous electronic base for national security and development. Hence, incited by security imperatives and also by recognizing the significance of technical advancements in the IT field, this Committee was later replaced by the Electronic Commission (EC) in February 1970 which was followed by the establishment of the DOE in June 1970 (Saraswati 2008; Gupta 2010). The EC was the primary policy-making body for electronics and computers whereas the DOE implemented those policies and together they regulated the policy environment for electronics and computer-related development in India (Subramanian 2000, p. 36). In its attempt to develop and expand an internally competitive software industry through finely customized export schemes, this policy phase is marked by the establishment of two large public sector computer companies, namely Electronic Computers of India Limited (ECIL) and the Computer Maintenance Company (CMC) and their collaborations with IBM and other transnational computer companies (TNCCs) in order to access the latest technologies. The Software Export Scheme of 1972 catered to the management consultancy firms which had diversified into software writing for domestic clients. These firms enjoyed a lower duty on computer imports and also received loans from the government for such imports of computers. The condition was to meet this loan within five years through foreign exchange generated from export of software skills. However, this policy was confronted with many logistic bottlenecks and failed to achieve the desired growth rate of software export. Nonetheless, the software export rose from Rs. 8.4 million in 1975 to Rs. 30 million in 1978 (Saraswati 2008, p. 1145).

The next phase of IT policy-making commenced with the Janata Dal coming to power in the Centre in 1977. The Minicomputer Policy of 1978 insisted on State intervention through selective and discriminatory licensing and at the same time regulation of the private sector activities within the IT sector. However, the continuous pressure from the domestic business houses reflected significantly in the way this policy was implemented:

For example, within the first two years of policy, over 40 licences were issued, undermining the economies of scale required for mass computer production and giving recipients of the licences no incentive to reinvest their profits into deepening capabilities via expanding productive capacity and R&D. Furthermore, emulation of the Taiwanese model required not only subassembly but local manufacture and supply of components and peripherals ... importation of Simple Knocked Down (SKD) kits from East Asia allowed, sustaining a subassembly system with little value-added. The DOE even allowed, by stealth, importation of more powerful computers, which was a market supposedly reserved for ECIL.

(Saraswati 2008, pp. 1146–1147)

Some other such measures were taken which were quite contradictory to the fundamental essence of the policy document. Despite the evident contradiction in its policy implications, the Minicomputer Policy in the long run influenced the growth of India's software industry. With no standardization in the fragmented hardware industry, hardware firms would not bundle software with their hardware as they did in Taiwan and Japan, but provided separate software services or none at all. As such, independent software firms began to service this burgeoning fragmented market, and hardware firms developed significant software revenue streams. This induced the growth of the domestic software industry, which rose from Rs. 2.3 million to Rs. 76.9 million between 1981 and 1985, in contrast to exports, which rose from Rs. 44 million to Rs. 280 million over the same period (Saraswati 2008, p. 1147).

This competition between the hardware and software market continued well into the next policy phase starting with Rajiv Gandhi's election as Prime Minister of India. Though the New Computer Policy was approved by the previous Prime Minister Indira Gandhi, it became statutory under the rule of her son (i.e., Rajiv Gandhi) and took effect (Subramanian 2000, p. 38). Between 1984 and 1986, the software industry became the thrust area under the New Computer Policy which was not only propelled by the potential of software export but also by considerable pressure from the business houses to lower the import duties on fully assembled computers and software packages. An Inter-Ministerial-Standing Committee (IMSC) was established to facilitate to ease the process of import restriction.

[T]he policy outcome was a reduction of basic customs duty on hardware from 135% to 60%, while customs duty on foreign software was reduced from 100% to 60%. While the excessively lenient reductions resulted in balance of payments problems and had to be modified in subsequent years, the policy increased the installed hardware base and further promoted the emerging software services industry.

(Saraswati 2008, p. 1147)

Rajiv Gandhi was a strong supporter of computerization and use of Informational Technology for nation-building. There were significant technological changes in the railways, banking and education sectors during his tenure (Gupta 2010). Thus, this policy phase can be characterized by wide-ranging computerization of public sector organizations albeit against strong resistance from the labour unions (Saraswati 2008).

A number of important policy initiatives were introduced by the DOE to exploit the export potentials of the software industry between 1986 and 1989. The first such policy was the Computer Software Export, Software Development and Training Policy 1986. Though maintaining the overall rhetoric of indigenous development, this policy eased the import restrictions on software packages moving from quota to tariff regime. This was followed by allowing business houses to enter the software development market which was restricted earlier under the Monopolies and Restrictive Trade Practices (MRTP) and also by offering attractive finance and marketing packages aiming at software export development (Saraswati 2008). In 1988, the Electronics and Software Export Promotion Council was backed by the Ministry of Commerce which was followed by the establishment of a software industry trade association called National Association of Software and Service Companies (NASSCOM) to provide further marketing support (Subramanian 2000, p. 39). The next major policy initiative was the International-Package-Switching-Services (IPSS) by the Department of Telecommunications (DOT) in 1989 which aimed at providing a telecommunication infrastructure at a fairly low cost to transfer domestically developed software to foreign countries. Around the same time DOE came up with its Software Technology Parks (STPs) project which besides providing advanced telecommunication infrastructure also made provision for other subsidies such as free water and electricity. STPs also implied that all telecommunications for software export came under the direct control of the DOE. STPs were a major policy initiative for the development of the software export market in India and have thrived ever since. As a result, there are currently 43 STPs across India, albeit in the midst of much dispute and debate over its role (ibid.).

Another important State initiative which is even more relevant for the purpose of this research is the establishment of the National Informatics Centre (NIC) in 1976. By 1975, there was a growing realization of the potential of ICT in improving government activities and hence overall development. As a result, NIC was conceived and set up with financial assistance from the UNDP. Starting as a miniscule initiative by the GOI, NIC has grown exponentially in the following decades to become one of the major government organizations to spearhead the growth of e-Governance and informatics-led development in India. 'NIC has leveraged ICT to provide a robust communication backbone and effective support for e-Governance to the Central Government, State Governments, UT Administrations, Districts and other Government bodies. It offers a wide range of ICT services' (NIC 2012). One of the milestone projects of NIC was the launch of NICNET, a Nationwide Communication Network, in 1987. NICNET engaged with:

> [G]ateway nodes at about 53 departments of the Government of India, 35 State/UT Secretariats and 603 District Collectorates to service ICT

applications. NICNET has played a pivotal role in decentralized planning, improvement in Government services, wider transparency of national and local Governments and improving their accountability to the people.

(NIC 2012)

NICNET was followed by the District Information System of the National Informatics Centre (DISNIC) which was an initiative to computerize all district offices across the nation (GOI, 2008). To date, 'NIC assists in implementing ICT projects, in close collaboration with Central and State Governments and endeavours to ensure that state-of the-art technology is available to its users in all areas of ICT' (NIC 2012).

Shifting policy framework in post-liberalization India

Given this historical overview of IT policy-making in India and the institutional framework for ICT-led developments within the public sector a few key issues can be underlined which have a direct influence on the later reform trajectory of IT policy and e-Governance. Firstly, quite contrary to popular belief the State played an important role from the inception of IT policies in 1970s. The role of State-led IT policies in the growth of the software industry in India cannot be entirely denied. It is in the backdrop of such a policy environment that the National Information Technology Task Force was established in 1998 which came up with the Information Technology Action Plan I (Software), Information Technology Action Plan II (Hardware) and Long Term National IT Policy (Task Force 2000). In 1999, a separate Ministry of Information Technology was established with a specialized Department of Information and Technology (Gupta 2010). Secondly, the influences of private or business sectors in IT policy formulation and implementation even in the pre-liberalized years are well established. Thirdly, the recognition of the developmental potentials of ICT tools dates back to the 1970s in India. However, the massive exploitation of ICT tools in governance reform and other developmental projects is fairly recent. The launch of nation-wide networks such as NICNET or DISNIC played an instrumental role in planting the seed of network governance in India. Fourthly, the role of International Organizations such as UNDP in interposing ICT tools in government activities can also be traced back to the 1970s (as noticeable in the formation of NIC); though such international donor intervention became rampant in the wake of the larger governance reform agenda after the economic liberalization in 1991. For example, international donor agencies such as the DfID, G-8, UNDP and the World Bank have been actively engaged in several policy and project initiatives under the framework of e-Governance for development (Sreekumar 2008; Gupta 2010). Lastly, navigating its way through the IT industry and ICT-led development, the Indian State (based on the recommendation of NASSCOM) tries to integrate private sector goals with social development goals. Hence the current policy focus in this field is on value-addition to IT as an industry and to take IT to the masses (Ahuja 2010, p. 2). It is under this broader framework of major policy issues and environment that the recent policies pertaining to e-Governance reform initiatives in India is discussed and examined in the following sections.

National Task Force on IT and Software Development 1998

The National Task Force on IT and Software Development or, as it is popularly known, the National IT Task Force was established in 1998 by the Prime Minister's Office. The Task Force was chaired by the deputy chairman of the Planning Commission and its main objective was to formulate a draft National Informatics Policy (Sinha 2006). There are many recommendations that the Task Force came up with in three Basic Background Reports. A few relevant recommendations were as follows:

- It recommended the 'preparation of Five-Year IT Plans by every department in central and state governments earmarking 1–3% of their budget for applying IT to streamline their functioning. It gave the various ministries and departments three months to issue all necessary instructions and amendments to procedures' (Madon 2009).
- At least 2 per cent of the departmental or ministerial budget was expected to be spent on IT development (Sinha 2006).
- There was a strong recommendation for international cooperation in terms of knowledge sharing and technical assistance in planning and implementation of IT projects (ibid.).
- It suggested reorientation of the civil service towards IT based on training and capacity building (ibid.).
- A Central Repository of Data in government was also recommended (ibid.).
- Citizen–IT interface was one of the focus areas of the Task Force which recommended wider penetration of IT for the masses through application in health, education, trade, taxation and so on (ibid.).
- It also recommended universalizing computer literacy through increasing use of IT and computers in education under the 'Operation Knowledge' programme (GOI 2008).

In sum, the National Task Force for IT and Software Development marks a paradigm shift in IT policy focus. The shift was from mere computerization to improved service delivery, a better investment climate and an all-pervasive use of IT for development. The outcomes became more important than the input which was reflected in subsequent policy frames.

Information Technology Act, 2000 and Information Technology Amendment Act, 2008

The Information Technology Act, 2000 (No.21 of 2000) received the Presidential approval on 9 June 2000. As per the legal document, it is:

An Act to provide legal recognition for transactions carried out by means of electronic data interchange and other means of electronic communication, commonly referred to as 'electronic commerce', which involve the use of alternatives to paper-based methods of communication and storage of information, to facilitate electronic filing of documents with the Government agencies and further to amend the Indian Penal Code, the Indian Evidence Act, 1872, the Bankers' Books Evidence Act, 1891 and the Reserve Bank of India Act, 1934 and for matters connected therewith or incidental thereto.

(GOI 2000, p. 1)

This Act was developed in direct response to the Model Law on Electronic Commerce, 1997. Commerce adopted by the United Nations Commission on International Trade Law in order to promote efficient delivery of Government services by means of reliable electronic records (GOI 2000, p. 1). The Act has a total of thirteen chapters and four schedules including a separate chapter on e-Governance. In principle this Act ratifies, (a) the legal acceptance of electronic communications and documents along with detail processes of attribution, acknowledgement and dispatch of electronic records, (b) legal recognition of digital signature along with details of authentication, certification and regulation of digital signature, (c) offences and penalties along with the establishment of a Cyber Regulation Appellate Tribunal and a Cyber Regulations Advisory Committee, (d) the role and power of different authorities involved in the institutional and regulatory framework of the Act. The Central Government holds considerable power under this Act to make rules and make changes to carry out the provisions in this Act.

The Information Technology Act, 2000 (IT Act, 2000) was a breakthrough in Indian legal history as it was the first cyber law to be formulated and enacted. However, being at a nascent stage of cyber law, the Act did not address many such issues that were deemed necessary to strengthen the legal framework. Hence based on the recommendation of the Expert Committee, the GOI presented an amendment document namely, the Information Technology Amendment Bill in 2006 (Naavi.org 2012). After much debate the Bill has been passed by the Parliament to become the Information Technology (Amendment) Act, 2008 (IT (A) Act, 2008).

The major thrusts of this Amendment Act were issues of cyber security, privacy, cyber terrorism, techno-legal information security and e-auditing. This also meant to refine the terminology, for example, substituting the term 'digital signature' with 'electronic signature'. It further provided to strengthen the Cyber Appellate Tribunal and to enhance the authority of the Central Government regarding security issues even though the word 'Regulation/Regulations' were omitted from the principal Act of 2000. The provisions for the intermediaries have also been revised under the Amendment Act.

The Information Technology Act, 2000 and the Information Technology (Amendment) Act, 2008, are both crucial in understanding the way e-Governance is gaining a foothold in the institutional framework of governance in India. There are a few key issues that arise from a careful scrutiny of these legal documents:

(i) These laws facilitate the overhauling process of communication and documentation within and with the government agencies in India through legalizing electronic data interchange. This has direct implications for communications and transactions between the government and citizen, between the government and business and also within different bodies, departments and agencies of the government.

(ii) The international framework plays an instrumental role in the development of the principal Act as the motive behind this law is described to be keeping uniformity with Model Law on Electronic Commerce adopted by the United Nations Commission on International Trade Law.

(iii) Another motivation behind the principal Act was 'to promote efficient delivery of government services by means of reliable electronic records' (IT Act 2000; 1). This fits within one of the basic principles of the e-Governance reform agenda and hence this Act paves the way to such reforms.

(iv) Similar trends are evident in the Chapter III on Electronic Governance under the Act. Through various provisions of legalizing electronic records, digital signatures, retention and dissemination of information in electronic format and so on this Act helps to standardize the process of information exchange within the public sector. Moreover, the provisions under section 7, that is, retention of electronic records promote transparency of information and harness easier structures of accountability with the government. For example, clause 1a and b in this section are particularly relevant in this regard. Even various sections of Chapter IV on Attribution, Acknowledgement and Dispatch of Electronic Records facilitate the same.

(v) The IT Act, 2000 also makes information on government rules, orders and regulations more easily accessible through rendering them available in electronic forms. This also enhances transparency with the government.

(vi) Under section 10 (Chapter III) and also under section 87 (Chapter XIII) the Central Government gets enough authority to set the format and manner of electronic communication including the digital signature and also to change rules through prior notification. However, there is much ambiguity in the way it outlines under section 9 (Chapter III) that any person cannot demand acceptance, creation or retention of electronic records or any electronic money transactions from any government authority. It leaves the question of governmental authority to different interpretations. The provision for a Cyber Appellate Tribunal in both the Acts (though with slight refinement of terminology) further hints at institutionalization of regulatory frameworks in electronic communications.

(vii) The IT (Amendment) Act, 2008, notwithstanding its major focus on privacy and security issues, make considerable amendments to the chapter on e-Governance in the principal Act. For example, 'for efficient delivery of services [to] the public through electronic means', this Act not only legalizes the privatization of service delivery mechanism but also legalizes the payment of fees for regular public services whereas the responsibility of deciding the scale of such charges lies with the Government (6A.(1), (2), (3) and (4)). Such a legal framework further encourages the model of public–private partnership widely adopted under the governance reform agenda.

(viii) Other amendments provided under the 2008 Act aid in the process of increasing transparency by legalizing e-audit (7A) and also the simplification of communication mechanism by recognizing contracts generated in electronic form.

(ix) By addressing the issues of cyber security and privacy and data protection, cyber law compliance and so on, this Amendment Act is supposed to affect the IT industry in India in particular and also bring massive changes in the corporate governance system within the country. These changes, in turn, have explicit and implicit impacts on the issues of transparency and accountability within the general governance structure where the private/corporate sectors have increasingly been involved.

Many view the introduction of such laws in the Indian context as a threshold in India's path to become a digital society.[1] Without delving deeper into the debate of digital society, these Acts can be understood as a legal step towards institutionalizing the changing nature of communications and interactions among different actors including public sector, private business and ordinary citizens. Hence they set the stepping stones of reform in the complex whole of governance structure in India by making legal provisions for e-Governance.

Five Year Plans and the changing discourse of e-Governance

Five Years Plans in India is one of the leading documents of policy directives which reflect the priority areas of development and strategies of intervention by the GOI. These plans are developed and approved by the planning commission of India where recommendations from both the state and central governments are incorporated. Analysing these planning documents holds immense significance to understand the overall policy framework as they point out key areas of strategic reform. The two most important documents to deal with governance issues are the Tenth and Eleventh Five Years Plan as both of them give special attention to governance in general and e-Governance in particular. Therefore both the Plans will be analysed in succession albeit only specific chapters on governance will be discussed in details.

The Tenth Five Years Plan (2002–2007) clearly demonstrates the significance of contemporary governance reform discourse in India's development planning as it devotes one full chapter to 'Governance and Implementation' (Chapter 6 of the Tenth Plan). It also expresses Indian policy-makers' allegiance to the 'good governance' paradigm at the very outset of the aforementioned chapter which states, 'Good governance is one of the most crucial factors required if the targets of the Tenth Plan are to be achieved' (GOI 2002, p. 177). The Plan starts off with a clear notion of governance that:

> [R]elates to the management of all such processes that, in any society, define the environment which permits and enables individuals to raise their capability levels, on one hand, and provide opportunities to realize their potential

and enlarge the set of available choices, on the other. These processes, covering the political, social and economic aspects of life impact every level of human enterprise, be it individual, the household, the village, the region or the national level. It covers the State, civil society and the market, each of which is critical for sustaining human development.

(ibid., p. 177)

While outlining the universal characteristics of 'good governance', this document recognizes the possibility of certain 'aspects of governance that are contextually driven and geared to address the local concerns' (ibid., p. 177). Here, there is evidently an attempt to balance universal notions with local realities that promotes context-specific policy reform. While disaggregating the concept of governance from that of development, the Tenth Plan demarcates features of poor governance followed by an alternative framework for conceptualizing governance. Exploring the contextual parameters of governance in India, it recognizes the presence of poor governance even in better developed states. These manifestations of poor governance can have direct correspondence with economic, political or civic aspects of governance. However, all these aspects together are based on a continuous process of intermediation between institutions, the delivery mechanism and the supportive and subordinate framework of legislations, rules and procedures. The continuous interplay between these predefined elements determines the alternative framework governance. Institutions are defined as 'adopted or created arrangements, both formal and informal, to bring about predictability, stability and efficiency in managing the social, economic and political transactions in any society'; delivery mechanism is viewed as 'including the executive apparatus adopted or evolved by the institutions for implementing the agenda and the objectives for which the said institutions have been created'; and, the supportive and subordinate framework for legislations, rules and procedures are said to be 'formulated for delivering and meeting the stated responsibilities of the concerned institutions' (ibid., p. 178). For efficient functioning of the system of governance, these three elements have to work in complete harmony. With the changing domestic and global contexts, these elements need to be capable enough to absorb changes and adapt accordingly. Therefore comprehensive policy framework and institutional capacity of the delivery mechanism become crucial in formulating and implementing appropriate projects/plans (ibid., p. 180).

The changing contexts in the domestic and global level can be manifold. For example in the domestic front, it could emerge from premature dissolution of coalition governments in changing political environment. Institutional changes have to adapt to these emerging contexts. Similarly, there are good reasons to devise new instruments that ensure continuity of basic policies on which there is consensus across political parties (ibid., p. 178). This Tenth Plan also accounts for changes in the global contexts by accepting the changing relationship between State, market and civil society in the context of market liberalism and globalization. It clearly acknowledges the extension of the market and the civil society domain at the expense of the State in some areas. It also underlines the area of their 'respective overlaps' (ibid., p. 181). This reformulation of roles of the State, the civil society and the market reflects unerringly in the governance reform trends in India.

The Tenth Plan admits that in the current situation it is impossible for the government to take a completely minimalist role. However, instead of being extremely proactive, the government focuses on certain key areas which would improve governance through efficient use of resources in the public sector and by strengthening personal and community capabilities geared towards sustainable development. These priority areas are: peoples' participation; decentralization; right to information; reforms of the revenue system; improving fiscal health of the Central as well as the State Governments by making necessary corrections in the subsidy and the pricing regime for public provisioning of services; inclusion of civil society as development partners; civil service reform; procedural reform (covering all aspects of government's interface with the public); formulation of programme/project in a more professional manner; project-based assistance to states and development agencies/institutions; synergy and coordination between different public and para-state agencies; stricter mechanism of monitoring and evaluation; rationalization of Central Sector Schemes (CSS) and Centrally Sponsored Schemes (CSSs) through convergence, weeding out and transfer to the states on Zero Based Budgeting (ZBB); empowerment of the marginal and the excluded; judicial reform; and using IT for 'good governance'/e-Governance. The underlying aims of all these thrust areas are improving the delivery mechanism, efficient resource mobilization and effective public expenditure (ibid., pp. 182–187). It is also important to list here some of the steps taken under the Tenth Plan to improve the quality of governance in India such as, the Right to Information (RTI) Act, 2005, an e-Governance Plan for 27 important areas to improve service delivery and digitization of information; National Rural Employment Guarantee Act (NREGA), National Rural Health Mission (NRHM) and other such initiatives to increase participatory governance; a new policy for Voluntary Organizations (VOs) by the Central Government to improve participatory governance, and the establishment of Second ARC in 2005 to prepare a detailed blueprint for revamping the public administration system.

Like its predecessor, the Eleventh Plan (2007–2012) also devotes an entire chapter to Governance (Chapter 10) and reasons that 'inclusive growth, reducing poverty and bridging the various divides that continue to fragment our society can only be achieved if there is a significant improvement in the quality of governance' (GOI 2007, p. 223). This chapter does not attempt to present any definition of governance and 'good governance' (which were already introduced in the previous Plan). It nevertheless specifies the concrete meanings of 'good governance' in the Indian context which are as follows: free and fair election with massive participation and a legitimate and responsible government; accountability and transparency at all levels of government and reduced corruption; effective and efficient delivery of public services particularly at the local level since key services such as primary education and health relies on the efficiency of the local governments; empowerment of PRIs; appropriate legal framework for protecting individual rights and rights of private entities; inclusive participation of disadvantaged and minorities groups (GOI 2007).

Keeping its allegiance to the 'good governance' paradigm, the Eleventh Plan proposes two specific measures. Firstly, 'the Department of Administrative Reforms and Public Grievances has proposed a framework for 'good governance' in the form of a Code Governance. The main components of this Code are: (i) improving service delivery; (ii) development of programmes for weaker sections and backward areas; (iii) technology and system improvement; (iv) financial management and budget sanctity; (v) accountability and transparency; (vi) public service morale and anti-corruption; (vii) incentivizing reforms' (GOI 2007, p. 224). Secondly, depending on the federal structure, this Plan proposes a state-wise index of 'good governance' measuring the performance of the states by a high-level expert group. This index can be used for giving incentives to perform and also to bring serious attention to governance issues (ibid., p. 224).

While maintaining the basic focus on achieving 'good governance', the Eleventh Plan takes major initiatives in a broad range of areas, such as, decentralization through strengthening and empowering PRIs; decentralization through introducing district level planning; decentralization by bringing CSSs under the PRIs; participation and harmonizing CBOs with PRIs; rehabilitation and resettlement; monitoring and evaluation; e Governance for better service delivery and programme design, implementation and monitoring; use of ICT in major flagship programmes; location-specific planning using geographical information system; partnering with VOs; corruption; civil service reform; police and judiciary reform; new regulatory structure with independent regulators. Additionally, the Plan identifies corruption as one of the major problems of governance and hence deems it extremely necessary to deal with this problem. As already discussed in the Tenth Plan, this Plan also calls for wider participation of private sectors and civil society organizations in matters of governance. Thus the responsibility of the government is to develop a business-friendly environment by promoting efficiency and to encourage VOs for developing citizen initiatives and monitoring government systems by promoting transparency (GOI 2007, p. 225).

Given the overview of the two consecutive Five Years Plans, the overall governance reform agenda espoused by the GOI over the last ten years become apparent. As both the Plan documents identify e-Governance as one of the priority areas, strategic reforms have taken place in this sector. The Tenth Plan identifies e-Governance as one of the important tools 'for achieving "good governance" especially with regard to improving efficiency, transparency and making interface with government user-friendly' (GOI 2002, p. 187). The basic aim of e-Governance is to use IT in the government functioning 'in order to bring about better governance which has been termed as SMART (simple, moral, accountable, responsive and transparent)' (ibid.). In the Tenth Plan, the focus on e-Governance was spread beyond connectivity, network and technology upgradation to re-engineering of processes and rules. In a quest to take IT to the masses, both private and public resources were to be mobilized under this Plan. Moreover, as sustainability, interactivity and standardization of e-Governance activities were prioritized under this Plan, the need for a comprehensive master plan for e-Governance with a specific time frame was asserted. Innovative, cost-effective solutions to develop G2C, government to business (G2B) and government to government (G2G) functionalities which will take local languages, local accessibility infrastructures into consideration were encouraged and promoted. A major step taken under the Tenth Plan was to adopt a NeGP in 2006 to improve service delivery mechanism to the citizens. This Plan spread across 27 major areas marks a significant difference from the earlier efforts of mere computerization.

In the Eleventh Plan, the initiatives taken in the field of e-Governance become more organized and comprehensive. Continued focus was on technology upgradation and process re-engineering for improved service delivery culminated into many important projects under the Eleventh Plan. Some of these projects are: (i) unique identifiers of citizens and businesses, 'to create a common platform for service/ programme delivery . . . a unique ID (UID) in the government to citizen (G2C) domain and Corporate Identity Number (CIN) in government to business (G2B) domain' (GOI 2007, pp. 231–232); (ii) Citizens Smart Cards Project to represent 'different entitlement groups for which free services or implicit/explicit subsidies are given' (ibid., p. 232); (iii) SWANs in 29 states and six Union Territories (UT) to establish 'an intra-government network with a minimum of 2Mbps connectivity from the State headquarters to block headquarters through the District headquarters' (ibid., p. 233). This project also provide connectivity for service delivery of different MMPs under the National e-Governance Plan; (iv) Common Services Centres (CSCs) Scheme to establish '100,000 broadband Internet enabled kiosks in rural areas which would deliver government and private services at the doorstep of the citizens' and the CSCs Scheme 'is the first step towards ubiquitous broadband reaching up to the village level' (ibid., p. 233); (v) connectivity for the last mile through BSNL and Universal Service Obligation Fund (USOF); (vi) SDCs across 29 states and six UT along with Disaster Recovery (DR), 'in order to provide shared, secured and managed infrastructure for consolidating and securely hosting State-level data and application. . . . The various MMPs, both at the Central level, State level and also the integrated services of the NeGP are expected to use SDCs to deliver their services. This infrastructure would have to be created during the Eleventh Five Year Plan' (ibid., p. 233). The SWANs, CSCs and the SDCs are the three most important pillars of the National e-Governance Plan. Besides these important areas of e-Governance activities, ICTs are also being applied in flagship government programmes such as National Rural Employment Guarantee Scheme (NREGS), Bharat Nirman, the Pradhan Mantri Gram Sadak Yojana/Prime Minister Rural Road Scheme (PMGSY), for the purpose of implementation as well as monitoring.

Taking a close look at the Tenth and Eleventh Five Years Plans establishes two important facts: first is that governance reform geared towards achieving 'good governance' standards has become an intrinsic part of government planning, and second is that e-Governance/application of ICTs in government functioning forms a major part of the governance reform planning. Hence it is important to analyse e-Governance as part of the broader agenda of reform including its other different dimensions. One of the crucial aspects of governance reform is the increasing influence of the market and civil society. This not only implies shrinking of the State but also hints at a growing partnership between the State, the market and the civil society in achieving developmental goals. The Tenth and the Eleventh Plans both reiterate this dimension of governance reform through myriad policy directions and project initiatives. In the case of e-Governance, such partnerships are envisaged to improve service delivery and renders government functionaries more citizen-centric. In all the e-Governance projects discussed in the Plan documents, the State plays the role of catalyst facilitating the coordination among all developmental partners. Through process re-engineering, e-Governance also promises to change the way government personnel, procedures and rules function at present. Along with simplification of the system, it also assists in increasing transparency, accountability and efficiency of the system while showing potentials to reduce the occurrence of corruption. E-Governance also aids in other priority areas of the government such as health, education, police and judiciary reform, revenue system reform, professional project formulation, monitoring and evaluation of projects/programmes and so on. Embedding e-Governance activities in major social flagship projects such as NREGS enables better implementation. Thus, the significance of e-Governance lies not only as a mere part of the governance reform programme but in its ability to permeate many other reform initiatives with equal impact.

One of the vital points which both Plans stresses is taking ICTs to the masses through increased sustainability, interactivity and standardization which further push for a master plan. Hence, the Tenth Plan introduces the NeGP including 27 MMPs and the Eleventh Plan continues to facilitate the successful implementations of these projects besides adding a few more under the rubric of NeGP. Being the single most important policy document for e-Governance initiatives in India, NeGP demands distinct attention.

From policy to an action plan: NeGP 2006

The National e-Governance Plan presents a holistic approach towards varied e-Governance initiatives taken at various levels in the country.

> During the 1980s and early 1990s, initial attempts towards e-Governance were made with a focus on networking government departments and developing in-house government application in the areas of defence, economic monitoring, planning and the development of IT to manage data-intensive functions related to elections, census, tax administration etc. These applications focused on automation of internal government functions rather than on improving service delivery to citizens.
>
> (GOI 2008)

There have been many isolated e-Governance initiatives in India ranging from the block level to the Central level they have not been particularly successful in yielding desires results. However, these experiences shaped the e-Governance strategy of the country in a considerable manner (GOI 2011b). The key learnings that these experiences underline are: need for political will at the highest level and a national vision for e-Governance; a dedicated team with a stable tenure; novel modes of public–private partnership; policies to address issues of security, privacy, etc.; need to develop support infrastructure for e-Governance, such as Data Centres, Wide Area Networks and the single window physical access points for delivery of government services which could be delivered at the doorsteps of the citizens; importance of pilots before scaling up; importance of re-engineering and change management along with issues of technology.

Taking these issues in consideration, the Department of Information Technology (DIT) and Department of Administrative Reforms and Public Grievances (DAR&PG) formulated the National e-Governance Plan which was approved by the Union Government on 18 May 2006. Comprising of 27 MMPs and ten components, NeGP is guided by one common vision, that is:

> Make all Government services accessible to the common man in his locality, through common service delivery outlets and ensure efficiency, transparency and reliability of such services at affordable costs to realise the basic needs of the common man.
>
> (NeGP 2006b)

The three main pillars of the NeGP are SDCs, SWANs and CSCs. Together they form the common support infrastructure of the NeGP. The SDCs functions as the Central repository of the State providing secure data storage which not only consolidate services, applications and infrastructure but also facilitate efficient electronic delivery of G2G, G2C and G2B services through CSCs supported by the SWANs (GOI 2008). There are also 27 MMPs, nine at the Central level, eleven at the state and seven at the integrated project level. Line ministries are responsible for the implementation of MMPs. Some of the notable Central MMPs are Income Tax (Ministry of Finance/CBDT), Passport VISA (Ministry of External Affairs), Immigration (Ministry of Home Affairs), MCA21 (Ministry of Corporate Affairs), Pensions (Department of Pensions and Pensioners Welfare), Aadhaar (UID) UID Authority of India (UIDAI) and so on and some of the state MMPs are Land Record, Police, Agriculture, Transport and so on. The CSCs Scheme falls under the category of Integrated MMPs.

In short, the overall strategy of NeGP can be characterized by centralized initiative and decentralized implementation, effective private sector participation, common infrastructure, policies, standards and framework to facilitate web-enabled Anytime, Anywhere access (Mathur et al. 2009). Implementations of grand plans in India usually demonstrate a different trajectory. In the case of NeGP as well, there could be wide gaps between the programme outline and the implementation processes. Nonetheless, the formulation of NeGP demonstrates the earnestness in the governmental attitudes towards e-Governance reforms.

E-Governance practices from the pre-NeGP era to NeGP experiences: a paradigmatic shift?

This section presents a brief overview of projects that were initiated in different federal states in India before NeGP came into existence and summarizes the lessons learnt from such varied project experiences. These lessons then serve as points of departure for the NeGP and can be reflected in few such instances as implemented under the Plan.

Computerization of Land Record by Department of Land Resources, Government of India

This project started from 1994–1995 with collaboration between the Union Ministry of Rural Development in collaboration with the NIC. It tried to implement a pilot project on Computerization of Land Records across eight states of India in a selected pool of eight districts. The project was already conceived in 1985. The basic aim of the project was to make the land and revenue administration more citizen-centric, transparent, efficient and reliable by enabling landowners to retrieve authentic computerized copies of ownership, crop and tenancy and updated copies of Record of Rights (RoRs) on demand. Through subsequent scaling up during planning phases, the project base grew extensively. During the Ninth Plan, funds were sanctioned for reaching out to 2787 *tehsils/taluks* which was further accentuated in the Tenth Plan by adding another 1615 more *tehsils/taluks* to the list. Different states have performed differently in the process of land record computerization, some have stopped manual issuance of RoRs, whereas others have completed data entry of RoRs and some others have made these data available on websites. However, despite attempts of scaling up and various recommendations the project is yet to penetrate the entire land and revenue administration of the country even after so many years. There are mainly two reasons attributed to the unsatisfactory outcome of the scheme; firstly, the lack of a holistic approach to deal with the entangled and complex nature of different administrative components and secondly, the inability to substantiate the existing land records with the dynamic field realities (GOI 2008).

Bhoomi, Karnataka

Following the Union Government's efforts of computerizing land records, many state governments undertook land record computerization projects. Among such state initiatives, Karnataka's Bhoomi project turned out to be one of the most successful attempts and hence the Union Ministry of Information and Technology has announced it be the national model for country-wide replication. Starting in 2003, Bhoomi has reached out to 6.7 million farmers through 177 public kiosks in Karnataka. The land records were extremely crucial for rural citizens as they contained data concerning ownership, tenancy, loans, title, crops grown, irrigation details and so on. Before, the rural land records were maintained by village accountants manually and therefore they held the monopoly to change and manipulate these data. This led to inefficiency, non-transparency and corruption in the system. Under the Bhoomi project, this inept system has made way to online delivery of land records and online request for the change of titles in exchange of a user fee. The strong political will at all levels, effective business process re-engineering, end to end computerization, well-built back-up mechanism, strong appeal to the rural mass, professional project management team and holistic approach covering planning, implementation and escalation are cited as some crucial factors behind the success and sustainability of this project. One of the main criticisms against the project is that on one hand it exhibits considerable bias towards rich and big landowners requiring bank loans or large sum of credits. On the other hand, by eliminating village middle-men it prevents small farmers and landless labourers access to bank loans and many other developmental schemes sponsored by the State (GOI 2008; Madon 2009).

Gyandoot, Madhya Pradesh

In the year 2000, Gyandoot tele-centres project was initiated in drought-stricken Dhar district of Madhya Pradesh to provide information and selected public services to the rural citizens. The project started off by installing computers in twenty village *panchayat* offices to which 15 more privately owned centres were added later. These centres were called *Soochanalayas* and were operated by the local rural youth called *Soochaks*. These centres were connected to the Intranet through dial-up lines and were also connected to the District Rural Development Authority in the Dhar Town. The services that were made available through these centres in exchange of a nominal user fee were: daily agricultural commodity price, income, caste and domicile certificates, lists of people below poverty line, public grievance redressal, Hindi e-mail, Hindi newspapers and so on. This initiative was not sustainable for many reasons such as poor accessibility of the centres, lack of awareness, user fees for public services; lack of support from local administration; lack of proper infrastructure; inadequate back-end processes and so on (Madon 2009; GOI 2008). Another major drawback of the Gyandoot project was that it got entangled into local power structures and social inequalities which defeated the basic motivations of a citizen-friendly e-Governance reform (Sreekumar 2008). Though the project could not raise much sensation, its failure holds significant lessons for future rural tele-centres initiatives. It points out the importance of basic infrastructure such as electricity, connectivity, e-readiness of back-end processes, etc. It also brings out the role of the local context in shaping the fate of an e-Governance initiative. Lastly, engaging citizens by simplifying the IT interface and by raising awareness is also considered to be an important prerequisite.

Lokvani Project, Uttar Pradesh

This project which was initiated in Sitapur district in Uttar Pradesh in 2004 was built on a PPP model by turning already existing cyber cafes into service kiosks and 109 tele-centres. The system was customized to suit the local contexts by taking into account the use of local language, the factors of illiteracy and lack of computer literacy. Though there were other public services online registration, disposal and monitoring of public grievances gained unprecedented popularity among the users. Hence, despite the infrastructural bottlenecks and other structural issues similar to Gyandoot project, Lokvani is touted as a success story due to the intense response to the grievance redressal component. Another reason for its sustainability is the successful implementation of the PPP model for which no public subsidies, loans or capital expenditure was required (GOI 2008).

FRIENDS Project, Kerala

This project started in June 2000 in the Thiruvananthapuram district in Kerala and was later replicated in other districts in 2001–2002. 'FRIENDS' (Fast, Reliable, Instant and Efficient Network for the Disbursement of Services) provides a single window opportunity for citizens to pay taxes and others dues to the state government through Janasevana Kendrams located across district headquarters. This project was launched despite the inadequate back-end computerization status of many government departments. Instead a hybrid system, combining front-end computerized service delivery with manual back-end processing was adopted. To ease the process, a government order was issued to confer similar status to payment receipts acquired from FRIENDS counters as that of receipts from the concerned departments. Given the success of the project further upgradation plans were conceived (GOI 2008).

Rural e-Seva, Andhra Pradesh

This project was initiated by district administration in 2002 in the West Godavari district. Rural IT-enabled kiosks operated by local entrepreneurs and self-help groups trained by District Rural Development Agency (DRDA) was set up to provide single window service solutions for rural citizens. The services included payment of government bills, issuance of certificates, application for government schemes and loans, accessing district authority bulletins and other public information, public grievance redressal and so on. The project was financially sustainable attributing to support from NIC and to low cost software built by local engineering students. Regardless of the successful pilot phase, the project nonetheless suffered from lack of administrative institutionalization and streamlining bureaucratic processes. The public services offered depended highly on the intention and enthusiasm of the incumbent of the District Collector position and thus rendered the entire project volatile (GOI 2008; Madon 2009).

These e-Governance initiatives by no means present an exhaustive account of all major e-Governance projects in India. They simply put forward the experiences, processes and methods associated with e-Governance projects in India. Although implemented as isolated efforts, all these projects, irrespective of their success rate, bring out a few significant policy lessons: they emphasize the need for political ownership at all levels and a national vision with holistic approach towards planning and implementation of e-Governance reform; the importance of basic infrastructure; need for seamless coordination between different sections of the government; the emphatic role of the PPP model; the need to disaggregate different components of e-Governance and phase out implementation; the significance of local context in both planning and implementation of e-Governance projects; the need to evaluate the actual needs of the citizens; the importance of prioritizing process re-engineering and change management over technical issues of e-Governance (GOI 2008; Madon 2009; Sreekumar 2008).

Based on these realizations, the idea of an integrated programme approach guided by a common vision, strategy and approach was exceedingly endorsed. The idea found more support as it was believed to heavily cut down on the total outlay for e-Governance initiatives by creating shared infrastructure, interoperable standards and by averting duplications and overlaps. Consequently, the NeGP was formulated by the GOI with a vision to create a seamless view of the government for the citizens. All the initiatives undertaken in the NeGP share its common vision, approach and strategy. Therefore, it becomes imperative to shed some light on the major initiatives undertaken by the NeGP. The NeGP can be described in terms of a three-tier structure (GOI 2011b). The first tier is represented by the CSCs which is the front-end delivery point for providing a range of services to citizens in a transparent manner, at a convenient location and at an affordable cost. Moreover, they create employment/entrepreneurial opportunities for local youth who are running these centres. The second tier of the NeGP is built by the common support infrastructure that links different components of governments with each other and with the citizens. This infrastructure is provided by the SWANs and SDCs. SWANs provide wide network support from all state/UT headquarters to the Blocks. This serves as a backbone of network in providing G2G and G2C services under the NeGP. The SDCs facilitate IT infrastructure to consolidate applications and data hosted by the state. The third tier is comprised of 27 MMPs which seek to transform selected high-priority services from manual to electronic mode of delivery. They are called 'Mission Mode' for their definite timeline, clear process re-engineering plans, specific service levels and an assigned project implementation team. MMPs are often portrayed as the future of governance in India.

To illustrate further, six out of these 27 MMPs are discussed in some details. Two projects are selected from each of Union, Integrated and state MMP categories. They are selected to demonstrate the wide-ranging scope of these projects and their multi-faceted relevance for different stakeholders. It is important to clarify that the selection of these specific projects is in no way intended to suggest any special preferential criteria. The objective is to grasp the nature, extent and processes of e-Governance reform under the NeGP.[2]

Income Tax

This Union Government MMP provides a set of 18 e-Services from the Income Tax Department to the tax payers all over the country. Some of the important e-Services under this project include online submission Personal Account Number (PAN) and Tax Account Number (TAN) application, electronic filing of income tax returns, online payment of taxes, status tracking and grievance handling of PAN/TAN applications, online tax calculator, downloadable e-forms, downloading *challans* and many more. The e-filing infrastructure has been fully operation and provides key services to taxpayers. PAN application receipt, digitization and issue of PAN cards have been outsourced to service providers. Primary Data Centre (PDC) in Delhi, Business Continuity Planning site (BCP) in Mumbai and DR site in Chennai have been established for consolidating databases and integrating project roll-out. Currently, The All India Income Tax Network (TAXNET) covers all 710 offices distributed in 530 cities across India and more than 13,000 users under a single national database (GOI 2011b).

UID

The Unique Identification project is an initiative to provide identification for each resident across the country and once achieved it will serve as the basis for efficient delivery of welfare services. It will also help different government departments to effectively monitor its various programmes and schemes. This project envisages making UID the single source of identity verification which will produce and issue Unique Identity numbers to all the residents of India and will provide authentication services. Under this project, the UIDAI will collect ten fingerprints, a photo and an iris scan (eye scan) of citizens as part of the biometric data collection exercise. The UIDAI will offer a strong form of online authentication, where agencies can compare demographic and biometric information of the resident with the records stored in the central database. It will support registrars and agencies in adopting the UID authentication process by assisting in defining the required infrastructure and processes. By such process of uniquely identifying citizens, the UID project, which is also known as *Aadhaar*, will help in sifting the actual beneficiaries of several public schemes. Hence UID is expected to help in the better functioning of developmental schemes such as NREGA, *Sarvashiksha Abhiyan, Indira Awaas Yojana* offered by the Union Government and other such schemes offered by the state governments by minimizing the possibility of identity frauds which will further ensure efficient utilization of funds allocated to these schemes. The long-term outcome of this project is the gradual reduction in total expenditure on overall developmental schemes by avoiding duplication and overlap by different departments. By creating a single repository of resident data with identity information the need to undertake fresh and frequent population surveys by individual departments can be averted. This will imply a more concerted and cumulative updating of the government databases and thereby a significant reduction in the overall government outlay in generating and maintain databases. For poor and underprivileged residents, UID facilitates entry into the formal banking system and enhances opportunities for availing public as well as private services. The UID also helps migrants to acquire unique identity and hence alleviate the process of mobility. UIDAI expects to issue UID numbers to 600 million (60 Crore) residents by the end of five years of its operations. Currently, the project is in the first phase of its implementation and the budget for the next phase has already been approved (GOI 2011b).

E-Courts

This Integrated MMP is envisaged to transform the Indian judiciary system with the use of ICTs. It has a clear-cut objective, which is 'to re-engineer processes and enhance judicial productivity both qualitatively and quantitatively to make the justice delivery system affordable, accessible, cost-effective, transparent and accountable' (GOI 2011b). The scope of the project is 'to develop, deliver, install and implement automated decision-making and decision support system in courts all over the country' by attaining 'digital interconnectivity between all courts from the *taluk* level to the *apex* court' (ibid.). The services to be offered under this project include, firstly, automation of case management processes for example case filing, registration, allocation, court proceedings, disposal, transfer of case, etc.; secondly, provision of online services such as certified copies of orders and judgments, case status, case diaries and so on; thirdly, information gateways between courts and government agencies such as exchanging information with police, prisons, government departments and distant production/examination of under trial and witness through videoconferencing; fourthly, monitoring of pendency in the courts by creating a National Judicial Data Grid. All these services are expected to equally benefit citizens, litigants, judges and advocates. During the first phase of implementation, the site preparation has been completed at 10,299 courts in 1,539 court complexes and 9,536 judges and 36,605 court staffs have been given special training (ibid.).

India Portal

The National Portal of India is an integrated MMP which offers a single window unified interface for almost 6,700 government websites in order to make seamless access to government information and services a reality. It coordinates between 35 states/UTs and 63 Central Ministries to develop and compile content on the website. The portal is available in Hindi and English and it serves as a central repository of documents, forms, services, acts, announcements, contract directories, schemes and rules. It has also provided special web interfaces for NGO partnership and RTI complaints and appeals. Besides acting as a one-stop source of government-related information, the portal also helps in launching and implementing various e-Governance initiatives endorsed by the Indian Government, facilitating public participation in the process of governance and in creating policies and standards of publishing information and electronic delivery of government information and services. The National Portal has 70,000 registered users and gets about 70 million hits per month from all over the world (GOI 2011b).

Agriculture

Over the years before NeGP, the Department of Agriculture and Cooperation (DAC) has taken up several IT initiative. The states/UTs have also taken up similar initiatives under the broader umbrella of DAC. Agriculture is a state MMP which strives to integrate all such IT initiatives with the Central Agri Portal (CAP) and the State Agri Portals conceived under the NeGP. The broader vision of this MMP is '[t]o create an environment conducive for raising the farm productivity and income to global levels through provision of relevant information and services to the stakeholders' (GOI 2011b). The project aims to improve the access of timely and relevant information and services by farmers throughout the crop-cycle, to provide location specific and latest crop management information, to improve government service delivery in agriculture, to better monitor and manage schemes under DAC and to facilitate private sector involvement for the benefit of farmers through integrated service platform. The services to be offered under this project include information on crops, farm machinery, training and Good Agricultural Practices (GAPs), forecasted weather, prices, arrival, procurement points, irrigation and marketing infrastructure, soil health, pesticide and fertilizers, drought relief and livestock management and other relevant information, electronic certifications for export and import, monitoring, implementation and evaluation of schemes and programmes. It will also provide an online mechanism for stakeholders' feedback. The project proposes to provide a multi-channel delivery of information, for example through Internet, *Krishi Vigyan Kendras*, government offices, *Kisan* Call Centres, Agri-Clinics, CSCs, mobiles phones and others. Implementation in the first phase is rolled out and the second phase is under progress. This project is expected to increase transparency in agricultural services, increase farmers' participation in information sharing through penetration of information at the grass roots level, enable customization and personalization of information suited to the local contexts and facilitate engagement of academic institutions in generating and disseminating information (ibid.).

E-District

This state MMP aims to support the administrative unit by enabling electronic delivery of high volume citizen-centric government services through back-end computerization. This initiative will ensure optimal exploitation of the three infrastructure pillars of NeGP, namely, SWAN, SDCs and CSCs to achieve the ultimate vision of the NeGP, that is, to deliver services to the citizen at his doorsteps. The back-end computerization is expected to reach out up to the sub-district/*tehsil* level to e-enable the delivery of such high volume services through CSCs in a sustainable and time-bound manner. Traversing through different components of the NeGP, this project promises to create significant linkages between the back-end and front-end mechanisms of service delivery. Although it is still in the pilot phase, this project is proposed to scale up and cover all districts in India. The five core services that e-District will initially offer are: issuance of different certificates such as birth, death, marriage, income, domicile etc.; social welfare schemes such as pensions, scholarships etc.; revenue court services; public distribution system; and ration card related services, RTI related services and grievance redressal. In the first phase of implementation, districts which have 70 per cent operational CSCs will be selected for pilot roll-out. E-District pilot projects have been initiated in 41 districts across 16 states to bring high volume services at the district level, which are currently not covered by any MMP under the NeGP. E-services are launched in 24 districts in eight states (six in Uttar Pradesh, five each in Madhya Pradesh and Tamil Nadu, two each in Assam, Bihar and West Bengal and one each in Jharkhand and Kerala). In Orissa, Mizoram, Haryana, Punjub, Maharashtra, Puducherry, Rajasthan and Uttarakhand the pilot project is being implemented at a high pace (GOI 2011b).

These MMPs under the NeGP demonstrate the overall environment of e-Governance initiatives. They depict a positive and decisive trend towards diversified yet holistic attempts of radically transforming the public service delivery mechanism and the system of governance. However, this large-scale enthusiasm can easily be marred by the several challenges that are encountered in the processes of implementation of these projects. Some of these challenges are already accounted for in the project planning, some are unprecedented hitches arising from the everyday practices of execution. In order to fully grasp these complex experiences of a project implementation process, a case study of CSCs has been undertaken across a few states of India. The findings of the case study will help in assessing the role of the NeGP in transforming governance in India. A similar intensity continues to reflect in the 11th Report of the Second Administrative Reform Commission (2008b) which concentrates on promoting e-Governance in India and lays out a number of recommendations in the field.

The 11th Report of the Second Administrative Reform Commission (ARC), 2008: a snapshot of practices and recommendations in the post-NeGP policy regime

The 11th Report of the Second ARC provides a holistic picture of e-Governance in India by connecting earlier experiences of e-Governance initiatives to the present status of e-Governance reform with a future policy direction added. The report also provides substantial links between the international practices of e-Governance and the Indian ground realities. Though greatly laden with recommendation, this document nonetheless presents a glimpse of governmental attitude towards overall e-Governance reforms in India. As it becomes evident from most of the policy documents discussed in this chapter, the GOI takes keen interest in e-Governance initiatives and there is a gradual shift in the way government functions. This shift is reflected in the continuous upgrading of the policy and legal framework attuned to e-Governance reform.

The Second ARC was established in 2005. Since then it has published many reports covering different aspects of the public administration system. Its eleventh report titled, *Promoting E-Governance: the Smart Way Forward*, published in 2008 tries to:

[A]nalyse the successes and failures of e-Governance initiatives in India and at the global level, in order to extrapolate the best practices, key reform principles and recommendations that can help the government to implement a new paradigm of governance in the country. This new paradigm would focus on the use of information technology to bring public services to the doorsteps of our citizens and businesses on the basis of revolutionary changes in our institutional structures, procedures and practices that would transform the relationships between our three levels of government, our businesses and our citizens.

(GOI 2008, p. i)

The Commission in all its previous reports has touched upon e-Governance while addressing different aspects of public administration and governance issues. This report takes e-Governance as the core issue. This report presents basic conceptual frameworks of e-Governance along with its different definitions by different International Organizations and also a definition more suitable in the Indian context. As the report talks about the importance of e-Governance in India and the status of e-Governance implementation in India, it does so by placing such experiences within the broader framework of the international scenario of e-Governance. In elaborating different aspects of e-Governance, starting from core principles to legal framework, from NeGP to knowledge management, this report not only describes the recent state of affairs in India but also lists a number of recommendations for each of these aspects. Before looking at those recommendations, it is worthwhile look at some of the basic features of e-Governance that this report highlights.

The Commission argues that 'the purpose of implementing e-Governance is to improve governance processes and outcomes with a view to improving the delivery of public services to citizens' (GOI 2008, p. i). Also:

While recognizing the potential of ICT in transforming and redefining processes and systems of governance, the Commission had suggested that e-Governance is the logical next step in the use of ICT in systems of governance in order to ensure wider participation and deeper involvement of citizens, institutions, civil society groups and the private sector in the decision-making process of governance.

(ibid., pp. 7–8)

The main goals of e-Governance, according to the Commission are: (a) better service delivery to citizens; (b) ushering in transparency and accountability; (c) empowering people through information; (d) improved efficiency within governments; (e) improve interface with business and industry (ibid., p. iii).

This report also recognizes the fact that 'the benefits of information technology have not been evenly distributed . . . that most of the time the benefits of e-Governance are also reaped by the affluent sections of society' (GOI 2008, p. iii). This calls for a 'concerted effort to direct e-Governance reforms towards the common man' (ibid., p. iii). In doing so,

E-Governance needs to transform all levels of Government but the focus should be on local governments since local governments are the closest to citizens, and constitute for many, the main interface with government ... e-Governance based administrative reforms in local governments can have maximum impact on citizens.

(ibid., p. iii)

The report promotes comprehensive e-Governance reform which goes beyond the mere introduction of technology as:

e-Government is not about 'e' but about 'government'; it is not about computers and websites, but about services to citizens and businesses. e-Government is also not about translating processes; it is about transforming them. e-Government is concerned with the transformation of government, modernisation of government processes and functions and better public service delivery mechanisms through technology so that government can be put on an auto-pilot mode.

(GOI 2008, p. v)

A comprehensive e-Governance reform includes four important pillars: people, process, technology and resources; which are framed as e-Governance imperatives in the report. Though the report gives much importance to the PPP model, it nevertheless reinforces the role of the government both as a leader and a facilitator. It also delineates elements of such a role where the State should be engaged in developing a national e-strategy, making ICT adoption and network readiness a national priority; in undertaking innovative projects that make a difference, to lead by example, adopting best practices; in reforming government processes covering areas such as revenues, expenditures, procurement, service delivery, customer grievances, etc.; in tracking, storing and managing information, promoting production of national content online and through electronic media; documenting 'successes' and 'failures'; in providing high priority to protection of individual rights, intellectual property, privacy, security, consumer protection, etc. and mobilizing the civil society; and finally in developing a supportive framework for early adoption of ICT and creating a regulatory framework for ICT-related activities (ibid., pp. v–vi).

Focusing on the policy initiatives in e-Governance the report reasons,

Creating the macro-economic environment for growth and innovation in ICT, including fiscal policies (cost, innovation, investment, and venture capital), legal and regulatory environment (competition, independent regulator, rule of law, intellectual property protection) and channelizing and mobilization of resources for ICT is an important corollary to e-Governance as is implementing an education policy for the right quantum and quality of manpower resources for a network-ready economy-curricula, ICT training facilities and wiring/networking of educational institutions.

(ibid., p. vi)

As there are differences within state in e-readiness, the international digital divide is further replicated within the Indian context. Hence, a concerted nation-wide initiative to bring uniformity in e-Governance implementation is much required. Therefore, in listing policy priorities, the Commission argues,

> Addressing the 'digital divide' domestically and internationally, giving signals to markets – articulating a national vision of ICT, according national priority to ICT, undertaking large projects, promoting innovation and risk taking through fiscal concessions and availability of venture capital; creating an investment climate for domestic and foreign investment in ICT sector; championing national interests in international forums etc. are equally important.
>
> (ibid., p. vi)

The Commission also identifies the lag between policy initiatives and accomplishments in India and posits e-Governance as a tool to bridge this gap. However, the Commission reinforces that 'in any e-Governance initiative, the focus has to be on governance reforms with the technological tools provided by ICT being utilized to bring about fundamental changes in the governmental processes' and in order be effective 'e-Governance projects have to be designed for specific contexts and environments' (ibid., p. 176). In this direction, it presents a host of recommendations covering different aspects of e-Governance reform which are summarized in the Conclusion of the report. These recommendations include: building a congenial environment; identification of e-Governance projects and prioritization; business process re-engineering; capacity building and creating awareness; developing technological solutions; implementation; monitoring and evaluation; institutional framework for coordination and sharing of resources/information; optimum use of PPP models; protecting critical information infrastructure assets; building a common support infrastructure; developing a robust legal framework for e-Governance; and knowledge management.

As it becomes evident from most of the policy documents discussed in this chapter, the GOI takes keen interest in e-Governance initiatives and there is a gradual shift in the way government functions. This shift is reflected in the continuous upgradation of the policy and legal framework attuned to e-Governance reform. There are many proposed changes in the process to be integrated into the formal policy paradigm. The proposed e-Service Delivery Bill 2011 which has already been presented in the Parliament is one such policy document which has the potential to usher in substantial shifts in the legal framework for e-Governance. Even though it is yet to become an Act, once ratified it would have serious implications for institutionalizing online public service delivery mechanism.

E-Service Delivery Bill, 2011: the future of e-Governance in India

The e-Service Delivery Bill is one of the important steps towards establishing a legal framework for the provision of electronic delivery of public services.

76   *E-Governance in India: an overview*

Undoubtedly, it envisages promoting efficiency, transparency, accountability, reliability and accessibility of public services to a wider mass. The key features of the Bill (Draft Bill, GOI 2011a)[3] are:

- It compels the Government to publish a list of public services to be delivered through electronic channels within 180 days after the commencement of the Bill.
- It also enforces the grievance redressal mechanism for such services.
- It sets a five years deadline for all public services to be delivered electronically with an additional buffer period of three years.
- The Bill sets clear guidelines for simplifying the delivery processes of online services and also provides for required assistance in availing these services.
- The Bill proposes for the establishment of a Central Electronic Service Delivery Commission along with its counterparts in the State Electronic Service Delivery Commissions to overlook the functioning of electronic service delivery specified under this Bill.
- The Bill also provides for penalties in case of non-compliance with the Bill and in case of failure to redress a complaint.

The Bill, once ratified, has the potential to introduce a radical shift in the way government functions and the core principles of the citizen-government interface. By providing strict deadlines for online service delivery and providing penalties for non-compliance, the Bill ensures efficiency and better accountability in the system. By making all public service delivery through electronic channels a mandatory provision, the Bill promotes accessibility and efficiency of the delivery mechanism. Finally, the 180 days deadline for publishing all possible services to be delivered through electronic means along with the provision of regular upgradation of such information enhances transparency of the system. Hence, the e-Service Delivery Bill could possibly overhaul the entire functioning of the public administration in India.

Conclusion: the hiatus between policies and practices

Insofar, this chapter has elaborated on the overall policy environment which has been formulated and initiated in harmony with the strategic reform in e-Governance. Such a policy environment is comprised of a legal framework designed for e-Governance; developmental initiatives in terms of new projects, schemes and plans; planning documents with clear policy directions; governmental reports and recommendations with e-Governance as a core focus and so on. All these policy and project initiatives view e-Governance as a crucial area of strategic reform in order to achieve 'good governance' in the Indian context.

The basic standards of 'good governance' that e-Governance reform is expected to attain are efficiency, transparency, accountability, reliability, equitability, responsiveness, inclusiveness and reduced channels of corruption. According to the governance reform agenda of Indian policy-makers, e-Governance, by introducing ICT in public service delivery mechanism, ensures promoting these qualities of governance and thereby enhances the level of governance.

Across all the policy documents the State recognizes the importance of non-State actors, such as the market and the civil society, in governance as well as the e-Governance reform agenda. The State plays the role of a facilitator and a leader whereas the non-State actors are treated as developmental partners. There is an emphasis on cooperation among these different partners and also an expectation that the market and the civil society should slowly take on many of the State functions. The increasing influence of the non-State actors become quite apparent across all policy documents, be it in legal provisions or in national schemes for e-Governance.

The agenda of reform in e-Governance also promotes the notion of citizen-centric governance which implies increased participation of the citizen not only in terms of accessibility of public services but also through active participation in decision-making. For example, one of the main aspects of the NeGP's vision is to make public services available to all citizens in their locality. Therefore, e-Governance reform facilitates the process of democratic decentralization and makes citizen participation an inherent trait of public service mechanism.

This holistic understanding of the overall environment of e-Governance reforms is often contradicted by the ground realities of such reforms. The everyday practices of e-Governance differ considerably from the policy documents and implementation guidelines. Such contradictions are evident even within initiatives that are running successfully and they create a hiatus between policies and practices. The challenge for a researcher or observer becomes how to interpret these gaps and how to evaluate their implications for the wider reform measures and governance institutions and practices. In dealing with these issues of hiatus between policy and practices a case study methods of analysis has been taken up to investigate one of the e-Governance initiatives undertaken within a grandiose national-level planning. The CSCs Scheme, which forms one of the main pillars of the NeGP, is an appropriate example of the massive initiative taken up by the GOI spreading across all the states and UT. The case study of CSCs examines to what extent this initiative reflects the policy outlines espoused by the Indian state, what are the gaps that exist in the design, implementation and actual reception of the scheme, and how far the original objectives of the scheme are being subverted and realized within the specific context. As the case study of CSCs is spread across the four regional states within India, it also captures the variations in the ways in which gaps between policy and practices are manifested within the same initiative. Together with the interpretive policy analysis approach, the case study of CSCs serves as the testing ground of the preliminary conjectures that form the basis of this research. The following chapter unfolds the case study and the resulting findings.

4 E-Governance in context
A case study

Introduction: CSCs and context-specific understanding of e-Governance

It is often observed that e-Governance projects in developing countries do not attain the desired outcomes despite the grandiose policy framework. Now the question arises how to analyse this gap between policy and practice. Should we term it as a failure of policy or of implementation? Rather than simply labelling it as a failure, we argue that these gaps between e-Governance policies and practices are functions of a process of adaptation in the context. In order to understand how these gaps actually come into place, one needs to debunk the processes of implementation and also the everyday practices of such projects so as to capture the processes of reception. For this purpose, a case study method was chosen for this research which facilitates the in-depth understanding of the processes and practices. The CSCs Scheme under the NeGP of India, which is one of the most significant e-Governance initiatives across the country, serves as the unit of this case study.

This chapter situates the e-Governance reforms within the contextual realities. In doing so it presents the findings from the case study of CSCs which is one of the crucial initiatives under the NeGP and rolled out across the country. India's federal structure gives its regional states relative autonomy and scope of innovation while implementing a national reform initiative both at the level of policy and practice. Hence the field narratives of the case study are elaborated here as regional experiences of the four sample states which are generated out of the same pan-national initiative. At the end, these narratives are compared and interwoven into a cohesive account of India's experiences of e-Governance reform. The objective of this chapter is to demonstrate how regional contexts play a catalytic role in coping with e-Governance reforms which in turn facilitate a context-specific understanding of e-Governance.

What are CSCs?: a comprehensive account of CSCs roll-out in India

CSC is the primary physical front-end of the service delivery mechanism which forms one of the three pillars of e-Governance infrastructure model as envisioned under the NeGP. The CSCs Scheme was conceptualized in May 2006 and was approved by the GOI by September 2006 with a budget allocation of Rs. 1,649 Crores which is shared by the Union (Rs. 856 Crores) and state (Rs. 793 Crores) governments. The objective of CSCs is to integrate private sector goals with the government's social objectives through a PPP model and thereby establish a sustainable business model for achieving vigorous socio-economic change in rural India through the use of ICT. The aim of the CSCs Scheme is to establish 100,000 rural kiosks across the country with an equitable distribution – one CSC for every six census villages – thereby reaching out to a network of 600,000 villages across the country.

The CSCs Scheme is not just about rolling out IT infrastructure but it also acts as an agent of socially inclusive community participation and collective action. CSCs are expected to create rural entrepreneurship and livelihood options by enhancing rural infrastructure and capacities, to strengthen participatory governance by ensuring transparent dissemination of information and efficient service delivery, to improve accountability of public services by eliminating intermediaries and establishing direct links between users and providers (the incremental value-addition of this scheme is well captured in Figure 4.1).

The CSC has Three-tier bottom-up implementation framework. The first level is comprised of the local VLEs who are equivalent to a franchisee and work as the kiosk-operator catering to the rural mass in a cluster of five to six villages. They act as a basic contact point for the citizen and both the public and private service providers. At the second level of implementation lies the private sector partner (franchiser) termed as the SCA. They build and manage the VLE networks and the business. They are positioned to be the prime driver of the entire ecosystem of the project. The state governments appoint the SDA at the third level to facilitate implementation of the scheme within the state, to select the SCAs within the state

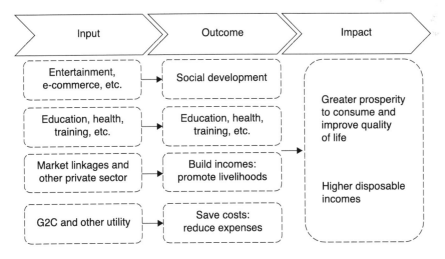

Figure 4.1 Matrix of rural development through e-Governance reform
Source: Author

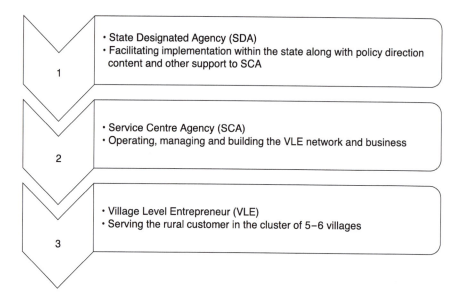

Figure 4.2 Three-tier implementing structure of the CSCs Scheme
Source: Author

and to provide policy and regulatory guidelines and other supports to the SCAs and to perform overall monitoring of the project.

The capital expenditure for setting up the CSC and other infrastructure are borne by the SCA. Even though no capital support is provided by the Government, government services (G2C) are expected to cover a part of the cash flow into the CSC. However, to attain sustainability in the face of delayed availability of G2C services, private services (B2C) could provide a viable business solution. Moreover, to overcome problems of financial viability and sustainability, a shared support is provided by the Central and the state governments in the form of a 'Guaranteed Provision of Revenue from Government Services' (GOI 2010a). By September 2010, a total of 84,830 CSCs had been rolled out across 30 states/UTs. In 21 states, more than 70 per cent of the roll-out had been accomplished whereas in Maharashtra and Uttarakhand, the implementation crossed the 50 per cent mark. However, due to lack of adequate numbers of G2C services, termination of some SCA contracts and other challenges, some of the CSCs which had been already rolled out became non-operational (ibid.).[1]

A total of 61,384 (72 per cent) of CSCs were connected by this time using multiple channels such as public services by Very Small Aperture Terminal (VSAT) and BSNL, Data Card, WILL or GPRS provided by private companies such as AirTel, Reliance and Tata Indicom. The scheme proposed to extend BSNL connectivity to all CSCs by June 2011. The CSC Online Monitoring[2] Tool has been developed to monitor the uptime performance of CSCs. By September 2010,

Table 4.1 Service status of CSCs

Name of the state	Government services available through CSCs
Andhra Pradesh	Certificates, information services on agriculture and cooperation department, utility services, online forms
Assam	Stamp vendors, certificates, pension, grievance redressal, jamabandi, utility services
Bihar	RTI service, certificates, NREGA services, grievance redressal
Gujarat	Land records, utility services, certificate, forms
Haryana	Certificates, social welfare schemes, Indira Gandhi Priyadarsini Vivah Shagun Yojna (IGPVSY), ration cards
J&K	Financial inclusion (banking correspondents)
Jharkhand	NREGA MIS data entry service, digitization of survey data, postal products, stamp vendor
Kerala	Utility services, agricultural services
Madhya Pradesh	MP online services, financial inclusion (banking correspondents)
Maharashtra	Land records, utility services
Orissa	Certificates, property tax, utility services, trade license
Rajasthan	Utility services, land records
Tamil Nadu	Electoral services, transport services, grievance redressal
Uttar Pradesh	Lokvani services, NREGA, land records, e-district services
West Bengal	Employment exchange registration, utility services, postal services, agricultural services

Source: GOI 2010b (adapted from NeGP Background Papers)

47,728 CSCs were registered under this tool whose performance could be monitored from various locations (ibid.).

A host of G2C and B2C services were provided in the CSCs by September 2010. There were many variations in such services from one state to the other.

The noteworthy B2C services that were offered by the CSCs included financial services, mobile recharge, Direct-To-Home (DTH) recharge, Railway Ticketing, Matrimonial services, e-learning, etc. The State Bank of India (SBI), Punjab National Bank and other commercial banks started using CSCs for delivery of financial products and services including banking and insurance (ibid.).

In April 2010, a Mid-Term Assessment of the CSCs Initiative (ibid.) was prepared by an independent market research team. The first step of this assessment was a Rapid Assessment Round (RAR) for which 347 villages were visited across 13 states. Out of these 347 villages, CSCs in 226 villages (65 per cent) were found to be operational. Sixty-two per cent of the CSCs which were found to be non-operational had not started services yet. One of the major reasons for CSCs not being operational was low footfall generated by the centre. The RAR observed that across all the states, villages with operational CSCs had almost double the population than where CSCs were non-operational. In some cases, there were delays on part of the SCAs to provide relevant support to the VLE, while in some cases the delay was caused by the termination of SCA contracts. In some states, incidence of insurgencies kept the traffic to the CSCs low. In states like Uttar Pradesh and Bihar issues of power supply and paved roads acted as limiting factors. The VLEs interviewed during the RAR were found to be well qualified as 98 per cent had completed secondary school or high school education, 54 per cent of them were graduates and above and 16 per cent were postgraduates and held even professional degrees. Only 64 per cent received any training for operating CSCs and most of these VLEs were not satisfied with the quality of training provided by the SCAs. One VLE had invested about Rs. 75,000 as capital expenditure in setting up the CSC, while only 20 per cent of VLEs were able to get any loan or other financial assistance such as credit schemes. On an average, a VLE was able to earn about Rs. 2,700 per month which denotes about a 13 per cent increase (from income before opening a CSC) in their monthly household income. Nonetheless it was contributing only approximately 35 per cent to their total monthly household income. Despite a low income generation, 67 per cent of the VLEs interviewed expressed their urge to continue with a hope of better return in the future (ibid.).

The IT infrastructure inside a CSC was found to be satisfactory in the RAR; however, physical space, power back-up and internet speed were found to be critical and required considerable improvement. In terms of services offered, IT/Telecom services were offered by 95 per cent of CSCs across states whereas 59 per cent of CSCs offered commercial and travel services. Financial and educational services ranked third (44 per cent) and fourth (38 per cent) respectively. Government services were offered by 30 per cent of CSCs and agricultural and health services ranked quite low in the list of services. Around 59 per cent of the CSCs during the RAR were able to generate traffic from five or more cluster villages and on an average a CSC experienced 13–14 footfalls a day. A large number of CSCs with higher footfall levels were found to be working beyond the requisite nine hours. Though some promotional activities were adopted by a number of CSCs, they lacked in innovation and depended mostly on village elderly to spread by word of mouth (GOI 2010a).

Based on these above-mentioned facts and figures, a qualitative case study of CSCs was taken up from November 2010 to July 2011 across four states of India.

Regional narratives of CSCs: an account of four sample states

Andhra Pradesh: a tale of political dilemma in a high tech state

In 2003, the Government of Andhra Pradesh (AP) started an initiative to convert Subscribers Trunk Dialing (STD)/PCO booths in rural and semi-urban areas into ICT kiosks which are called Rural Service Delivery Points (RSDPs). The service provider of RSDPs was AP Online which is a joint venture company between the Government of Andhra Pradesh and Tata Consultancy Services. Another initiative called Rajiv Internet Village (RIV) by the Andhra Pradesh government started in 2005 in order to establish 11,000 ICT kiosks in rural areas excluding the RSDPs. Given this context in rural AP, CSCs started in the state in 2008. Besides opening new centres under the CSCs Scheme, many of the RSDPs and RIVs had been converted into CSCs and the process was still ongoing at the time of the field trips. At that time the SCAs operating in the state were CMS Computers Ltd (in 11 districts) and Sreeven Infocom (in three districts). Sreeven was relatively new as they signed the contract only after contracts with two SCAs – 3i Infotech and TIMES – operating previously had been terminated. Therefore, the centres operating under these SCAs became non-functional and delayed the roll-out plan of the CSCs Scheme in the state.

The G2C services offered in the state varied from one district to another. For example, Visakhapatnam had more G2C services than any other district. In general, the most widely available G2C service was electricity bill payment on revenue share basis between AP Online and the SCA. The other common G2C services were BSNL bill payment and public service commission *challans*. The district of Visakhapatnam offered revenue services such as income certificates, land record certificates, residence proof and birth and death certificates. These revenue services under G2C had started online in this district since March 2011. The main B2C services in the state were railway reservation, mobile recharge, post-paid bill payment of mobile connections, DTH services, private insurances and Western Union money transfer services.

One of the centres visited in Visakhapatnam district earlier used to come under the Madhurawada *gram panchayat*; however, since 2008 Madhurawada was relocated under the Greater Visakhapatnam Municipal Corporation (GVMC). Despite being known as such it is surrounded mainly by villages and so the CSC here caters to these surrounding villages. The centre was run by two VLEs in partnership namely, Lakshmi and Karuna. Both of them were part of the state government run self-help groups for STD booths and were selected through interviews for the RIV centre in 2004. This RIV centre was integrated into the CSCs Scheme in 2008. Both Lakshmi and Karuna had a BA degree. The centre had two desktops and two printers. One was a laser printer which also had a scanner. One of the desktops, along with a colour printer, was given by the Andhra Pradesh government and the other system and the laser printer were bought by the VLEs. They had a BSNL broadband connection and had the online monitoring tool installed. The centre was open from 9 a.m. to 7 p.m. every day except on Sundays. They experienced power cuts only during summer months which usually lasted one to two hours a day. They did not have an inverter or generator, but they used an Uninterruptible Power Supply (UPS) device which gave them back-up for four hours. The space for the centre is given to them by the Andhra Pradesh government on Rs. 800 monthly rents.

The G2C services they offered were electricity bill deposits, BSNL bill deposits, public service *challans*, revenue services including land record, income certificates, birth and death certificates, residence proof and so on. For revenue services, the citizen will come to the CSC and apply online and in return get an acknowledgment receipt with a delivery date. Then the VLEs will collect the certificate from the *tehsil* after all the required inspection is done. They mentioned two problems regarding G2C services. Firstly, the government had opened a call centre for electricity bills since last year affecting their revenue collection which was even doubled by a collection centre very close to their centre. Secondly, there was no Joint Collector for the last three weeks (at the time of the visit) whereas the new Collector joined only three days previously. This coincided with many transfers in the local revenue office. As a result, revenue services offered through CSCs were arrested temporarily causing delay in the process and eventually agitation among the customers. Besides these two problems, there was also high demand among the citizens for especially two more G2C services, namely, road tax and driving licences.

Among B2C services they offered railway reservations, mobile recharge, DTH services and LIC insurances. They earned about Rs. 10–15 thousand per month. During March to June, due to the school and college admission season, their income might go up to Rs. 30 thousand a month. However, before the introduction of the revenue services they faced severe problems in terms of survival.

Other centres visited in Visakhapatnam district had more or less similar narratives which experienced considerable popularity of the centres due to the availability of revenue services. They also showed the influence of age-old bureaucratic processes (in terms of transfer of personnel, delay in the services and so on), the inertia within the system (existence of parallel system, duplication of procedures, dominance of intermediaries, etc.). For example, one of the VLEs in Visakhapatnam district revealed her initial challenges in getting the centre running. In her own narrative:

> I started the centre as a RIV [an Andhra Pradesh Government Initiative] in 2004. In those days the electricity department was collecting the payment on their own despite the availability of the kiosks. I personally visited the relevant offices and fought for its withdrawal. I had to struggle a lot in the initial days. . . . Now since the revenue services have been introduced; there has been a steep increase in the number of customers. Most importantly, people do not have to go to Mandala [local administrative unit] revenue offices and deal with the brokers anymore.

The second centre in Vizanagaram district came under the Mandala headquarters as well as the *gram panchayat* of Jami. The name of the VLE was K. Srinivasa, who had a BA degree. He started the centre under the RIV scheme in 2006, which was later converted into a CSC in June 2009. He had two desktops along with the printers, one of which was bought by him and the other was given by the state government. He had BSNL broadband connectivity and he had no complaints about it. However, he was facing some problem with the server which was run by the SCA (CMS Computers Ltd in this case). Power cuts were frequent during the summer months. Therefore he had arranged for an inverter which lasts up to six hours. The space for the centre was privately acquired by Srinivasa on a monthly rent of Rs. 1500. The online monitoring tool was not installed and he did not seem to have much clue about it.

The only G2C service that this centre offered was electricity bill deposit. However, there was another electricity bill collection centre, only half a kilometre away from the centre. Since this centre catered around 10–15 villages, the VLE still got enough electricity bills to deposit. Among B2C services, this centre offered mobile recharge, DTH recharge, railway reservation and LIC insurance. The LIC was quite popular among the villagers around. The VLE earned about Rs. 3,000 per month which is not enough for survival. According to him, without availability of some G2C services, especially revenue services, survival of the centre will be a serious concern.

In total, five centres were visited in AP: three in Visakhapatnam and two in Vizanagaram. Given the difference in services, these two districts exhibited quite different stories as far as the CSC implementation was concerned. Nonetheless, some generalization can still be drawn on the basis of the conversations with SDA and SCA representatives in Hyderabad, district coordinators of SCA, VLEs and also some interactions with the villagers. There was discrepancy in the way CSC had been implemented in different districts. For example, Visakhapatnam was much ahead of other districts in terms of providing revenue services and therefore was touted as a success story. This again emphasized the significance of G2C services in the effective implementation of the CSCs Scheme. VLEs where G2C services were consistently available were making profits. There was a prominent presence of women VLEs among the centres visited. Villagers admitted to the convenience of availing services from the CSCs over government administrative offices. There was evidently a lack of coordination between different governmental departments which evidently slowed down the implementation process. Most of the governmental departments in the AP were much advanced in terms of e-readiness and also have their services already available online. But there was visible reluctance on their part to bring these services under the purview of the CSCs. Due to some malpractices by previous SCAs, there was a general air of mistrust among government departments about SCAs, which became problematic for the current SCAs in particular and for the PPP model in general. AP Online, which is a joint venture of the Andhra Pradesh government and TCS, was proving to be a rival for the SCAs as they had to share the commission of most of the government services available online. The state government had similar initiatives before such as RSDPs and RIVs. This overlap between state government schemes and the schemes like the CSCs initiated by the centre created much confusion and in some places even conflict zones. Due to strong resistance from RSDPs, some CSCs could not be opened while some were even caught in impending court cases. In some isolated cases, there was also active yet indirect resistance from intermediary brokers operating in public administrative offices. Delay in the availability of G2C services were causing frustration and agitation among VLEs. During the field visit, a group of VLEs from Nizamabad district were in fact voicing their frustration and protesting in the SCA headquarter in Hyderabad. This general state of affairs of the CSCs Scheme implementation is indicative of a larger dilemma that AP appeared to be grappling with at the time – whether to push its success story of a high tech brand of urban growth or to focus on a more populist state rhetoric of inclusive development.

Gujarat: efficiency, growth and e-Governance

The e*GramVishwagram* project was initiated in 2003 in Gujarat by the state government. Given the success of the project, the GOI decided to integrate these e-Gram centres within the CSCs Scheme. By February 2010, 13,695 existing e-Gram centres were integrated into the CSCs Scheme and CSCs monitoring tool was being installed in all of them. Since e*Gram* started before CSCs, it followed a little different implementing structure than the standard CSCs structure. Each e-Gram/CSC is situated in the village *panchayat* office and the VLE is known as a Village Computer Entrepreneur (VCE). Then there is the Technical Support and Training Service Provider (TSTSP), which in addition to providing technical and training support and assistance to roll-out G2C and other e-Services, monitor and implement integration of e*Gram* with CSC. They have a team of district level and *taluka* level coordinators. The TSTSP teams visit each centre every month and present a monthly Management Information System (MIS) report. There is a smooth communication chain from the state, to district, to *taluka*, down to the village level and monitoring of the project is very high from bottom to top, mainly through videoconferencing.

As of December 2010, all 13,695 village *panchayats* had been equipped to provide a host of G2C and B2C services through VSAT broadband connected PCs (along with printer, UPS, Web Cam, VoIP Phone). G2C services offered at the time of the visit included birth certificate, death certificate, document for caste certificate, income certificate, tax collection receipts, land right records services (RoR), application forms of various development schemes through Gujarat Portal, ITI application forms, data entry work for government departments like health, etc. and electricity bill collection. Some rolled out B2C services during this time were: ticketing of railways, airlines, utility bill payments (telephone, mobile, DTH, etc.), market linkages for agriculture commodities, desktop publishing (DTP) work.

The centre visited in Gandhinagar district was in the *gram panchayat* of Vavol which was only about five to seven kilometres from the Gandhinagar Secretariat. The name of the VCE was Jawesh Rawat. The *talati* and some villagers were present at the kiosk which was situated in the Vavol *panchayat* office. Jawesh was giving only two G2C services at the moment; namely, land record certificates (RoR) and electricity bill deposit. The birth and death certificates were also issued. He roughly makes 200 copies of land record certificates a month. Only these two G2C services earned him about Rs. 5,000 a month. In the last year the connectivity had improved considerably due to broadband instead of the earlier dial-up connection. Therefore, he would now focus on B2C services, such as e-ticketing for railways, online application forms, telephone bills, insurance premium, DTH, etc. He had been running this centre for four to five years. Despite an initial few years of hardship due to infrastructural and technological issues, he had been able to sustain himself quite well, while in the last year things have improved considerably. The strategic location of the centre and the support from the *talati* and *sarpanch* helped him gain the credibility among the villagers.

Talati and villagers all had the same opinion that this centre eased their life in many ways. First, getting certificates through ICT tools made the system efficient and quick. Moreover, it saved them the trouble of travelling to the *taluka* office (which is about five kilometres away) where things moved rather slowly. Villagers were looking forward to the B2C services such as railway ticketing, online application forms for educational and employment purposes, telephone bills deposit, some limited banking facilities, insurance. These services together would make their lives self-sufficient within the village. The *talati* believed that there are a lot more services which can be made available through this platform and which might be difficult for the villagers to imagine at present.

The other centre visited in the Gujarat Industrial Development Corporation (GIDC) area was located in the Santej *gram panchayat.* It is almost equidistance from Ahmadabad and Gandhinagar in the GIDC area. There were many factories on the way to the villages. Being within an industrial belt, the village experienced a huge influx of workers from other parts of India, especially Uttar Pradesh and Bihar. The centre was as usual located inside the *gram panchayat* office and has been run by the VCE, Jivanji Thakur for two-and-a-half years. He finished his Bachelor's degree. Here also the most demanded services were land record certificates (RoR) and electricity bill deposits. Being in the industrial area helped the centre in two ways. Firstly, the influx of labourers increased the number of electricity bills along with the larger commission on the higher electricity bills of the surrounding factories. Secondly, since most of the villagers were into agriculture, they all had their own land. At the wake of rapid industrialization, land prices have gone up many times leading to frequent land dealings which in turn increased the demand for land record certificates.

Beside these two G2C services, he also did entries for birth and death certificates and other data entry jobs for the *panchayat* office. The villagers who were interviewed said they did not have much idea about how the process worked. Nevertheless they did not feel uncomfortable availing these services as they trusted Jivanji and also the fact that he sits in the *panchayat* office. Jivanji earned up to Rs. 15,000 per month. He earned most through land record certificates. However, in his opinion in a small village where land is not so important, it would be difficult for the VCE to earn that much.

The centre visited in the Rajkot district was in *gram panchayat* Mota Gundala, which was 70 kilometres from Rajkot city and 12 kilometres from Jethpur block town. The name of the VCE was Kalpesh who was pursuing a Bachelor's degree. At the moment he was solely dependent on the electricity bill deposits which come in every alternate month. The land record with thumb impression used to be available in the centre, but then it started taking too long to arrive from the *taluka* office. Therefore, villagers started going to the *taluka* office on their own. There is a high demand for this certificate and they hope after the entire process is digitized (end to end solution), it would ease their current problem and also improve the VCE's conditions who is struggling to sustain himself. Even though he was providing some B2C services such as mobile recharge, there was hardly any demand for such services from his centre. He was awaiting and looking forward to the Mahatma Gandhi National Rural Employment Guarantee Act (MGNREGA) data entry work. Overall, Kalpesh seemed low on motivation and opened the centre only four to five hours a day.

According to the district level coordinator who was present during the visit, Kalpesh also took the minutes of *gram sabha* meetings that take place every three months and put them online so that they can be further accessed at the district and state level. He also projected government programmes and schemes to the villagers through the facilities available in the centre. The *talati* said the VCE also helped with official work at the *panchayat* and he insisted that his work pressure could be minimized by various services accessible via this centre. The level of education and awareness appeared to be low in the village and hence the demand from the centre was also low. The main demands of the villagers were for RoR and electricity bill deposits.

Certain general observations could be drawn on the basis of conversations along all the levels of citizens/customers, VCEs, TSTSP team at district and state level and the representatives of the SDA. The state government has played and is still playing a very active role despite adopting the PPP model. Given the strong role played by the Gujarat government, there is commendable coordination between government departments which in turn made the implementation smooth; the bureaucracy appeared to be extremely organized and efficient, which also reflected not only in the implementation of the project but also in the neatness of the information available on the project; there is a strict centralized monitoring mechanism of the entire project. For example, a state representative in Gandhinagar commented:

> Now every state department has an IT budget for hardware, software and staff training. The Gujarat Informatics Limited (GIL) [which is part of the Department of Science and Technology, Government of Gujarat] works for the capacity building within the state government and also manages regular training programmes for the staffs. For Class 3 staffs sixteen hours of training and for Class 1 and 2 staffs one hundred hours of trainings are being provided since last seven years and the process is still on.

Such measures not only showcased the efficiency of the bureaucracy but also the priority of the state government for such reforms to be successful. The prominent presence of the state government was also manifested in availability of the sites which were centrally controlled so as to keep up the speed of connectivity. CSCs/e-Gram centres thrived more on the G2C services; the general traffic to the centre was consistent, the location was convenient and the VCEs were making profit. Though there were problems of connectivity in the first few years since its inception in 2003, by 2009 all connectivity issues were resolved.

The Gujarat model of CSCs implementation was a success story of ample bureaucratic efficiency. Though availability and relevance of many services through these centres in remote areas were of questionable nature,[3] narratives of Gujarat marked the presence of centralizing trends of bureaucracy, dominance of public agencies within the PPP model and a clear top-down mandate as some important factors behind the most successful roll-out status among the four sample state.

Rajasthan: technological leapfrogging confronting primordial social fabrics

In Rajasthan the CSCs Scheme was initiated in May 2009. As of August 2009, 500 CSCs were commissioned with a future target of total 6,626 CSCs in the State of Rajasthan. In August 2010, 1,831 CSCs were rolled out. According to the Report of Department of Information Technology and Communication of the Government of Rajasthan, by end of July 2011, there are 1,984 VLEs who are providing a pool of G2C and B2C services in all 33 districts of Rajasthan.[4] One unique feature of CSCs in Rajasthan is that the Government of Rajasthan decided that women would be given priority for selection as VLEs in the state. At the time of the visit, there were two SCAs operating in the region; namely, CMS Computers Ltd and Zoom. The SDA was RajComp and in every district there was a District e-Governance Society which played an active role in implementing the CSCs Scheme across the state. One of the major reference points for the CSCs implementation team in Rajasthan was the successful implementation of the e-*Mitra* project which was geared towards the urban centres in the state. However, the CSCs Scheme was much more extensive and complex in its scope and hence challenges facing the CSCs were also different and far more dynamic in nature.

The centre in Jaipur district was located in a village market in Khejroli which is about 65 kilometres from the city of Jaipur and took about two hours to travel to. The location of the CSC was very good as it was a busy market place. Santosh, the VLE and some villagers were around and available for interview. However, the person who runs the centre was the VLE's husband and he was not available that day. Santosh was 10th passed and her husband has completed the first year of graduation. Santosh seems uncomfortable talking in front of strangers and she did not have much idea about the operation of the kiosk. According to her there was not much work to be done in there only except during the period of electricity bill deposits which takes place every alternate month. During this period she comes to the kiosk to lend a helping hand to her husband. Santosh's father-in-law had a garment's shop under the same roof. A small portion of that was allotted for the operation of the kiosk. It had enough space to sit three to four people comfortably. The kiosk had one desktop computer along with a printer. The online monitoring tool was installed and the centre was considered to be well operational in terms of opening hours and transactions.

Most of the villagers in the surrounding area claimed that they pay their electric bills through the kiosk. It actually becomes quite crowded and they have to sometimes stand in the long queue during the bill deposit period. Nonetheless, they consider it to be a better option and want more G2C services such as land and revenue records (RoR), caste certificates and so on to be available through the kiosk. They have to go to Chomu which is about 22 kilometres away and government offices always required multiple rounds for the work to be done. For example a respondent in the Jaipur district of Rajasthan reasoned:

> I submit my electricity bill through the kiosk. It is much easier as I do not have to travel much to do this and waste half of my day. Though there are sometimes long queues in front of the kiosk during bill deposit period, it is still quicker. I wish the RoRs' for Land Records and Caste Certificates were also available here. Now, we have to travel all the way to Chomu which is about 20 kilometres away for all these services. You can see the state of local

transport here. It is not so easy to travel such distances. On top of that, our work is never done in one trip. We have to make several rounds of trips to the administrative offices, bribe inconsequential people such as gateman, peon, etc. and face unnecessary harassment for getting simple things done.

In Udaipur district the pre-selected CSC could not be visited on account of 'bad roads'. However, this reason was cited by the accompanying project team and was not verified with any factual evidence. Instead a different centre at Sarada block, which was based at a *tehsil* level and was situated right opposite to the block administrative building, was visited. This centre was about 62 kilometres from Udaipur city. The VLE, Mukesh had a Bachelor's degree in Information Technology. The franchise for the kiosk was acquired in the name of his sister, but she got married and moved, and hence he took over. He had a job in the local *panchayat* office and was also working as the block coordinator for the CSCs VLEs in Sarada block.

There was quite a rush in the kiosk at the time of the visit. There were two systems along with the printer. The kiosk also had a photocopy machine which attracted a lot of customers, especially given its location opposite the block administrative office. According to the VLE, the earning from the centre was not enough to sustain him, only because of his job in the *panchayat* office and his photocopy business that he can somehow manage. He also reiterated that the good location and his personal contacts in the block administrative office and *panchayat* proved to be very helpful in promoting his centre.

Mukesh's problem was a little different from the previous VLE in Jaipur district. Since this kiosk was situated right opposite the *tehsil* office, villagers would feel reluctant to come to his centres for most of the G2C services, except the electricity bills. So for him unless and until G2C services are channelled only through CSCs, it would be difficult for him to tap the villagers for those services.

Based on the conversations among all the levels of citizens/customers, VLEs, SCAs and SDA and also interviews conducted during the VLE workshop (organized by the State Department of Information Technology and Communication and attended by VLEs across the state, representatives of the SCAs and the SDA) in Jaipur (which was attended for two full days) certain general points could be drawn about the experiences in this state. There was high demand for G2C services, but the only consistent G2C service available across the state during the field visit was the electricity bill deposits; the footfall varied from one month to the other. For example, in Rajasthan electricity bills were deposited every alternate month. Hence, there was a rush in the centres during the bill deposit dates. Most villagers who have used CSCs recognized that it was more convenient than going to crowded government departments and also saved the time and money spent on their trips to administrative offices. However, some of the villagers interviewed within the public service camp in a village school almost five kilometres away from the nearest CSC were not even aware of its existence. Incidentally, most of these villagers were women whose husbands were migrant labourers in some other states. Noticeably, though most of the CSCs franchises (VLE contract) were given to women as a result of the special policy drive of the state government, most of the VLEs at the ground level were found to be actually male relatives of these women. The CSCs visited reflected the same trend. Even during the workshop only a nominal number of women VLEs were present. There was a problem of connectivity across the state which was mostly dependent on BSNL and there was an apparent lack of coordination between the SDA and BSNL, particularly at the lower level of bureaucracy despite several attempts of negotiation. The bottleneck allegedly laid in reluctance among the ground level employees owing mostly to their lack of awareness about CSC. The lack of coordination between government departments was visible in a number of cases. For example, there were some centres which faced problems in collecting electric bills, because there was already the same service available at the electricity board very close to their kiosks. Despite repeated requests, this did not stop and the VLEs were losing out on their customers. There was also a problem of power supply for which it becomes almost imperative for the VLEs to arrange for back-up power sources, such as an inverter or generator. This definitely turns out to be an additional financial burden for most of the VLEs. There was a considerable amount of confusion among VLEs about the financial management system run by the SCAs, however, the problem of sustainability was their major concern given the slow arrival of G2C services. In terms of the G2C services, VLEs also faced the problem of credibility as they were perceived as merely a private franchise lacking the authenticity of public offices. There was a growing frustration among VLEs as some of them had taken a loan to set up the kiosk and were now running the shop at a loss. Another noteworthy observation witnessed in a few cases within the state was an underlying tension between the field coordinators of the SCAs and the District E-Governance Society which were the local implementing bodies of the state government.

Field narratives of Rajasthan underline the process of implementation fraught with an entanglement of infrastructural, bureaucratic and socio-cultural problems. On one hand, there was strong push towards labelling it as a flagship governance reform programme of the state government by embedding other developmental goals (such as rural development, decentralization, women's empowerment, etc.). On the other hand, an inept bureaucracy, low-levels of economic development and infrastructure and an archaic patriarchal social structure grappled (sometimes inadvertently) with the meta-narrative of those reform strategies.

West Bengal: reform caught under political transition

In West Bengal, the CSCs Scheme was initiated in 2007 by the name of *Tathya Mitra* with a target of 6,797 centres across the state. According to the West Bengal *Panchayat* and Rural Development Department sources, as of 31 May 2010, 5,211 CSCs had connectivity and were operational. The main SCAs which were selected in the beginning of the project were SREI *Sahaj* e-Village Limited and Reliance Communications Limited. They had a target of 4,937 and 1,860 centres respectively. However, at the time of the visit only SREI was working as the SCA, since the contract with Reliance was already terminated in response to their poor performance. CSCs in West Bengal were offering only two G2C services in March 2011, i.e. electricity bill deposit and BSNL bill deposit. Most of the other services offered were mainly B2C. The main B2C services offered were; internet surfing, digital photography, DTP, computer education, e-learning courses, railway ticket reservation, mobile phone top-ups, insurance premium deposit, photo capturing for MGNREGA job card, etc. The online monitoring tool had been installed in more than half of the operating CSCs in the state by SREI by May 2010.

This first centre visited in the state was in the North 24 Parganas almost at the outskirts of the city of Kolkata. The *gram panchayat* was called Ganganagar and the name of the VLE was Biswajit Mazumdar. He had been running this centre for three months. There was one computer and one printer in the kiosk. The online monitoring tool was installed. He ran a parallel business as a private cable TV service provider. He came to know about this franchise through personal contacts of his father in the local electricity board office. The only G2C services he offered was electricity bill deposit. On a daily basis he deposited around 30 bills. There are two problems that he mentioned about this G2C service. Firstly, he was receiving some of the factory electricity bills for huge amounts which he refused. The reason being, his commission on the bill amount remained fixed irrespectively and hence he concentrated only on household electricity bill deposit. Secondly, a lot of his customers came after the due date which he is not allowed to submit. Therefore, he would have preferred a commission in a certain percentage of the bill which would increase his profit share for the larger bill amount and also he would have liked to be allowed to submit the bills beyond due dates. He could not deposit BSNL telephone bills as the locality has the same exchange as Kolkata and that was not integrated into the system as yet. The B2C services that he provided were mobile phone top-ups, railway reservation (which was temporarily suspended during the time of the visit). But he did not seem to be too keen on B2C services as he had his own business to look after. When asked, he said he was running at a loss. Nonetheless, since he has just started he would rather give it some more time to take-off and wait for other G2C services to arrive.

The centre in Howrah district belonged to block Uluberia II and *gram panchayat* of Baribaon and the area was known mostly as Rajapur. The centre had a very good location inside the premises of the Block Development Office. The VLE, Imran Kazi was very young, enthusiastic and a student of BA final year. He had been running the centre for the last two years. He had two laptops, two printers and also a photo printer. He had both an inverter and a generator, but he said the inverter had been more than sufficient. He was connected through VSAT. He would have liked a broadband connection which is currently beyond his affordability. He came to know about the CSC franchise through a newspaper advertisement and went to the Howrah district office to apply. West Bengal government's Department of *Panchayat* and Rural Development requested the erstwhile Block Development Officer (BDO) to provide Imran with some space inside the block office premises. Accordingly, Imran got this office space with a No Objection Certificate from the BDO. Since then he has to get the lease agreement every now and then depending on the agreement he has with the BDO.

Like most other VLEs in West Bengal, Imran also offered electricity bill deposit as the only G2C service. On a monthly basis he deposited 500–700 electricity bills. Initially this was not the case. He used to get only about 250 bills per month. However, recently the nearby electricity board office had been removed which increased his business. Though he earned the most from electricity bill deposit, Imran also focused on some B2C services. He offered about five e-learning courses which cost Rs. 1,000 per month each, insurance from different companies, online form download and fill-up, result publications, printouts, etc. The current BDO gave him some work on MGNREGA data entry and other office work including printout for his office. However, Imran thought this is only temporary and could change any time if there was a new BDO. According to Imran, he ran the centre on a no-profit no-loss basis. He would like to have more G2C services such as voter card, pan card, driving license, ration card, birth and death certificates. There was, in his view, high demand for these services and this would definitely make the kiosk profitable.

Although a total of eight centres were visited in West Bengal almost all the VLEs narrated similar experiences. Therefore, an attempt has been made to summarize the issues on the basis of the experience in all centres and conversations with all stakeholders related to CSCs in the state. Though the project had been initiated in 2007, there were hardly any G2C services available in the state. There appeared to be a problem of e-readiness in most of the government departments which delayed the process of channelling G2C services through CSCs. As one of the field executives from the SCAs in West Bengal commented:

> There should be as many G2C services as possible in the CSCs. Government services might not be very profitable (for the VLEs or the SCAs) but they help increasing the popularity and credibility of the CSCs. Public response [for G2C services] is very high.

There was a temporary problem on the *Sahaj* Portal during the field visit which was attributed to system upgradation. There was mounting frustration among VLEs regarding G2C services. The B2C services and especially e-learning was quite popular among the citizens. There was a talk of turning CSCs into local banking agents. Beside the online monitoring tool, there was lack of strong monitoring mechanism at the state level. There was more room for training for the VLEs.

The implementation process of CSCs was marked with political uncertainties looming large in the state as it was on the brink of a regime change. A state assembly election was due within two months and the fall of a long-standing government by the Left Front was widely predicted. Consequently, all administrative processes were experiencing a lull which resulted in delays for most G2C services. There was an air of apprehension across all groups of actors involved in the project which was further accentuated by the frequent incidence of political violence across the state. Amidst these broader environments of political instability e-Governance reform took a back seat.

E-Governance reform and regional contexts: a comparative perspective

The regional narratives above show how e-Governance reform unfolded differently in each of the sample states. This section tries to pull together these unique narratives into a comprehensive comparative analysis of the CSCs Scheme across four sample state. Firstly, it provides a cursory yet compact account of differential status of implementation in these states (see Table 4.2).[5]

Moving beyond this implementation status, now we will examine how the contextual realities of each state affect the process of e-Governance reform in general. The contextual realties are manifested through myriad political, cultural and social factors. However, in comparing the e-Governance reform in these four states a set of four criteria are deployed here. They are namely, policy drive, the status of bureaucracy, political will and the local socio-political dynamics. They demonstrate how each of these factors played a crucial role while implementing a national project thereby leading to different outcomes in different states. These criteria of analysing context-specific e-Governance are in no way extensive, but they nonetheless quite straightforwardly explicate the importance of the context in harnessing the governance through e-Governance.

Policy drive

Given the federal structure of India, the state governments enjoy relative autonomy in policy-making in a number of areas. This led to different kind of policy-orientations in different states. In the case of CSCs, the diverse nature of IT policy and particularly e-Governance orientations of the state governments in all four states influenced the implementation process in a significant manner. For example, Gujarat and AP have made much progress in developing the physical infrastructure and wider IT environment due to a consistent track record of favourable IT policy environment in the states, whereas in Rajasthan the policy focus on IT infrastructure and e-Governance is fairly new. These differences reflect in the way CSCs are rolled out in these states as Rajasthan's infrastructural issues act as a deterrent in the level of IT penetration among the masses. Conversely, in AP, despite an initial thrust on the IT sector during Chandra Babu Naidu's tenure (1995–2004), IT took a back seat in the state policy framework after his electoral debacle. This attitudinal shift was quite evident in the interviews with all the state officials in AP and the slow pace of implementation of the CSCs in the state was partly attributed to this policy shift.

In another instance where a state policy was found to be conducive for the effective outreach of CSCs, Gujarat government's strategy can be cited. The state's initiative to establish e-Gram centres in each *panchayat* office building proved to be a successful strategy as it ensured more visibility of the project, more accessibility for village populations as well as increased the credibility of the VLEs despite their private franchise status. In addition, the co-existence with the *panchayat* office led to better cooperation between the public and private partners on one hand, and to higher state-monitoring of the project on the other. Even though Gujarat shows an

Table 4.2 Comparative status of the CSCs in the four sample states

Status of CSC implementation Categories of evaluation	Name of the states visited			
	Rajasthan	Gujarat	West Bengal	Andhra Pradesh
G2C services	Electricity bills	Birth certificate Death certificate, document for caste certificate Income certificate, tax collection receipts Land right records services (RoR- 7/12 and 8A) Application forms of various development schemes through gujarat portal ITI application forms, data entry work for government departments like health, etc.	Electricity bill deposits BSNL bill deposits	Electricity bill deposits
B2C services	There were no standardized B2C services across centres. The most common were railway reservations, mobile top-ups, print outs, photocopies	Electricity bill collection E-Ticketing of railways and airlines, Utility bill payments (telephone, Mobile, DTH, etc.) Market linkages for agriculture commodities DTP work	Utility bill payments (mobile, DTH, etc.), e-learning courses, railway reservations, private insurances	Railway reservations, utility bill payments (post paid mobile, DTH, etc.) Mobile top-ups Private insurances, Western Union money transfer services

(*Continued overleaf*)

Table 4.2 Continued

Status of CSC implementation	Name of the states visited				
Categories of evaluation	Rajasthan	Gujarat	West Bengal	Andhra Pradesh
Connectivity	BSNL Broadband (there were many complaints of low connectivity)	VSAT Broadband (no problem of connectivity, however, controls on availability of websites)	Not standardized, some were connected through VSAT, some through Broadband. Ones with broadband did not have much problem of connectivity	BSNL Broadband (connectivity was not a problem)
Infrastructure	The space was usually arranged by the VLE, everyone had at least one PC and a printer. One of the main problems was electricity as everyone could not afford an inverter or generator	Gujarat had the most standardized infrastructure in terms of location in *panchayat* office, technical equipments, connectivity and other facilities	Space was organized according to the contacts of the VLE, some were in BDO or *panchayat* office and some were privately acquired, every centre had one PC and a printer, other systems and equipments were arranged by the VLE	Most of the centres were acquired by VLEs privately, each centre had one PC and printer given by the state government and the rest were arranged by themselves
Status of VLEs	VLEs without any other private business of their own were finding it difficult to be sustainable	With G2C services, most of the VLEs were in a comfortable position, some even earning quite well	It seemed to be a mixed experience, without much G2C, some VLEs were fighting for survival. While some others were doing well relying only on B2C services	Except Visakhapatnam, VLEs were fighting for survival which led to deep frustrations, sometimes invoking strong agitation. Another problem was conflict with other projects run by the state

Role of the state government (SDA)	State government played an active role through the SDA in motivating the VLEs as well as coordinating among different departments	The state government played the most active role in all levels of implementation and operation of the project	The role of the state government seemed to be much in the background	There seemed to be some kind of reluctance within the state government in implementing CSC
Role of the private sector (SCA)	Despite some problems, SCAs worked closely with the state agencies in implementations of CSCs	Role of the SCAs were more of a facilitator to the SDA	SCA played a very active role in the project implementation	SCAs were trying to play an active role albeit in a not so pronounced way
Status of the PPP model	Both SDA (public) and SCAs (private) seemed to have an equal stake, hence more of a cooperation between public and private partners	State had much stronger role despite the adoption of the PPP model	SCA, the private partner, had a more visible presence than the public agency in the PPP model	There was a lack of cooperation between the governmental departments (except the SDA) and the SCAs, which was a hindrance to the PPP model within the CSC project framework
Citizen awareness and participation	General awareness was low. Demand was high for G2C services which attracted most of the traffic to the centres. However, the availability of G2C services were limited	General awareness and participation were both quite high	General awareness level was substantial yet the participation did not match the level of awareness	Both awareness and participation was high in centres where revenue services were available

Source: Author

intense state control over the PPP model, nonetheless such a strategic policy position of the state government was effective in increasing the outreach of the initiative.

The status of bureaucracy

A direct impact of the state government's policy orientation reflects on the functioning of the bureaucracy. The status of the bureaucracy is represented by both its capacity to absorb change and its attitude towards change. E-Governance reform hinges heavily on both these aspects. Barring Gujarat, in all the other sample states either of these aspects was missing which further impacted the implementation process of the CSCs. For example, in West Bengal the capacity of the bureaucracy was a major hindrance towards channelling government services through CSCs even with much infrastructural advancements. There was severe lack of coordination between different governmental departments as well as between public and private partners. In Andhra Pradesh, where the e-readiness and capacity of the bureaucracy was a non-issue, coordination and cooperation between departments posed considerable challenge. The departmental initiatives were mostly run by a champion-driven vision and innovations which did not trickle down to lower levels of the bureaucracy. A similar trend was evident in Rajasthan as well where the non-cooperation of the lower bureaucracy across departments was one of the main bottlenecks experienced by the CSCs team in the state. One of the reasons behind such non-cooperation was aversion to change. The local bureaucracy in village areas enjoyed considerable authority without much need of any accountability. Introduction of public services through CSCs challenged this sphere of authority not only through digitization of services but also by demanding greater transparency and accountability in public service delivery mechanism. In Andhra Pradesh as well, the VLEs where CSCs were running successfully complained about such non-cooperation from local bureaucracies in the initial stages. In Gujarat, bureaucracy appeared to be more adept to e-Governance reform. For example, the organized and efficient functioning of the bureaucracy was already witnessed even before making the field trip to Gujarat. This was evident in the way the field visits (of just an ordinary academic researcher) were planned and coordinated as well as communicated in an efficient and systematic manner. In the case of CSCs, where the centres were well integrated into *panchayat* operations, the local bureaucracy as well as village *panchayats* facilitated the process of implementation. Another factor which made much difference in the case of Gujarat was the pressure from higher political authority. This factor brings us to the next criterion of political will.

Political will

The idea of a political will is closely related to the role of state political elites and interest groups which are again a by-product of the federal structure of the Indian State. This criterion is also closely related to the policy domain as the political elites and interest groups within the state exert enormous influence on the policy orientation of the state governments. In case of e-Governance reform also this political will plays a crucial role and it was time and again reiterated during the interviews with the experts as well as state officials. For example, in the case of West Bengal, the political leadership of the erstwhile Left Front government found itself in the midst of controversies and political opposition (within and outside the party rank and file) in the face of their pro-growth developmental stance. This led to a general environment of suspicion and ambiguity around reform policies and practices of which e-Governance was also a victim. Especially, during the field visits in West Bengal in March 2011 with state assembly elections approaching in two months (May 2011), either CSCs, or e-Governance in general did not seem to appear on the priority list of the political leadership in the state. A similar narrative was encountered in Andhra Pradesh, where IT is considered a jinxed topic for much of the political leadership particularly after the decline of Chandra Babu Naidu. During his tenure as a Chief Minister massive policy reform was introduced in the state with much hype and publicity. Andhra Pradesh made significant progress in the field of IT and e-Governance and the capital Hyderabad was often touted as the Silicon Valley of India. However, Naidu's defeat in the 2004 assembly election was attributed to the backlash of his reform strategies that focused more on technology-driven Hyderabad-centred development at the expense of the rural mass. Hence, the political leadership since then maintained the rhetoric of pro-poor social policies. Though e-Governance continued to receive state funding, it did not remain on the priority list of the politicians. Quite the contrary, e-Governance received much attention of the highest leadership in Gujarat and Rajasthan, even though both these state were not quite at the same level of e-Governance development. In Gujarat, political leadership put e-Governance reform in their top checklist of the overall development agenda of the state. Consequently, they took several policy measures to incapacitate the bureaucracy and embed e-Governance reform to the lowest unit of state administration. The clear mandate from the political leadership and the pro-active demeanour of Chief Minister Narendra Modi provided the much-needed impetus for the reform and hence accelerated the pace of reform albeit with some significant criticism. Hence, the Gujarat government's initiative of e-Gram was already advancing at a fast pace when the CSCs Scheme was conceived at the national level and acknowledging the success of the state initiatives CSCs were incorporated into the e-Gram centres. In Rajasthan, the political leadership has now arisen to the significance of e-Governance reform in improving public service delivery model. This reflects in the earnest effort of the policy-makers of the state and the subsequent push to the bureaucracy in implementing CSCs in the state as well as other measures to improve public service delivery mechanism.

Local contextual dynamics

Local social as well as political factors also play a role in the implementation processes as they have the potential to leverage the role of the political elites, the policy framework as well as the bureaucracy. In the local networks of power involving administrative personnel, village leaders are key players in any effective reform process. For example, secondary literature on many e-Governance projects in India has displayed how these power networks worked against the sustainability of the initiative (Sreekumar 2008; Panda 2007). In the case of CSCs, local social as well political circumstances act as both an impediment and an incentive in different states. Some of the political factors particular to the states and their role in CSCs implementation process are already mentioned in the discussion on the other three criteria. Furthermore, in states like Andhra Pradesh and West Bengal, the volatile political situations acted against the roll-out of e-Governance reform. In Andhra Pradesh, the separatist movement of Telengana affected the general reform agenda in a significant way as it preoccupied a considerable amount of political and administrative attention, thwarting the pace of institutional reform. This coincided with other forms of protest within the CSCs project itself. During the time of the visit, the VLEs of Nizamabad district demonstrated in the capital against the slow roll-out of public services through CSCs and the reluctant attitude of the state government. Reportedly, similar protests had taken place on earlier occasions as well. Another point of contestation in Andhra Pradesh CSCs was the existence of similar Internet kiosks from previous initiatives of the state government. These kiosk operators not only took legal measures to prevent the rolling out of CSCs in their locality, some also took recourse to violent measures. As a result, many CSCs in Andhra Pradesh remained non-operational in spite of being officially opened. In West Bengal, political violence in some of the district was on an upswing (as observed during the field trip) accounted to Maoist insurgency, political rivalry between the incumbent allies and the opposition parties. The state assembly elections were impending and the exit of the long-standing Left government was almost imminent and there was a general air of massive political and institutional change riding on the success of the regional party the *Trinamool* Congress. However, the process of change was fraught with much aggression and violence on both sides. This wider regional political situation led to a sense of instability within the political institutions which was only likely to increase given the future change of the state cabinet. The volatile regional political contexts rendered not only the process of CSCs implementation difficult at a bureaucratic level but also in the everyday practices of the centres. In many places centres could not operate due to such incidence of political violence. Another example of political influence was witnessed in West Bengal, where some VLEs got their contracts through their political connections at the local level. During an interview, one of the field executives mentioned that some of the *panchayat* heads and BDOs were known for such favouritism, in some cases there was action against them but most of the time it continued as business as usual. In Rajasthan, regardless of the highest political will, the local contexts at times played out quite differently. For example, despite the state policy women VLEs were hardly visible on the scene and this went quite openly without stirring much ire among the officials and politicians. The gender inequality within the state of Rajasthan was acknowledged in the rhetoric of state policy, however without insistence on enforcement of the same policy. In another instance, the tension between the local representative of the private sector players and their public sector counterparts added to the complexities of the implementation process. For example, in Jaipur the field executive of the SCA and the official of the district e-Governance office shared a mutual understanding of the local situation and admitted to the shortcomings of both the public and private partners, whereas in Udaipur the situation was quite the reverse as the partners were busy blaming each other. The local contexts display even more diversity in the ways local *panchayats* or block administrative units extended their hands to the CSCs. In Gujarat they were mostly supportive, whereas in other states the situation differed on a case-to-case basis even within one district. The entrepreneurial qualities of the individual VLE and their personal relationships to the local elites also added to the diverse CSCs narratives across regions.

These comparative regional narratives do not intend to merely evaluate the performance of the state in implementing e-Governance reform. Instead, they demonstrate how each region differed in their experiences of the same reform initiatives. The above-mentioned criteria are only symptomatic of a few main factors behind such diverse trajectories of e-Governance reform and in bringing in the significance of local contexts in the national framework of public policy orientation and strategic reform. These contexts-specific narratives also hint at a few broader analytical questions. To what extent could e-Governance facilitate governance reform? Is efficient bureaucracy a prerequisite for successful reform? How does the agency of the actors affect policy processes and institutional structures? Hence, the policy prescriptions, project implementations processes and new institutional set-ups emerging in the form of internet kiosks – all together pose a larger analytical challenge to explain how structure and agency confront each other and ultimately e-Governance reforms bridge the state and society.

Conclusion: questioning technological determinism

As we argued in the beginning of this chapter, context-specific understanding of e-Governance is extremely crucial in evaluating how these reform initiatives are affecting the overall quality of governance. Regional narratives from the field which include experiences of the public and private sector, of VLEs and citizens, brings out the wide range of understandings of the same project and the comparison between these narratives further enrich the analysis of these regional differences. The significant learning that comes out of this analysis is that any reform in e-Governance need to consider issues not only related to technology (ICTs in this case), but also issues of politics and culture. In most of the policy paradigm, we observe an ardent faith in the potential of technology to alter governance, to alter life in general. However, this technological determinism moves our attention from the complex relationship between technology on one side and politics and culture on the other side. It is the constant negotiation between these forces that determine which technology we produce and adopt and how we consume and receive these technologies. It is also important to remember here that this relationship between politics, technology and culture is universal even though the specificities and the way they actually play out will differ from one context to the other. It is with this broader understanding of e-Governance reform that we should move ahead to explore how e-Governance in India fares in leveraging the state–society dynamics.

5 Negotiating politics, technology and culture

Introduction: ramifications of e-Governance on the quality of governance in India

The endeavour to study e-Governance in India started with a simple aim to understand the effects of strategic reform on the quality of governance in the country. Consequently, this research is based on four basic points of departures (four theoretically informed conjectures) which serve as the link between e-Governance reform and the overall quality of governance. Now, having analysed the primary and secondary sources on e-Governance policies and practices in India, it is imperative to infer a few general patterns of e-Governance and draw concomitance to those conjectures.[1] For this purpose, in this section we revisit the four basic postulations on the basis of the general observations drawn from the analysis of policies and practices of e-Governance.

One of the key assumptions behind studying e-Governance reform is that as a strategic reform it improves the life-conditions of the citizens and thereby improves the level of governance. The findings clearly indicate there has been a major shift in the policy paradigm of e-Governance. In the drive to take IT to the masses the legal framework has been reformed, a national strategy has been adopted with a vision to take services to the doorsteps of the citizens. As it becomes evident through the case study of the CSCs Scheme, there is a high demand among citizens to avail public services without hassle, to acquire information about services without interruption and to voice their concerns and grievances without intimidation. E-Governance initiatives such as the CSCs and other MMPs under the NeGP strives to provide for these needs of the citizens. Field narratives from the CSCs show how citizens can actually benefit and how their experiences in availing public services can improve through the scheme. It minimizes the time to avail services, reduces the trips to government offices, curtails the frequency of bribes and cases of nepotism. Thus, it can be argued that e-Governance initiatives create avenues for citizen-centric governance and hence have a positive impact on the level governance. However, what remains uncertain is to what extent these potentials that ICTs offer could be fully realized in the current circumstances. As we witnessed the inertia and ineptness of bureaucracy, mere populism or lack of political will on the part of the governing elites and the problems of inadequate infrastructure stand in the way of optimum utilization of these technologies. Lack of a proper understanding of citizens' needs adds to this problem. Without such a need assessment, technology often becomes ornamental instead of enabling.

The second major assumption about e-Governance is that as a strategic reform it caters to the overlapping benefits of all political and non-political actors and as a result improves the quality of governance by bridging the gap between different power positions within the society. According to the policy network of e-Governance (see Figure 2.3) there are five major stakeholders, namely International Organizations, State or the public sector, market or the private sector, citizens and civil society. The role of the State has been to co-opt all the major players into the broader framework of e-Governance reform. The secondary literature on IT policies in India and primary sources on the same uniformly suggest the strong presence of International Organizations such as the World Bank, the UNDP, DfID and so on under the broader agenda of 'good governance' and e-Governance for development. All the major policy documents in India are fraught with the idea of e-Governance reform to achieve 'good governance' and also with examples of best practices as espoused by the major International Organizations. These organizations actively engage in the policies and processes of e-Governance in India. The World Bank representative interviewed as part of the expert group confirmed the support that his organization provides to the central as well as the state governments in terms of technological solutions and policy advice. The private sector goals are also integrated into most of the e-Governance initiatives taken up by the State. The overarching model on which the NeGP is constructed is the public–private partnership (PPP). Similarly one of the guiding principles of the CSCs Scheme is to integrate the developmental role of the State with the market orientation of the private sector players. As a result all the CSCs are run by private companies (SCAs) to provide both G2C and B2C services through individual rural entrepreneurs (VLEs). Hence, through a sole initiative it creates opportunities for livelihood in villages, plugs in to private resources to build infrastructure in rural areas and brings a single-window front-end service delivery channel to the rural mass. In terms of civil society organizations, no particular instance was found during the case study. However, a few such organizations were visited in Delhi and there are more such specialized NGOs in other parts of the country. They mostly worked in the field of digital empowerment, e-Governance promotion, social and legal aspects of IT/ICTs. They provided consultative support to the State on different policy and implementation issues. Furthermore there is a continuous emphasis within the public sector for capacity building and better coordination among different departments and wings of the government. The varied examples from the case study reveal the manner in which the State relentlessly tries to accommodate all the interest groups and devise policy solutions. In each particular instance, the CSCs implementation clearly demonstrates how successful policy outcomes and hence better levels of governance could be accomplished by proficiently assimilating conflicting interests. Nonetheless, one of the important findings from the CSCs case study is that where the state takes more control over the process, the roll-out tends to get faster.

However, this top-down approach runs against the guiding principle of NeGP and the project objective of CSCs as well. In the wider context of governance reform debate this also becomes problematic as it promotes centralizing tendencies within the state and bureaucracy and defies the logic of decentralization and partnership models between state, market and civil society sectors.

The ability of macro-policies to accommodate embedded values and norms within a local context is directly linked to the quality of governance. This broader assumption fits perfectly well into the e-Governance policy responses in India. The ability to adapt into the everyday life of citizens is one of the guiding principles of the CSCs Scheme. Using local language has been one of the policy guidelines for e-Governance in India. For example the Tenth Five Year Plan clearly describes:

> Creation of softwares for establishing an interface with the diverse Indian languages used in India poses a real challenge. In the Tenth Plan the endeavour will be to develop suitable software and technologies to enable people to interact and use computers in local languages. Internet accessibility and content creation in local languages will be promoted.
>
> (GOI 2002)

The use of local languages is evident in the interfaces with citizens under the CSCs Scheme and use of software in local languages was also encountered within the CSCs visited.

The designing of the CSC Scheme as rural tele-centres/ Internet kiosks exhibits innovation on part of the policy-makers to suit the Indian context of mass illiteracy and to deal with concomitant digital divide. The VLEs under the CSCs Scheme act as a link between the illiterate masses and the public authorities. These VLEs were found to be competent in dealing with this responsibility. The educational qualifications of VLEs were found to be quite satisfactory as described by the Impact Assessment Survey (GOI 2010a). The same trend was reinforced during the case study as all the VLEs interviewed had completed school and 15 out 22 (68 per cent) had a university degree. There was also special training imparted to them for running the kiosks from the SCAs. However, the quality of these trainings did not appear to be adequate given the holistic requirement for running these centres. To address this need the erstwhile DIT, GOI has approved (with funding) an initiative to certify VLEs of the CSCs Scheme under the Department of Electronics and Accreditation of Computer Courses (DOEACC) Society's Course on Computer Concept (CCC). VLEs receive the course certificate by successfully passing the exam and an authorization from the DOEACC Society to impart the same training to citizens. This initiative envisages to facilitate VLEs to further train citizens in their locality and to enhance their own service capabilities and income. It also helps in standardizing the digital literacy level of VLEs across India which is recognized by government departments. Under the same initiative a pilot in a few selected states was also approved on a Women's Literacy Scheme by giving special incentives to trained VLEs for imparting skills under the CCC to women in their locality. This initiative, though embedded in the larger framework of the CSCs Scheme, started rolling out only in 2011 and hence could not be encountered or studied during the field visits.

The intention of the broader policy framework is reflected in the numerous efforts to deal with illiteracy, digital divide, education, health, financial inclusion and so on. As part of the broader goal of community development, CSCs create livelihood opportunities for village youth; encourage women's participation through various associated initiatives, build concrete village infrastructure. Beside central initiatives, state governments under the federal structure of India adopt several measures to cater to the specific need of its populations. One of the prominent examples of such measures was the Rajasthan government's policy to introduce the scheme of village level women entrepreneurs (VLWEs) under the CSCs Scheme. This measure helps to promote women's involvement in the project in an otherwise strictly patriarchal state. There are many such examples which enhance the adaptability of the scheme across the diverse contextual realities of India and hence the resilience of the system of governance.

The above-mentioned instances bring out the larger policy orientation of the State while designing the larger schemes and rolling out certain special initiatives for particular social groups. However, the actual ramifications of these initiatives in the local social and cultural contexts remain a matter of concern. For example, despite holding the CSCs franchise women were hardly visible in the everyday practices of the scheme in Rajasthan, whereas in Andhra Pradesh, given the preference given to earlier self-help groups, women VLEs marked a remarkable presence in the state. This further demonstrates how the general fabric of culture and society, status and education of women, dominant power relations tend to perpetuate through emerging structures. Also the local context of politics and bureaucracy play a crucial role in the everyday practices of the scheme. For example, in Rajasthan, West Bengal where local governing bodies were not aligned with the scheme's objective, it created considerable hindrances for the VLEs either due to their non-cooperation or sometimes active resistance. Strategic reforms through e-Governance possess the potential to confront the existing system of power and dominance. Hence, reactionary politics and resistance are only inevitable. Under such circumstances, the challenge remains not only in innovative policy design but also in following them through with further innovations in implementation strategies albeit keeping the significance of local cultural and political contexts in mind.

The final major postulation is that capacity of the state machinery to absorb institutional change resulting from strategic reform and to deliver policy results manifests in the improved quality of governance. This impels us to look at the supply side of the public service delivery. The policy papers, the government practices experienced during the case study and expert interviews suggest that public sector reform is one of the major focus areas of the e-Governance initiatives. There are special projects undertaken for this specific purpose under the NeGP. The CSCs Scheme strives to integrate ICT-enablement with business process re-engineering and change management that will change the face of public administration. There are regular trainings, capacity development and sensitization programmes to make the public servants more aware of the benefits of the

ICT tools for their own work. However, examples from the CSCs Scheme shows that where there has been simultaneous change in the bureaucratic capacities, the project goals have been more effectively fulfilled. For example, in Gujarat there was seamless coordination between different departments, clear line of authority and responsibility shared within all levels of bureaucracy and a strong political will at the highest level. All these factors make Gujarat one of the successful implementers of the CSCs Scheme. Evidently, this establishes a strong relation between the higher state capacity and improved level of governance. However, to what extent successful roll-out of kiosks can be synonymous with actual capacity building of the public sector is a matter of contention.

Most of the literature and policy documents on e-Governance persistently discuss the need for business process re-engineering and change management within the public sector. These terms are borrowed mostly from management jargons and thereby promote corporatization of the public sector. While partnering with market forces help in raising the resource base for public initiatives, imitating management principles in governance of a nation-state raises serious concern. Balancing between different and sometimes opposing interest groups with varied power positions renders the latter a process fraught with contradiction and far more complex than corporate governance. This complexity are accentuated by the postcolonial contexts where most of the political institutions carry a legacy of the colonial past and therefore requires much manoeuvring while accommodating the needs and aspiration of diverse populations, particular in a multi-cultural society such as India. Thus, incapacitating the public sector in India requires a deeper understanding of the entangled nature of politics, technology and culture within the wider purview of strategic reform in e-Governance.

Politics of governance reform and e-Governance in India

As e-Governance reform in India demonstrates substantial impact on the level of governance, it would be appropriate to locate e-Governance in the broader context of strategic reform which in turn falls under the rubric of a transnational agenda of governance reform. It has been reiterated since the beginning of this research that a major shift has taken place in governance discourse since the end of the Cold War which has reconfigured the relationships between state and society in most postcolonial and post-communist states. India has been no exception in this global trend. Although the initial push came from a transnational agenda of 'good governance', the domestic politics in India was also conducive for such ideas to flourish. Stagnant economic growth, problems of poverty, inept state bureaucracy, growth of regional parties and development of a strong civil society – all contributed to the burgeoning interest in wider reform in the system of governance. Thus ensuing currents of 'good governance' or governance reform agenda followed after the economic liberalization in the early 1990s and manifested in major policy reforms across different sectors. All these reforms have not only significantly changed the way the state functions but also impacted the nodes of state–society interaction leading to considerable rise of market and civil society in the matters of governance.

E-Governance as a major sector to facilitate the wider goals of development and good governance thrived within such shifting contours of reform discourse. E-Governance reform encapsulated not only the technological promises to improve the interaction between State and society (including market, civil society and citizens) but also the political potential to address the parameters of 'good governance', such as transparency, efficiency, predictability and so on across all sectors. Therefore, e-Governance slowly and steadily moved into the national agenda of policies and planning which manifested in new legal frameworks, growing emphasis in policy dialogues and ultimately in a national planning strategy. The burgeoning interest in e-Governance reform reflected many trends of the wider agenda of governance reform. Firstly, it emphasized a market concept of equality among citizens by empowering them with increasing access to public services and information. Secondly, e-Governance reforms propagated such concepts of equality by projecting the State as a services provider and citizens as consumers and clients. Thirdly, e-Governance reform in India is widely based on a PPP model where private sectors take on many roles previously performed by the State. Fourthly, such reforms revolve around the concept of citizen-centric participatory governance with seamless and increasing interaction between state and extra-state spheres. Fifthly, with its ability to reach out to the remotest corner of the country, e-Governance contributes to the process of decentralizing administration. Finally, e-Governance reforms cater to both technical as well as developmental capacity of the state. All these characteristics of e-Governance render it a coveted sector for strategic reform. Hence, post-Cold War trends of governance reform made a strong presence in the policy framework of post-economic liberalization India and e-Governance lay at the forefront of such reform discourse. However, it is important to remember that by no means is e-Governance the only sector to witness this impetus for strategic reforms. On the contrary, e-Governance reforms in India are only symptomatic of emerging currents of governance reform within the broader context of the post-liberalized Indian political economy.

Connecting technology and governance: a means to an end or an end in itself?

E-Governance is promoted as a strategic reform because of its probable positive impact on the overall quality of governance. The above observations clearly show how e-Governance can lead to better levels of governance. However, this research also emphasizes that this connection between the technology (ICT in this case) and governance is not automatic, but is in fact mediated through other factors such as politics, society, culture and contexts. As Sreekumar reiterates:

> The idea that ICT is inherently a liberating technology, and hence e-Governance, is a new way of transcending inept and inefficient bureaucratic systems, which empowers 'end users', appears to be completely inaccurate in the rural societal setting. . . . [Therefore] E-Governance delivered simply as an improvement in the pragmatics of governance exemplified in the

efforts to make service delivery quicker or more accessible, would probably end up in reproducing technological practices, which hinges for its existence on the crucial technology component rather than its social dimensions and would help the consolidation of and centralization of power in the hands of those who directly or by proxy own, control or manipulate the technology.

(Sreekumar 2008, p. 185)

Therefore a holistic understanding of e-Governance needs to closely examine the relationship between technology and governance by putting governance at the intersection of politics, technology and culture. This brings us to a rhetorical question that often forms the underlying assumption of most of the e-Governance initiatives: Is e-Governance a means to an end or is it an end in itself? Although, most of the literature stress the fact that e-Governance is not a panacea for better governance and only one of the tools for improving governance, often in practice technological determinism overshadows the political dimension ensconced in the concept. The other aspect of this problem is that a certain standard of governance seems to be a prerequisite for technological innovations to sync into the system. Though there is no fix formula to set these prerequisites, they are usually a mix of political, social and cultural fabrics embedded in a context. The other issue is that e-Governance reform often violates standards that it should ensure by default. All the issues posit an intertwined problematic indicative of a caveat in the conceptualization of the link between technology and governance and thereby need some close introspection.

The first issue engages in asking to what extent ICTs are treated to be a means to attain broader goals of governance. As mentioned at the outset e-Governance is usually promoted as a means to achieve 'good governance'. As a matter of fact, both 'good governance' and e-Governance parameters in India draw heavily on Western standards of technology and governance. Hence in a modernizing quest to catch up with higher technological advancement, the local political, social and cultural dimensions more often than not take a back seat. As already discussed (in Chapter 1) in correspondence to the 'good governance' paradigm, this developmentalist approach towards technology also suffer from a hegemonic universalism. The inability to account for the gap between such universal ideals and realities of developing countries are considered to be the most important reason behind massive failures of e-Governance projects in transitioning societies (Heeks 2003). In this approach the incorporation of the latest technology in service delivery and building of technological infrastructure in rural areas becomes an end in itself, an empty yet symbolic signpost of development. This study takes a critical stand against such a modernizing notion of governance, albeit its initial research goal of connecting the developmental jargon of governance with the social science perspectives of the notion. This study argues that, strategic reform of e-Governance improves the quality of governance when it purports to trickle down into everyday practices of social and political life. That is to say, it is not enough to introduce new technologies, but there is further need for innovation in institutions and practices to use these technologies in particular contexts.

The catalytic nature of the context points towards the other related issue which questions what are the prerequisites of a context-specific and effective e-Governance initiative. There are no simple answers or no readymade recipe for success. However, besides understanding the complex dimension of e-Governance, some structural factors are also required for realizing the potential of e-Governance. A few examples of such factors would be an efficient and supportive bureaucracy, a strong leadership, legitimacy of rule and ruler, deeper understanding of citizens' needs and the local context. Although this list does not include all such factors, nonetheless the absence of any of these can pose a serious challenge to e-Governance reform. The analysis of e-Governance reform in India has already illustrated in detail how these factors vary from one region to another thereby reflecting on the varied pace of reform in these regions. For example, Andhra Pradesh started on a high note on e-Governance reform in the state in the late 1990s; however the pace of reform was baffled by the electoral demise of the government that spearheaded such reform. It also stated a clear public mandate against the leadership and their reform policies. This is a clear example where despite an efficient bureaucracy and a visionary leadership was not enough to gain legitimacy among the citizens as their needs were not catered to through such a reform agenda. In another case, Gujarat has made substantial advance in taking IT to the masses in rural areas amidst intense criticism against the government for massive human rights violations and for subjugation of minority communities in the state. Though this research do not investigate the reasons of the Modi governments' electoral success vis-à-vis the Naidu governments' electoral debacle, the trajectories of e-Governance in these states nonetheless raise important questions in this direction. Similarly, in case of West Bengal the overall reform agenda professed by the Left Front experienced a major setback by ousting of the longest-standing government in the state. Whether the reform was one of the reasons behind this demise or there were other underlying factors need a separate and deeper analysis. Nevertheless, these examples show e-Governance, or any strategic reform for that matter, cannot inevitably mend the legitimacy deficits unless they take all the relevant political, social and cultural factors into consideration.

Another point of contestation in e-Governance reform is the way such reforms are introduced and consolidated. This is a problem in general with the entire governance reform agenda as they often reinforce the characteristics of governance that they espouse to eliminate themselves. For example, even though increasing transparency of the public service is one of the aims of e-Governance reform, the way e-Governance policies are incorporated are far from being transparent. While discussing the conceptual tension within the 'good governance' agenda, Jenkins (1995) has focused on the ability of the state and political elites in India to adopt non-transparent strategies for consolidating policy reform. According to him:

> These include strategies to soften the edge of political conflict by promoting change amidst the appearance of continuity, and to arrange accommodation among groups who perceive reform as a threat. In other words, governance

capacity of democracies need not rest solely on the transparency of decision-making or relationships.

(Jenkins 1995, p. 38)

Mahadevia (2005) in his analysis of Gujarat economic reform raised similar concerns and label it as 'reform by stealth', where public debate over policy priorities were consciously avoided. He further linked these trends of policy reform with the rise of communal politics in the state. Therefore, a vast literature on the political economy of India post economic liberalizations focus on the issues of Hindu nationalism, identity politics as simultaneous developments besides policy reform (Jayal 2001; Corbridge and Harriss 2000; Mooij 2005; Ruparelia et al. 2011). While applying these concerns in the field of e-Governance, the basic argument remains that with an overwhelming fascination with efficiency of service delivery, other criteria of e-Governance such as accountability and transparency are often overlooked. The pursuance of efficiency often relegates citizens to mere customers and turns the state into just one of the service providers without much heed to the notions of justice and social inclusiveness. As a result, governance just becomes a techno-managerial fix of increasing efficiency. These biases are ingrained in neo-liberal ideals of 'good governance' and hence unavoidable as long as e-Governance reforms are merely viewed as a tool to achieve those ideals. This not only calls for changing the ways policies are framed but also the way policy processes and policy impacts are analysed. This implies stepping out of the 'good governance' paradigm and scrutinize the politics of reform taking place in the real political context.

The real political context unfolds in the relationship between the governed and those who govern, this includes not just a few policy-makers and the citizens but an entire policy network (see Figure 2.3). All the actors in this network, in their particular context and capacity, assert their agency in accordance to their particular preference and interests. Therefore, without denying the differential power distribution, this research demonstrates and claims how these myriad agencies taken together can bring in change in the system of governance.

Hybridizing e-Governance reform in India: contradiction or consolidation?

The basic analytical framework of this research conceives e-Governance as an independent variable with a probable impact on the level of governance. The above observations exhibit how e-Governance reforms are slowly taking root in the Indian political contexts. On the one hand, the neo-institutional model of governance explains how institutional designs and elite strategies together facilitate the process of consolidation of these reform measures. The elite strategies which Jenkins (1995) calls 'political skills', Mitra (2006) refers to as 'room to manoeuvre' are embedded within the political structures of Indian democracy. The capacity to contain political conflict manifests in the constitutional design, in the federal structures and also in elite competition. On the other hand, the social constructivist approach elucidate how local contexts as characterized by a mix of political, social and cultural factors have the potential to subvert the technological impact on governance by generating reactionary forces within the system.

However, e-Governance is an emerging field of reform initiated in India in the recent past. Its absolute impact is far from being properly understood let alone being fully realized. There is a clear paradigm shift in the policy discourse turning it towards favourable conditions for e-Governance reform initiatives. Yet, State-led e-Governance reforms in India are going through a process of transition which is confronted with strong resistance from the society. This constant tussle between structure and agency mark the process of change with conflict and rupture which cannot be fully captured within the neo-institutional or social constructivist approaches of understanding e-Governance reform. Hence, the concept of hybridity adds to the basic propositions of this analytical model discussed above. In its transitory phase e-Governance initiatives go through a process of hybridization and generate hybrid institutions and practices which are far from policy prescription yet grounded in local cultural contexts. On one hand, the CSCs Scheme stands out as one such example of hybrid e-Governance institutions that emanates from the hybridizing tendencies of the State to leverage the relationship between state and society. On the other hand, everyday practices of the same scheme show further processes of hybridization by state and society to better accommodate local interests, norms and needs.

The CSCs Scheme is a State-driven top-down initiative to combine private sector interests with developmental goals. The designing of CSCs are done in a manner to address the issues of illiteracy, digital divide, rural employment, rural infrastructure and service delivery to rural masses. In its own right it is a hybridizing political strategy on part of the policy-makers to accommodate conflicting interests of market, of donor agencies, of local political elites and of citizens. It not only shows how elites adapt the imported categories of governance reform into the innate political contexts, it also exhibits how the hybridity of already existing institutions in turn facilitate the elite strategizing tendencies. As, for example, the federal structure of India helped the national elites to minimize the possibilities of opposition by deflecting reform through regional political structures. The policy drive of the regional governments differs from each other. As on one hand Gujarat shows a dominant role of the state government within the general rhetoric of the PPP model, on the other hand the Andhra Pradesh government took a rather reluctant stance in influencing the reform. However, at the same time the overall implementation in all the states indicates that despite stressing the PPP model, state elites and state institutions work as the driving force behind this mammoth initiative. Furthermore, CSCs can easily pass on to the pool of hybrid institutions that already exist in the Indian context. Like its predecessors, the Internet kiosks help harnessing the gap between alien standards of e-Governance and the Indian reality. Thus, the process of e-Governance policy formulation and implementation in India are produced through a continuous yet non-linear process of hybridization and further produce hybrid institutions. In this way, the neo-institutional model of elite strategy attains a new analytical edge through the conceptual prism of hybridity.

The regional narratives demonstrate the different course that the same scheme took in the particular contexts. The relative autonomy of the states within the federal structure of the Indian polity not only ensured smoother consolidation of reform policies but also led to different strategies by stakeholders in the face of such reforms. These differential experiences also attest the context as the catalyst. The policy focus, the political will of the highest leadership, the mindscapes of the local bureaucracy and finally the minute details of political, social and cultural fabrics of these states affect to what extent and how e-Governance reforms are absorbed into these regional contexts. There are instances where the state takes innovative hybrid policy measures to integrate e-Governance reform with other social dimensions as in the case of the Rajasthan government's policy to promote women VLEs or VLWEs. This particular policy again goes through a process of hybridization when the male relatives of these women beneficiaries take over their responsibilities. Here, the cultural values of patriarchy embedded deeply in the social structures subvert the top-down policy solutions. Nonetheless, this policy also led to a hybrid institutional space within CSCs in Rajasthan, where some women VLEs co-existed alongside their dominant male counterparts. Similarly visibility of women VLEs in Andhra Pradesh can also be attributed to the hybridizing tendency of the state government's policy to integrate self-help groups into the CSCs Scheme. The scheme also gives ample opportunity for VLEs to improvise the institutional space by asserting their entrepreneurial skills. Therefore, even though the public services were more or less standardized across CSCs in a particular state, the private services varied substantially from one centre to the other. The educational qualifications of VLEs, the local politics of selecting VLEs, the personal relationships of VLEs with local bureaucracy and village *panchayat* leaders – all were differently played out in different contexts leading to a continuous process of hybridization and hybrid institutional structures and spaces. The broader political contexts and the organization of bureaucracy from upper ranks to the lowest levels also differed not only from one state to another, but sometimes from one district to the next. These varied trajectories are sometime produced through the deliberate assertion of stakeholders' agency as they engage in actively negotiating the processes of e-Governance reform. At other times they are merely unintended by-products of such processes of assimilation and consolidation. Subsequently, the practices of e-Governance reforms differed considerably from the policy dictum. However, such gaps between policy and practices did not necessarily denote a contradiction in the reform process but rather the consolidation of the policies by negotiating through contextual realities. Here, hybridity strengthens the social constructivist approach by adding a productive political agency to all the stakeholders who in continuous interactions with each other not only overcome the legitimacy deficit but also gradually shift the structural parameters of governance.

Thus, through hybridizing e-Governance reform conjures up the neo-institutional model of governance with that of the social constructivist analysis of technology. In doing so, e-Governance brings governance and technology as two intertwined themes under the same analytical frame. It explicates how reform practices that not only differ from the original policy plan or design and that often exhibit contradictory trends in varied local contexts could possibly get consolidated into the local context. This process of consolidation could imply the perpetuation of the existing power structure and dominant culture in the society or it could also imply gradual shifting of power dynamics albeit without overtly challenging the structural set-up. Therefore, rather than simply evaluating the gaps between policies and practices of reform hybridity serves as a heuristic device to critically understand the entanglement of different forces within the broader structure of governance that work together (or against each other) that ultimately lead to significant changes in the overall system of governance. Hence, contradiction and consolidation might take place at the same time while a reform initiative is introduced whereas the latter will ensure the sustainability of the initiative. However, whether it would bring in any improvement in the system of governance will be determined by how successfully these reforms can elicit legitimacy in a democratic set-up.

Manoeuvring legitimacy with strategic reforms: a democratic dilemma

Democracy is broadly understood as rule of the people which is also linked to governance as suggested by the institutionalism thriving on both the rational-choice and sociological models. In the rational approach, where the preferences are exogenous, political actors turn individual needs and resources into collective action through bargaining, lobbying, coalition formation, etc. This is an aggregative model of democracy which is built on a set of institutional arrangements, civil and political rights and regular free and fair elections (March and Olsen 1995). For the sociological approach, that emphasizes endogenous nature of preferences, individuals act more according to the appropriate norms rather than personal interests. This is an integrative model of democracy which is based on participatory processes furthering democratic identities (ibid.). There are, of course, many more forms of democracy such as representative democracy, deliberative democracy and associative democracy, and so on. The scope of this book does not allow us to dwell further on the types of democracy or to select between these different forms of democracy. The purpose of enquiry limits us to the notion of legitimacy as ensconced within the system of democracy. As pointed out above legitimacy can be derived through many sources, such as free and fair election, exercise of one's rights, efficiency or simply the 'capacity to get things done' (Mitra 2006). The last concept of efficiency makes considerable demand on public policy dimensions of the governing mechanism. It is this relationship between efficiency and legitimacy that leads to strategic reform initiatives. However, within a democratic set-up this relationship becomes further complicated with an additional attribute of accountability. Strategic reforms are often used as tools to enhance legitimacy of the rule of the institutions of governance. Taking on the indicators set out earlier for the analysis of e-Governance reform in India, this section will see how these strategic reform initiatives grapple with these dual aspects of legitimacy.

Let us first start with the notion of efficiency. Public service delivery in a democracy often suffers from inept bureaucracy; slow pace of formulation and implementation of policy goals as articulating and accommodating diverse interest groups becomes a major challenge. A pertinent question therefore arises: Is democracy and efficiency impossible to achieve at the same time? This impels us to ask a further question: What is efficiency made of? Does it simply mean the ability to get things done in a stipulated time? Or does it mean reaching out to all sections of society? If we consider all these aspects, then efficiency of public service delivery should be evaluated through the participation of citizens and active involvement of other actors, availability and predictability of services and adaptability of the system to suit the contextual realities. Do e-Governance reforms ensure all these above criteria? There is no simple and readymade answer. Use of ICT in public service delivery definitely has the potential to increase the accessibility of services by reaching out to remote corners of the country, to increase predictability of time and quality of services by enabling technological solutions. However, when the mere technological upgradation takes precedence in such reform initiatives, adaptability of the system to local contexts and needs takes a back seat. This lack of sensitivity towards local needs in terms of public service, and the complex challenges of enforcing technological solutions to public service often result in partial enforcement of policy goals if not complete distortions. As the CSCs Scheme experiences demonstrate, the initiative was rolled out without taking stock of what is really needed by the citizens and what capacities required on the part of the entire system of public administration. Hence, the most persistent complaint across most CSCs visited were the delay in making a range of public services available through this window. In fact, for example, one of the experts interviewed in Delhi opined that:

> CSCs are just a waste of time as they try to merely introduce technologies into public service delivery and end up creating parallel and often duplicate mechanisms for the similar public services. This only creates confusion for the citizens and additional burden for the administrators.

One of the defending arguments against such an allegation is that any strategic reform programme goes through a long cycle of challenges before projecting any significant result. While this might be a valid argument given the complex interplay of politics, technology and culture in implementation of e-Governance reform, nevertheless articulation of such complexities in policy formulations and a concomitant strategy to deal with them should receive the utmost priority of political authorities. Otherwise the potentials of technology-induced public service delivery will be undermined and it will only create a parallel system of administration instead of making the existing system more efficient.

The other aspect of legitimacy is accountability. In e-Governance reform in India accountability becomes a complex issue given the involvement of many actors and an active PPP model of implementation. International donor agencies that influence the framework of governance reform in general in the country do not follow a direct line of accountability with the citizens and the same holds true for most civil society organizations. However, these organizations often serve as a monitoring agency or a watchdog for the performance of public service delivery and helps in pointing out the concerns and problems of the community to the policy-makers and administrators.

In the case of a large-scale pan-India initiative such as CSCs or other integrated MMPs, the federal structure and resultant involvement of central as well as state governments could create overlapping structures of accountability within public administration within the same project. The private partners in e-Governance reform are often accountable to their public counterparts (through contractual agreement) and also the network of VLEs that they employ, particularly in case of CSCs Scheme. In many cases as witnessed during this study the partnership between the public (SDA) and private (SCA) partners were fraught with disappointment, mistrust and frustration. The delay in providing public services also created frustration and agitation among VLEs and they were not sure who they should turn to for recourse. Being a private franchise also created considerable hurdle for CSCs to gain public trust. The only exception was visible in Gujarat where the location of kiosks within the *panchayat* office and the strong mandate from the state government worked in favour of the initiative. Although the prominent push by the public sector establishes a direct accountability structure, it does not ensure transparency in the process which is a closely related to the notion of accountability. Narratives of Gujarat points out this issue where the state government exerted enormous amount control over the initiative in terms of regulating the sites, supervising the VLEs and also managing the private partners. There was a preoccupation with technology for its ability to enforce a centralized surveillance mechanism rather than focusing on its empowering capacities.

This brings us back to the problematic questions of what is more important for attaining legitimacy efficiency or accountability, or both. Also, how can one tackle both the issues at the same time? The skilful manoeuvring of both efficiency and accountability can ensure sustaining legitimacy of a regime while keeping the process of democratic consolidation intact in a postcolonial set-up. Strategic reform in e-Governance is deployed by political elites in order to improve the quality of governance which shows substantial potential for both the above principles. These reform strategies have already marked a distinct shift in the policy and legal framework in India. However, whether e-Governance reform will remain just a populist political strategy or it will actually aid in the process of reforming the governing mechanism traversing the entanglement of politics, technology and culture is yet to be fully realized.

Conclusion: researching governance through the prism of e-Governance

Although the basic aim of this study is to understand how strategic reform affects the system of governance in a democratic set-up, its preoccupation with e-Governance reform takes the analysis further by unraveling the relationship between technology and governance. Drawing closely on the policies and practices of e-Governance in India, this study views e-Governance as a hybridizing experience grappling with the intermingling issues of politics, technology and culture, as embedded in the wider context of the society which further produces hybrid institutions and practices of governance.

The novelty of this research lies not only in its subject matter but also in its methodological approach. As far as the subject matter is concerned, while analyzing the impact of strategic reform on the level of governance, the study takes up e-Governance reform which is an under-researched field of enquiry within social sciences. Even within the studies of technology and governance, e-Governance has attracted only limited serious academic attention. Most of the studies on e-Governance reflect either techno-managerial perspectives, or institutional management approach, or policy outcome studies or developmental perspectives. In dealing with e-Governance as part of a research on governance theory, this study demanded some methodological innovations. In analyzing the entire spectrum of e-Governance reform – starting from the policy formulation to implementation, from reception of reform initiatives to consolidation of reform – the study deploys a novel combination of the neo-institutional model of governance from political science, a social constructivist approach from sociology and an analytical category of hybridity from postcolonial and transcultural perspectives on politics. This interdisciplinary theoretical and methodological approach enriches the context-specific understanding of governance as viewed through the lens of e-Governance where technology, governance and cultures are relentlessly enmeshed within the everyday practices of reform.

As has already been mentioned throughout the discussions in this book, governance as a concept not only transcends scholastic boundaries of social sciences but also captures the fancy of development practitioners to civil society activists, from policy-makers to political leaders. Given such widespread interest in and engagement with governance, the term at times tends to lose the conceptual clarity. This ambiguity around the notion of governance often stem from the fact that experts working on governance in their respective fields talk passed each other rather than talking to each other. The development consultants working in the ambits international aid and development community formulate their own idea of 'good governance' and espouse prescriptive governance reform agenda for universal application across all developing countries. Policy-makers and political leaders in the developing countries, either under the pressure from donor agencies or in an attempt to incorporate into the global neo-liberal economic network, promote these governance reform agenda in their respective political contexts at least rhetorically. Since policies are being viewed more and more as the key to institutional/governance reform in developing countries, the donor agencies in recent times have shifted their attention from direct intervention to policy facilitation. As a result, the International Organizations like the World Bank or the UNDP frequently serve at the advisory committees of policy-making and planning in developing countries. The policy prescriptions and solutions that emerge from this spectrum are usually coded in an ideal type construction of governance and a quick techno-managerial fix to achieve this ideal. However, undoubtedly these ideals of governance are far-fetched from the realities of the receiving countries and are thereby doomed to fail almost without exception. What is worse is that such governance paradigm being a far cry from reality often leads to counter-productive forces by reiterating the evils it wants to eliminate to begin with. The lack of transparency in governance reform policy processes in India already explicated this point. The civil society, though fiercely promoted by this popular governance reform agenda, often finds itself at loggerheads with both the State and the market over the implications of 'good governance' paradigm for the ordinary citizens. Hence the position and role of civil societies in the system of governance becomes further complicated given their complementary yet contesting relationship with the State. Amidst all these cacophony of ideas and agendas the academic engagement with governance becomes even more pertinent as the need to re-establish governance as a political and social problematic instead of a mere development jargon is ever more pressing. Still, this does not imply ignoring the debate that emanates from these other perspectives on governance. Instead the aim of this research is to address this very debate in regaining the centrality of governance as a political and social concept.

The burgeoning preoccupation of the international development community with governance is symptomatic of a wider trend of shifting from government to governance as experienced in different political contexts of the developed and developing nations. This shift in the developed nations was brought through the popularity of New Public Management theories of public policy and public administration. The result was the emergence of policy networks of different actors reducing the influence of the public sector. In the developing counterparts, the shift was an immediate outcome of the changing domestic and foreign political environment of the post-Cold War times. The manifest impact was the popularity of 'good governance' or governance reform agenda focusing on the expansion of market and civil society and the reduction of the sphere of the State. As these governance reform agenda has become rampant throughout most post-colonial and post-communist societies, it becomes extremely important to unravel the impact of these reform agendas on the State institutions and on the society at large. However, the realities of the developing countries do not necessarily reflect this trend even while adapting State institutions to this broader governance reform agenda.

In order to understand why such a gap still exists despite consistent deliberations by international donor agencies and national policy, we need to turn to the concept of governance as a social and political problem. At this point, it is worthwhile to briefly point out the major connotations of the term in the social science research. Governance is predominantly a field of study in the discipline of political science albeit conceived differently by the sub-field of public policy, international relations and comparative politics. However, one common theme that runs through all these different fields of study is that they all view governance as a broader concept than government and engage with institutions as the site of interactions between different actors. In this way, most of the governance research is governed by an overarching panoply of institutionalism and focuses on how institutions affect actors and their behaviour and how institutional change occurs. Hence, governance as a concept dwells on the interaction of the institutional structures with the agency of the actors. In other words, it can be described as the interface between State and society (see Figure 1.1). This conceptualization of governance conjures up all the actors in its fold at the same time: the State, the market, the civil society and the citizens. It is within the institutional spaces created by the State that market, civil society and citizens interact with each other and as well with the State. While the State institutions determine these interactions, the institutional set-up also gets transformed through these interactions. Taking this view of governance facilitate understanding the conceptual tension within the 'good governance' definition of governance and its techno-managerial solution of governance reform. At the same time it is important to keep in mind that academic and developmental perspectives on governance are not formulated in complete separation and isolation. In fact there are enough instances of overlap. For this purpose, the related concepts of efficiency, accountability and legitimacy (already discussed in the Introduction) become crucial as they lie at the overlapping zones of these different conceptualizations of governance. In the political science literature on governance, legitimacy of rule sets the basic premise of governance in a democracy, whereas efficiency and accountability (though not always mutually inclusive) serve significantly to manipulate the legitimacy of rule and thereby the nodes of democratic governance. Similarly, all these concepts are integral parts of the governance reform agenda which takes democracy as a necessary but not a sufficient condition for 'good governance'. These intersecting concepts associated with governance discourses further reveal the complex and interconnected nature of governance as a concept which can easily traverse scholastic boundaries. The flaccidity of these concepts also hints at the difficulty in analytically separating the techno-managerial perception of governance from its academic roots.

This brings us back to the basic aim of the book that was explicitly laid out in the beginning, that is, how strategic reform of a techno-managerial variety influences the notion of governance that hinges upon the relationship between State and society. In finding answers to this basic research question a neo-institutional model of governance (see Figure 2.2) has been adopted as it explains why and how strategic reforms affect the level of governance. To deepen the understanding of strategic reform, the focus has been narrowed down to a specific sector of reform that is e-Governance in this case. E-Governance can be described as the use of ICTs in leveraging the relationships between State and society and is comprised of two distinct yet interrelated dimensions such as technological and political. It is the interaction between the two that determines how e-Governance is going to influence the quality of governance. Therefore, in addition to the neo-institutional model of governance, governance research will attain further analytical depth by turning to the relationship between technology and governance. The relationship between technology and governance has been studied here from a social constructivist interpretation of technology. The social constructivism of technology defies technological determinism and argues that the impact of technology is not automatic and neutral. Rather the impact of technology is mediated through social processes and practices. Now the use of a social constructivist understanding of technology in a neo-institutional model of governance can raise some scholarly doubts. However, our analysis of the e-Governance reform in India can provide a simple answer to such apprehensions. While e-Governance policies and projects are planned by policy-makers and political elites, the appropriation of these new technologies are shaped by the different stakeholders depending on their respective subject positions within the system of governance. A social constructivist approach is therefore necessary to understand how ICTs initiated by the State are received by the society. Here the society includes all the stakeholders affected by the e-Governance reform. Such an approach not only explicates the relationship between technology and governance but also affirms how this relationship is mediated though an array of political, social and cultural factors. In other words, social constructivist analysis of the e-Governance reasserts the context-specific analysis of governance.

The underlying assumption of governance presupposes a differential distribution of power between those who control the State and those who inhabit the society. Technologies of power and governmentality (Foucault 1980) ensure the legitimacy of the rule despite the hiatus between the governed and those who govern. Based on this view of power and governance, sanctions and welfare become a two-track strategy of the elites to ensure the legitimacy of the rule (Mitra 2006). In this way, e-Governance becomes a strategic reform aimed at attaining better governance through welfare. However, such a power dynamics does not imply seamless reception of dominance by the powerless. For that reason, the neo-institutional model of analysing e-Governance as a strategic reform and the political, social and cultural factors as discussed within the social constructivist approach towards e-Governance – all together hint at the notion of agency inbuilt into the understanding of governance. This notion of agency is assigned to all the actors, or in other words stakeholders, who implement and are implicated through e-Governance reform. It is through the analytical category of hybridity that this research illustrates how each stakeholder exerts their agency to negotiate the State-initiated e-Governance reform and in turn affect the institutional arrangements of e-Governance.

Researching governance through the prism of e-Governance often runs into the risk of shifting the focus of analysis. In other words, while originally e-Governance reforms were intended to serve as an analytical tool to ameliorate research on governance, it could well be taken as the end in the process of enquiry. Although this study on e-Governance reform in India might have a few policy implications, these are not simply the ultimate aim of this research. Instead of just focusing on the policy outcome of e-Governance policies, this book takes on a broader aim of unraveling governance through strategic reform. Hence the implications of this study spills not only beyond the study of e-Governance but also beyond its specific geographical contexts of India which we will explore in some details in the concluding chapter.

6 Conclusion

Transcending the Indian context: from area studies to theory of governance

In studying the impact of strategic reform on the level of governance, it has been asserted time and again that the context of reform is of prime significance in fully capturing its implications. For this purpose the analyses of e-Governance reform – starting from policy formulation to policy implementation, from project design to reception of project, from introduction of reform to consolidation of reform – in this research has been firmly grounded in the context of India's governance. One of the broader assumptions behind understanding India's governance through e-Governance is that governance is a key to the resilience of the democratic system in India. The theoretical and methodological dispositions have been arranged accordingly to demonstrate how India's governance has been affected by e-Governance reform and further contributed to the resilience of the system albeit the process is still on-going. However, does it imply that the findings and observations derived from the Indian context will be confined only to the understanding of India's governance? Does the understanding of India's governance say anything of governance that can spill beyond its context? Does this research have any implications for theories of governance in general? These are the questions that compel us to transcend the context to find out the general theoretical implications of this research, in other words, to move beyond area studies to theory-building.

There are two distinct yet related aspects of this research which can be linked to the broader issues of governance research; first the theme or subject matter of the study and second, the methodological approach adopted to analyse the theme. The first aspect that deals with the theme of this research relates to the issue of e-Governance and its ramification for governance research. The concept of e-Governance hinges upon the relationship between technology and governance as it deploys ICTs in harnessing the interplay between State and society by refurbishing the public service delivery mechanism. As the term suggests e-Governance is comprised of a technical as well as a political dimension, which together aim to transform governance. Therefore, e-Governance can be studied both as the politics of technology as well as a technology of politics. On one hand, the politics of technology shows how the broader political context of neo-liberalization and the concomitant agenda of governance reform push the recent upsurge of e-Governance in most developing countries in the last two decades. Furthermore its focus on the Indian context leads to general understanding of governance reform agenda and its subsequent impact on the postcolonial and post-communist societies of the developing world. This reflects in the way policies of e-Governance are formulated and initiated through policy networks (see Figure 2.3). The national, regional and local politics further influence the way such technologies are percolating through the system. On the other hand, e-Governance as a strategic reform serves as a political tool in the hands of the elites to control the system of governance. Therefore technology policies have been an important area of enquiry for political scientists and sociologists. Social Construction of Technology, Sociology of Science and Science and Technology Studies (STS) studies have analysed the myriad ramifications of technology from a sociological and philosophical perspective. However, this research views the relationship between technology and governance from the disciplinary approach of political sociology. Though social, culture and contexts have been added to the analytical frame, the focus still remains on politics. In this way this research on e-Governance not only shows how strategic reform aids the system of governance but also elicits important observations on the relationship between technology and governance. Undoubtedly, such insights go much beyond the Indian context and contribute to the larger research on governance.

The second aspect of the research that displays wider connotations lies in the theoretical and methodological approach of the study. In evaluating the impact of strategic reform on governance, a dynamic neo-institutional model based on elite strategy (see Figure 2.2) has been deployed. This model forms the analytical grid of this research. However, as the specific strategic reform selected in this case is e-Governance, this model needed to be strengthened with further dynamism which could facilitate understanding the interplay of technology and governance. Here, the social constructivist approach to understand the relationship between the two has served this purpose. However, both the neo-institutional and social constructivist approaches leave a few gaps in their analysis despite the prevalence of agency and context in their methodology. The neo-institutionalism as being an essentially Eurocentric theoretical model presupposes a methodological individualism which might fall short of fully analysing the postcolonial and other developing societies. Similarly, social constructivism of technology, though focusing on political, cultural and social dimensions, explicates the transformative processes more in terms of policy deficits. While these analyses successfully point out the problems of universalism in particular contexts, they also contain the risk of indefinite relativism. Such approaches could turn the governance of a postcolonial society either into an exotic aberration or a unique case in itself without much scope for generalization. To counter this epistemic gap, a transcultural perspective of politics has been introduced in studying e-Governance. A transcultural methodology of politics serves two purposes in this study; first it demonstrates how even a seemingly local phenomenon is entangled within the broader political, social and historical trajectories; second it provides an analytical toolbox to understand the process of such entanglement and its implications. From this methodological stance, e-Governance is understood as part of a wider political context of neo-liberal agenda of governance reform which has been proliferating across developing countries in the last two decades even though its local consequences differs considerably from one context to the other. Unlike the modernizing developmental theories, these local variations are not analysed in terms of deviation or exoticism. Instead, a transcultural methodology helps understand the local manifestations of e-Governance in their own rights. Based on this methodological perspective, this research makes use of the analytical category of hybridity.[1] Hybridity aids in our analysis of e-Governance in many ways, such as, by explicating the application of e-Governance as a hybrid political strategy of reform by the elites; by unravelling the political agency of the different stakeholders through hybridization of e-Governance institutions and practices at the local contexts; by demonstrating how e-Governance as a strategic reform leads to hybrid institutions which can further enhance the level of governance; and by adding explanatory value to the structure-agency dynamics with the matrix of governance. Thus, hybridity serves to analyse how broader theoretical models takes root in the local contexts through multilayered processes of entanglement. In a postcolonial context, hybridity can explain how legitimacy is generated by bridging the hiatus between imported institutions and inherited social norms.

So, evaluated both on the bases of its subject matter and methodological outlook this research transcends much beyond its specific context of India. Without disregarding the significance of the context-specific analysis of governance, this research illustrates general theoretical implications: firstly in terms of its analysis of the shifting discourses of governance and the global context of governance reform and its influence on changing societies; the concomitant impact on how e-Governance makes a prominent entry in the transnational and national agenda of governance reform; how the relationship between technology and governance plays out in the context of postcolonial societies and finally; how the interdisciplinary methodological approach could address the entanglement of politics, technology and culture in the complex whole of governance. In this concluding chapter, some of these broader issues raised by our study so far will be discussed so as to connect its relevance for the general understanding of governance.

Shifting discourses of governance

Governance as a concept as well as in practice hinges on the power relation between the governed and those who govern. The analysis of this power relation is best explained in the writings of Michel Foucault[2] who eloquently elaborates on the nature of power in the social body that surpasses the juridical-legal aspect of the state. While conceptualizing power as productive, technical and positive he subverts the mere repressive nature of power and focuses mostly on the mechanisms through which the meta-power of the state need to be rooted in the entire gamut of existing networks of power relations invested in the society, starting from the body, to family, to kinship, to knowledge, to technology and so on. It is this understanding of power relations that holds the state–society relationship in the modern state. Hence, on one hand governance becomes contingent upon the adaptability of political institutions to accommodate these wider networks of power relations and embedded values of the society and on the other hand to initiate strategic reform (Mitra 2006). This becomes even more important for postcolonial and post-communist societies where political institutions are mostly imported or lacking in 'collective memory' (ibid., p. 6).

Having established the significance of strategic reform in leveraging governance, it is also imperative to take note of the fact that approaches towards such reforms have shifted in the last two decades which also hints at the shifting discourse of governance. The strategic reform in the public sector since 1980 marks a clear shift from the principles of bureaucratic hierarchy[3] to development of policy networks (Kjaer 2004). This reform process which is sometimes referred to as the New Public Management (NPM) is typically characterized by privatization, decentralization and ushered in policy networks geared towards efficient public service delivery and, more importantly, a changing role of the state and changing relationships between public, private and civil society organizations.

The shift in the nature of state authority which marks a move from hierarchic government to network governance, and then to meta-governance and decentred governance, can be traced through three separate waves of change (Bevir and Rhodes 2010). The first wave which is termed as the Anglo-governance school focuses on the public sector reform of the 1980s driven by the neo-liberal reform strategy of the state. As an outcome of these reforms the role of markets, quasi-markets and networks increases in public service delivery which was further intensified by the global changes such as the emergence of transnational organizations or the rise of regional institutions such as the European Union. Consequently, the state power and authority becomes simultaneously dispersed among different networks ranging across local, national and supranational levels of governance. The second wave of meta-governance disputes this dispersal of state authority albeit its recognition of burgeoning influence of markets and networks. In the wake plurality of networks, the state's role of direct governance shifts to meta-governance of different modes of interventions through indirect steering and guiding of chains of somewhat self-governing stakeholders. A clear attempt to bring the state back is evident in this phase. However, this meta-governance is countered by a third wave of decentred governance which focuses on human agency and social construction of individual practices. Within this wave, governance is constructed through individual actions of a plurality of actors embedded in their beliefs rooted in diverse and overlapping traditions. Rather than the state the point of departure becomes the 'various traditions that have informed the diverse policies and practices by which elite and other actors have sought to remake the state' (ibid., p. 82). In developing their analysis of decentred governance, they also firmly refute generality as they argue that governance is contingent upon the agency of the actors ensconced in culture, context and history.

A similar notion of decentred governance is found in the idea of social-political governance which tries to develop a new conceptual framework to analyse the emerging patterns of interactions between the government and the society. This form of interactive social-political governance implies 'setting the tone; creating the social-political conditions for the development of new models of governing in terms co-management, co-steering and co-guidance' (Kooiman1993, p. 3). These social-political forms of governance and governing of course spreads way beyond governments to include continuous yet shifting interactions between social actors, groups, state, market and civil society organizations. The notion of decentred governance or socio-political governance finds empirical manifestations in the contexts of developed as well as developing nations. Studied from diverse theoretical paradigms (ranging from system-theory to public administration and public management theories, from communication theory to the theories of state and theories of inter-organizational networks) these shifting notions of governance focuses on the patterns of interactions between state and society; growing complexity, dynamics and diversity of the societies; and the issues of governance, governability and governing at analytical as well as empirical levels. One of the important aspects of this changing discourse of governance is that it views governance as a social quality to be shared by public and private actors and as a mix of different kind of interactions between a multitude of actors growing out of increasing complexity, diversity and dynamisms of modern societies, though the nature of this mix (as a continuously changing element) varies depending on the context and level of governance and in turn affects the process of governing itself. This changing pattern of governance does not totally write off the traditional role of governments, it rather points out the limitations of the role of the state and its traditional government interventions. The awareness of this limitation on the part of the state only reshuffles the role of the government rather than shrinking it (Kooiman 1993, 2003). As Kooiman explains:

> In diverse, dynamic and complex areas of social activity, no single governing agency is able to realize legitimate and effective governing by itself. Such governance is achieved by the creation of interactive, social-political structures and processes, stimulating communication between actors involved, and the creation of common responsibilities next to individual and separate ones. There is a need to restructure governing responsibilities, tasks and activities, based upon differentiation and integration of various concerns and the agents representing them.
>
> (Kooiman 2003, p. 4)

There are different ways of interpreting the shifting notion of governance in recent times. However, the trends of this shift can be summarized in the following four points: (i) fiscal crisis within the government, (ii) growing citizen demand for better quality of services along with a responsive government, (iii) lack of trust in the competence of public agencies and (iv) failure of a state to deliver on its developmental role (especially in the context of developing countries) (Ramesh and Fritzen 2009). These trends implicated the size of the state, locus of authority and the distribution of authority between state and other sectors which in turn brings the focus on the 'good governance' agenda which basically develops some universal scales and measures the performance of different countries along these scales and also on public administration and management which has gone through severe reform in recent years. Though the shifting discourse of governance has unleashed in developed and developing societies (albeit in different times and contexts) the dominance of the 'good governance' paradigm, in recent times it has had far more implications for ideas, institutions and practices of governance in changing societies. As we witnessed in the case of India, the above patterns of shift in the concept and connotations of governance was definitely echoed throughout the policies and practices of governance reform in general and e-Governance in particular.

Politics of governance reform and changing societies

Governance in the international development paradigm is basically understood as a condition of development. The overall theoretical or philosophical underpinning of such an understanding is guided by neo-liberalism that has been on a growing binge since the 1980s in the changing contours of international politics after the end of the Cold War. To understand how the 'good governance' paradigm coincided with the already changing notions of governance, it is important to look at the emergence of 'good governance' in changing societies. It is observed that:

> [A]s the neo-liberal view started downplaying the state and overvaluing the 'market', and the trend was to decentre the state from its monopoly status in social control, the idea of 'governance' gained in prominence, connoting a plurality of rules replacing the state's monopoly.
> (Chakrabarty and Bhattacharya 2008, p. 2)

This shift from the government to governance theories emphasizes a process-oriented view of state and politics over the structure-oriented hierarchical approach that intends to improve the technical expertise of the government and hence tries to depoliticize the act of governing. There are three dimensional views of 'good governance': firstly, as a set of principles based on a checklist of criteria for public management; secondly as a complex process of interaction between state, market and civil society based on a mix of policies, values and institutions; thirdly, as a regulatory capacity of the state inevitable for effective realization of the principles and processes (ibid.). The other two related themes which became popular at the same time in most of the changing societies was that of democracy and economic development which was also instrumental in moving from a planned socialist economy to a neo-liberal market economy.

This new agenda of 'good governance', though based on the premise of early liberal theories puts emphasis on a market concept of equality which strives for empowerment of citizens by making them economically self-sustaining and enabling them to enter into market transactions. The cooperation of private agencies and NGOs are crucial for this purpose (Joseph 2001). Under this new-found concept of equality and active participation of different actors, citizens are often viewed as end users or customers whereas the government acts as the service providers. Improving the quality of these services and reaching out to a wider base of customers with the help of the private and non-governmental stakeholders are the central objectives of the governance reform projects.

The neo-liberal turn in developmental policy-making and its inevitable link to the 'good governance' agenda became a common state of affairs within most changing societies from the late 1990s onwards. Consequently, e-Governance reform became a popular sector of strategic reform in most of these countries for its specific alignment with 'good governance' goals. The exploration of the Indian experience where 'good governance' has become a buzzword across sectors of policy-making and development assistance to academic research, demonstrates the processes through which this transnational agenda of governance reform has become a national parlance.

E-Governance reforms in changing societies: mapping the trends

E-governance is a key policy priority for the international development community and hence it has been promoted by these organizations across all postcolonial and post-communist countries in the last two decades or so. This does not mean that e-Governance reforms are only confined to these countries, but the context of its emergence and increasing prominence were markedly different in developed countries.

There are different kind of e-Governance projects which can be categorized under different stages of growth, such as e-Administration, e-Services and e-Participation (Bhatnagar 2009; Heeks 2001; Madon 2009). In the first stage, most projects are undertaken for internal improvement of government by computerization and automation of processes, in the second stage a citizen interface is established by providing information and some services through ICT platforms and in the last stage of development active participation of citizens in policy-making by electronic voting and petitioning are attained. In most of the developing countries, e-Governance projects fall under the first two stages that focuses firstly, on upgrading the government functioning, gathering micro-data about communities and citizens and secondly, on improved service orientation by using ICTs (as part of the neo-liberal turn in public policy deliberation) to simply routine administrative procedures (Madon 2009). As part of the second orientation, there has been an upsurge in the multipurpose rural tele-centres across changing societies which are typically run by private local entrepreneurs and provide government information and services (birth and death certificates, caste and income certificates, land registration certificates, regular bill payment and so on) to rural communities other than customized private services.

The findings from the Indian case demonstrate both the above trends in terms of policy-orientation and in the kinds of e-Governance projects that are being rolled out in the country so far. The tele-centre experience as explicated by the CSCs Scheme case study also indicates a few trends that most of the changing societies have been confronting in the case of such reform strategies. Firstly, e-Governance initiatives add developmental value to government, to citizens and businesses, and to societies at large by providing cost saving and better administrative coordination, by providing improved services, by simplifying administrative services at saved time and cost and by improving general standards of governance respectively (Madon 2009). Secondly, e-Governance projects in developing parts of the world underscore the significance of intermediaries unlike its developed counterparts. In developed countries, there is a direct digital connection between the government and individual. However, in developing societies like India and South Africa, human intermediaries play a crucial role in the disbursement of public services (Heeks 2001; Madon 2009). However, in the wake of more and more e-Governance projects the old intermediaries of local administrations are being replaced by a new group of intermediaries such as private entrepreneurs or (as in the case of CSCs) VLEs. Irrespective of their designation (as old or new), these intermediaries are instrumental in ensuring a fair and equitable distribution of resources and services across communities. In some cases, the existence of two parallel groups of intermediaries might lead to a conflict of interests and result in hostilities in the local context. This brings us to the third dimension of e-Governance reform in changing societies, that is, the impact of local social and cultural fabrics on e-Governance projects (Madon 2009). As was seen in the case of CSCs, local contexts in terms of gender codes, existing social networks and dominant power relations all played an important role in the process of its implementation and which were not part of the original policy design.

Given these overall patterns of e-Governance projects in changing societies which also surfaced in the Indian experience, this book attempts to unravel the general framework of context-specific understanding of governance. Moving beyond its specific subject matter of e-Governance reforms this book also attempts to introduce new conceptual tools in theorization of emerging models of governance.

Emerging models of governance: innovations or subversion?

E-governance has made its mark as a policy priority and an area of strategic reform in the national policy environment of India. A comprehensive understanding of policies and practices in e-Governance in India also leaves us with a few insights in general theorizing about governance. These findings can be captured within a continuum of innovation and subversion which by all means is a dynamic process. Being a comparatively new area of reform, e-Governance demands a fair amount of innovation starting from policy formulation to project planning to implementation. Innovations in this regard are urged from political elites, from bureaucracy, from market forces and from private entrepreneurs as well. Such innovations ensure not only better use of technology but also a broader level of acceptance of new technologies in the society. The issue of acceptance leads us to the other side of the continuum, that is, subversion. As a social constructivist perspective reveals, technology is never neutral. The production and consumption of technology is determined by the dominant ideology of the state and the existing relations of power in the society. Since governance presupposes the existence of different power positions in leveraging the relationship between state and society, it inexorably recognizes the socially constructed relationship between technology and governance. Hence, a parallel process of subversion runs through the entire gamut of e-Governance reform. On one hand, policy-makers, being driven by the dominant ideology of neo-liberalism, seek to push ICTs into governing mechanisms as a flagship model without much recourse to the actual needs of the diverse groups of citizens. On the other hand, a group of bureaucrats, being dominated by a deterministic view of technology, overlooks the reactionary potentials of technology and still another group tends to resist and subvert the intended goals of these initiatives. At another level, intermediaries of local administration attempt to subvert the consumption of technology by exerting their power and to further keep their sphere of dominance intact. Even among the citizens, different groups perceive and receive these initiatives depending on their respective subject positions in the wider networks of social relations and hierarchy (Feenberg 1992, 1999; Sreekumar 2008).

This continuum of discursive and non-linear yet constant process innovation and subversion determines the contours of the relationship between technology and governance and also the shifting patterns of governance across societies. Some of the overarching trends of this relationship and its influence on the system of governance are discussed in this book. However, its claims to generalizations are balanced by its allegiance to the significance of contextual specificities. Thus, even when we find e-Governance to be a complex interlocking of politics, technology and culture, we restrain in generalizing the nature and meanings of such entanglements.

An interdisciplinary approach to e-Governance: methodological implications

One significant aspect of this book is undoubtedly its interdisciplinary approach to understand e-Governance in India. From most of the theoretical perspectives (be it neo-institutionalism or social constructivism), we encounter certain gaps within the strategic reform initiatives as they often fall short of their desired goals which might be considered as failures. Then such failures are attributed either to the reform initiative or to inadequacy of the particular societal context. This way of analysing any reform, particularly in changing societies, is not just confined to e-Governance but extends to strategic reform in general. Even though they provide some kind of explanations for a reform initiatives and its outcome, they do not present a holistic understanding of the entire process of reform. Hence we need an interdisciplinary approach.

In our analysis of e-Governance in India, the neo-institutional model of governance explains why strategic reforms are necessary for governance, why certain reforms are favoured over the others and what they imply for postcolonial democracies. Social constructivism cautions against technological determinism while evaluating the potential and actual effects of ICTs on existing systems of governance. Finally, the transcultural perspective (which again push for an interdisciplinary approach in social sciences and humanities) borrowing the notion of hybridity from Postcolonial theories helps to focus on how there has been subtle shifts in governance practices despite the gaps between policy goals and outcomes, how these shifts represent a 'third space' in terms of governance institutions (that are substantially different from its predecessor but far from the predicted counterparts) and how these continuous yet non-linear processes of shifts are determined by the negotiation between structure and agency, between different power and subject positions.

This interdisciplinary approach adopted in this book presents an experimental methodological design by combining not only different disciplines but also diverse theoretical perspectives. However, without denying further room for improvement, it is hoped that this design could serve as a point of departure for other studies not only in the field of e-Governance or governance but also in other fields of social sciences where interdisciplinary approaches have become a *sine qua non*.

Further research

E-governance is a burgeoning field of strategic reform to achieve higher standards of governance. Undoubtedly, its popularity has increased in developing countries in the last two decades as a direct outcome of the governance reform or 'good governance' paradigm. Given its recent upsurge and emerging nature, the academic study of e-Governance is at a very nascent stage. Furthermore, most of the studies done on the topic are either rooted in the development literature or in the techno-managerial field of information management or purely technological study of IT system development and upgradation. These studies focus mostly on the technical and administrative side of e-Governance. The sociological and political implications of e-Governance are relatively under-researched topics so far. Some literature with critical analysis of e-Governance projects do exist and has been extensively consulted for this research. However, there is clearly a deeper need to understand the policies and practices of e-Governance for its myriad implication in political, social and cultural fabrics of the society and its impact on the institutions and practices of the state.

Furthermore, as being closely connected to the field of technology, the evolution of e-Governance is fast and ever-changing. For example, in the Indian context the next step of e-Governance is towards mobile governance which intends to take advantage of the extensive usage of mobile phones among the Indian population. Recognizing its growing importance, the DIT, GOI has published the *Framework for Mobile Governance* in January 2012. Therefore, there are constantly emerging new fields of enquiry in which e-Governance reforms could be studied. The e-Governance, or in other words the use of ICTs, is transforming the local governance which also needs more academic attention. Gender and ICTs and its impact on local governance, the problem of digital divide, e-Governance and rural development are some of the related and relevant research fields that this book briefly touches upon without going much deeper into their analysis.

In a final note, it can be said that this book explores e-Governance as a strategic reform for its impact on the overall quality of governance. While doing so it draws on an array of political, social and cultural issues which lie much beyond the scope of this study. However, grappling with these interconnected themes, this study attempts to indicate the many ways that e-Governance research can lead to. Furthermore, by drawing balance between universal versus context-specific understanding of governance and by devising an experimental interdisciplinary methodological design, this book holds the potential to expand the relevance of this research to other societies beyond India.

Methodological appendix

Case study

Case study of the Common Services Centres (CSCs) Scheme as being implemented under the National e-Governance Plan of the Government of India across 29 states of India is being conducted, on the basis of a selected sample of some already operational kiosks.

Objective of the case study

How far the better level of governance could be achieved in a particular social context through a planned intervention of e-Governance initiatives?

Strategic sample

1. Rajasthan
2. Gujarat
3. West Bengal
4. Andhra Pradesh

Timeline of field trips (September 2010–August 2011)

- October 2010–August 2011: Expert interviews in different places
- November 2010 – Rajasthan
- December 2010 – Gujarat
- March 2011 – West Bengal
- July 2011 – Andhra Pradesh

132 *Methodological appendix*

Appendix table 1 Sources of data

A. Case study = 107				
Groups of respondents	*Rajasthan*	*Gujarat*	*West Bengal*	*Andhra Pradesh*
VLEs	6	3	8	6
SCAs (private sector)	3	2	3	4
SDA and other public sector representatives	6	4	1	2
Citizens	16	22	11	9

B. Expert interviews = 12

- Policy-makers: 2
- Technocrats: 4
- Academic experts: 3
- Civil society experts: 2
- International organization: 1

C. Policy documents and different project documents

D. Secondary literature

Source: Author

Qualitative interviews and focused group discussion (FGD)

Most of the interviews were purely qualitative and therefore the course of one interview varied considerably from the other. However, the overall attempt was to focus on certain issues depending on the group which would in turn help evaluate the indicators. Some interviews were taped; some were documented through field notes. The interviews usually lasted from 20 minutes to one hour, sometimes even more. In the case of villagers, mostly FGDs were deployed. The number of focused group members varied from 5–12 from one state to another. Other than FGDs, villagers were interviewed while they were availing services in the kiosks, or in marketplaces and *panchayat* offices around the CSCs. Questions varied depending on the group of stakeholders. Some sample questions are elaborated below. However, it is important to remember, as part of the qualitative interviews the course, sequence, presentation and framing of these questions varied from one person to the other.

For villagers (including *panchayat* members, school teachers):

1 Do you know about CSCs (different names in different states were used)?
2 How did you come to know about them?

3 What do you think they do?
4 How often do you visit a CSC and why?
5 Do you know what all the services are available here?
6 Are you satisfied with the services you get here? You want any more services?
7 How do you perceive CSC? Is it a public or private enterprise?
8 Why do you choose to go to a CSC, if at all?
9 How can you be sure of availing public services from this individual who is not a public servant?
10 Do you think that you need the help of middlemen any less in acquiring government services?
11 Will it be fine with you if these CSCs are removed from your village?
12 What do you think are the most pressing needs of your village?

For VLEs:

1 How did you come to know about the CSC franchise?
2 Why were you interested in being a VLE?
3 What are the procedures you had to follow to become a VLE?
4 How long have you been running this kiosk?
5 What did you do before leaving for this?
6 How did you promote your centre?
7 Do you have an online monitoring tool installed in your system?
8 What are the services that you are currently providing and what are the most demanded services? Can you classify these services under G2C and B2C categories?
9 Are you planning to start any services on your own other than waiting for further G2C services?
10 What is your educational qualification? Did you get any training before starting off the centre? Do you think that training was enough or would you like to get some further training?
11 How are your relationships with SCA coordinators? Do you see them often?
12 Do you know any other VLEs in your surrounding area, district or state?
13 Are you satisfied the way the centre is functioning? Do you earn enough to survive?
14 What do you think about the future of your business here? And what do you think about the future of such centres anyway?
15 What are the main problems you are facing in running the kiosk?

For SCA:

1 How did you get the contract for CSC in the state?
2 How do you select and train VLEs?
3 How is your experience with government collaboration?

4 There seemed to be a lot of misunderstanding as far as the financial system is concerned. Are you aware of it? If yes, how is it been tackled?
5 How do you visualize the future of CSC?

Along with these interviews, there have been prolonged conversations with SCA field coordinators who accompanied almost all of the field visits. These conversations were not taped and were carried out in a casual manner in-between other interviews. However, all these conversations were extremely insightful as some of these coordinators were more than willing to share their problems, frustrations and hopes without any inhibitions.

For SDA:

1 What do you think are the main strengths of CSC?
2 How is CSC different from other e-Governance projects?
3 What do you think are the main hindrances in its implementation?
4 How do you describe the role of state government in CSC?
5 How have the partnerships with the private partners in e-Governance been so far?
6 What is the general state of e-Governance in the state and why do you think it is relevant?
7 Do you think there has been any significant change in the e-Governance scenario in the state post-NeGP?

For experts:

1 How long have you been associated with the field of e-Governance? How did you become interested in this field and how did you acquire expertise in this area?
2 What is e-Governance according to you? How is it different from common understanding of governance?
3 Why do you think there is such a buzz around e-Governance these days?
4 What is the status of e-Governance in India, in your view?
5 To what extent is it a technological and to what extent is it a political issue? What should be the state of balance between the two?
6 How do you describe the role of public, private and civil society sectors in e-Governance in India?
7 Do you think in India e-Governance is driven by a more State-centric top-down approach?
8 Do you think there has been any significant change in the e-Governance scenario in India post-NeGP?
9 What is your take on CSC? Do you think it is different from other government projects of e-Governance? If yes/no, why? Do you think it would be sustainable in the Indian context?
10 Do you think PPP is a suitable model of implementation in the Indian context? What do you think about the accountability of private partners?

11 Do you think an e-Governance project (e.g. CSC) has the potential to tackle the issues of corruption, transparency, accountability, participation and efficiency?
12 In your opinion, what are the main issues of hindrances in India to successfully implement e-Governance reform?
13 To what extent do you think ICTs can really improve the level of governance in India?
14 How would you compare the Indian experience of e-Governance with other developed and developing countries?
15 What is your take on the issues of digital divide and e-Governance reforms in India?

Glossary

Challan The requisite form filled to pay cash, cheque, demand draft in a bank, tax department, government office, etc. This also means in simple terms official receipt of payment.
Crores A term to represent ten million (10,000,000), used in Indian English when expressing large numbers.
Dalits A political label under which formal Untouchable caste in India are described.
Gram Sabha Village council meeting
Janasevana Kendrams People Service Centres
Kisan Farmers
Panchayat Local self-governments in India
Panchayati Raj Institution of local self-governments in India
Sarpanch Head of the panchayat
Sarvashiksha Abhiyan Mass Education Campaign
Soochaks Informer
Soochanalayas Information Centres
Talati Village accountant
Taluk A revenue unit at the village/district level
Tehsil Administrative unit at the district level

Notes

1 Introduction

1 Following Mitra (2006) 'changing societies' are taken to represent societies in which formal institutions are mostly of exogenous variety and lack roots in the inherent social structure. This feature of changing societies put them in sharp contrast to the post-industrial, stable democracies at large.
2 Strategic reform in the context of this research can be defined as a broad sectoral reform which emerges as a deliberate shift in the policy regime initiated by the elites as strategies of welfare in order to harness legitimacy of the rule.
3 Ideal type is an analytical construct which represents a 'methodological utopia' to denote conceptual purity without any claim to reality. *Stanford Encyclopaedia of Philosophy* in http://plato.stanford.edu/entries/weber (accessed 21 September 2012).
4 Stakeholder in this case implies those affected by the institutions. Though many critics see stakeholder as developmental jargon ripped off any political essence, this term is used here to bring in all the actors affecting and affected by the strategic reform initiatives of the state.
5 Both Postcolonial and transcultural perspective are mentioned at the same time for two specific reason. Firstly, transcultural perspective (far from representing a consolidated and unified school of thought) involves emerging ideas to counter the Eurocentric bias in the current system of knowledge across disciplines. In this quest, they draw heavily on Postcolonial studies and literature with which it shares the overall objective of challenging Eurocentrism. Secondly, this piece of work relies on the analytical value of the term 'hybridity' which gained its explanatory rigor in the writings of Postcolonial scholar Homi Bhabha. Later, this term also gained some prominence within the transcultural studies.
6 James Scott used this concept in his book by the same title *Weapon of the Weak: Everyday Forms of Peasant Resistance* (Yale University Press, 1985) to understand how subaltern peasants in Malaysia could exercise their agency in their everyday practice to resist ideological and material hegemony.
7 The word conjecture is used here instead of the word hypothesis. The main reason behind this choice of word is the qualitative nature of this research. Hypotheses should generally be either proven or rejected on the basis of the available data. As there were no substantial quantitative analyses deployed here, the use of the word hypothesis could have been misleading. Hence, though formulated in a similar fashion conjecture is here used to denote the basic assumption that this work started with. However, they are much more refined than general assumption as they are based on earlier scholarly work and empirical studies.

138 *Notes*

2 Methodology

1 Value rationality which can also be termed as substantive rationality in Max Weber's terminology in the context of this research can be described as actions which are determined by the conscious belief in the value (of some ethical, religious, political nature) in itself without much consideration for some utilitarian ends. Reading Max Weber in http://www.colorado.edu/Sociology/gimenez/soc.5001/WEBER04.TXT (accessed 21 September 2012).
2 Barnett's discussion on constructivism in this article is predominantly aimed at International Relations discourses. Nonetheless, he lays out the fundamentals of social constructivism in a concise and succinct manner.
3 These ideas on transculturality were extracted from the webpage of Cluster of Excellence: Asia and Europe in a Global Context, pertaining specifically to Research Area on Public Sphere in http://www.asia-europe.uni-heidelberg.de/en/research/b-public-spheres/overview/what-are-the-key-terms-we-use-and-what-do-we-mean-by-them/transculturality.html (accessed 17 June 2012). Though this book is not about the public sphere, these extracts were thought to be explaining the relevance of transculturality for our work in a comprehensive manner.
4 For more information on the methods of data collection see Methodological Appendix.

3 E-governance in India: an overview

1 A Digital Society is based on information and communication technologies. The other related concepts are information society and knowledge society. For more details, see IITE Policy Brief: 'Digital Natives: How Do They Learn? How to Teach Them?' UNESCO Institute for Information Technology in Education, September 2011 in http://iite.unesco.org/files/policy_briefs/pdf/en/digital_natives.pdf (accessed 23 September 2013).
2 The facts and status of the MMPs under NeGP are accessed from different documents published by the Government of India.
3 The draft Electronic Delivery of Services Bill 2011was available from the Department of Electronics and Information Technology, Government of India on http://deity.gov.in/sites/upload_files/dit/files/Electronic_Delivery_of_Services_Bill_2011_16thNov_Legal_17112011.pdf (accessed 23 September 2013).

4 E-governance in context: a case study

1 The status updates are extracted from the GOI documents (Background Papers, 2010b) that present the status of CSCs as of 30 September 2010. This date is carefully chosen to match with the commencement of field trips in November 2010 onwards. Some other survey data were available from a Mid-Term Assessment of the CSC Initiative presented by IMRB International in February 2010.
2 Online monitoring tool: The Web Based Online Monitoring System For CSC provides a Decision Support Mechanism by monitoring the CSCs which are rolled out by SCAs in their area to provide B2C and G2C services. For more information see: http://www.csclive.in/ and http://www.negp.gov.in/index.php?option=com_content&view=article&id=107&Itemid=687 (accessed 21September 2013).
3 During the focused group discussion in this village, another major issue that came up was that of provision of education. One of the teachers from the village school was part of the focused group and the school building (which was visited later) was adjacent to the panchayat office. Though the school was equipped with computers and other technological accessories, their actual use in educating the students did not come out very clearly. Other physical infrastructure of the school also appeared to be quite inadequate.

4 For more information see: Government of Rajasthan: http://doitc.rajasthan.gov.in/e_CSC.asp (accessed 1 September 2011).
5 On the basis of the field observations and critical scrutiny of project documents a comparative account describing the differential status of the four states in the implementation of the CSCs Scheme is documented in this table. This table summarizes different status of the CSCs implementation in the four sample states. The categories of evaluation in this table are selected carefully according to their relevance to the overall level of governance. An attempt has been made to combine purely technical criteria such as infrastructure and connectivity with that of more qualitative aspects of governance such as participation and awareness level. However, it is important to acknowledge that this comparative table does not present an exhaustive account of different issues involved in the CSCs implementation in these four states. Nonetheless, this comparative account provides some crucial insights into how differential implementation status and strategies can possibly reflect on the level of governance in these particular states.

5 Negotiating politics, technology and culture

1 Given the qualitative nature of this study, the findings only indicate a difference in quality of governance rather than showing a quantitative scale of the level of governance.

6 Conclusion

1 Hybridity is usually deployed in political science literature to denote special categories of state which lack the pure characteristics of either democracy or autocracy and hence fall inbetween in the measurement scales of democracy. In this research a hybridity is used to understand the transcultural perspective on politics. Even though essentially the term denotes an impurity of concepts in both the cases, unlike democracy theorists, transcultural understanding of hybridity renders all conceptual categories as essentially impure.
2 *Power and Knowledge: Selected Interviews and Other Writings 1972–77* (Harvester Press, 1980) elaborate this concept in much detail particularly in the chapters titled Truth and Power, and Power and Strategies.
3 Weber's concept of bureaucracy: 'Bureaucratic coordination of activities,' he argued, 'is the distinctive mark of the modern era. Bureaucracies are organized according to rational principles. Offices are ranked in a hierarchical order and their operations are characterized by impersonal rules. Incumbents are governed by methodical allocation of areas of jurisdiction and delimited spheres of duty. Appointments are made according to specialized qualifications rather than ascriptive criteria. This bureaucratic coordination of the actions of large numbers of people has become the dominant structural feature of modern forms of organization.' in http://www.cf.ac.uk/socsi/undergraduate/introsoc/weber12.html (accessed 28 October 2013). Weber's conceptualization of bureaucracy should be seen in terms of his ideas on rationalization of organizations and also in terms of his ideas on authority and domination.

Bibliography

Abdellatif, Adel M. May 2003. 'Good Governance and Its Relationship to Democracy and Economic Development'. *Paper presented at the UNDP-Global Forum III on Fighting Corruption and Safeguarding Integrity*. Seoul

Abrahamsen, Rita. 2000. *Disciplining Democracy: Development Discourse and Good Governance in Africa*. London; New York: Zed Books

Ahrens, Joachim and Philipp Mengeringhaus. 2006. 'Institutional Change and Economic Transition: Market-Enhancing Governance, Chinese-Style'. *The European Journal of Comparative Economics* 3(1): 75–102, accessed 21 September 2013, http://eaces.liuc.it/18242979200601/182429792006030105.pdf

Ahrens, Joachim, Rolf Caspers and Janina Weingarth. 2011. *Good Governance in the 21st Century: Conflict, Institutional Change, and Development in the Era of Globalization*. Cheltenham, UK: Edward Elgar

Ahuja, Shirin. October 2010. 'Information Technology in India: The Shift in Paradigm'. *Paper presented at the Where in the World? Conference*. Budapest

Alampay, Erwin (ed.). 2009. *Living the Information Society in Asia*. Singapore: ISEAS Publishing Institute of Southeast Asian Studies

Alcantara, Cynthia Hewitt de. March 1998. 'Uses and Abuses of the Concept of Governance'. *International Social Science Journal* 50(155): 105–113

Appadurai, Arjun. 1996. *Modernity at Large: Cultural Dimensions of Globalizations*. Minneapolis: University of Minnesota Press

Avegerou, Chrisanthi. 2001. 'The Significance of Context in Information Systems and Organisational Change'. *Information Systems Journal* 11: 43–63

Avegerou, Chrisanthi, C. Ciborra, A. Cordella, J. Kallnikos and M. Smith. 2005. *The Role of Information and Communication Technology in Building Trust in Governance: Towards Effectiveness and Results*. Washington, DC: Inter-American Development Bank

Bagga, R. K., Kenneth Kenniston and Rohit Raj Mathur (eds). 2005. *The State, IT and Development*. New Delhi: Sage Publications

Bailey, A. 2008. 'Issues Affecting the Social Sustainability of Telecentres in Developing Contexts: A Field Study of Sixteen Telecentres in Jamaica'. *EJISDC* 36(4): 1–18

Bandyopadhyay, D. 1996. 'Administration, Decentralisation and Good Governance'. *Economic and Political Weekly* Nov 31(48): 3109–3111 and 3113–3114

Banguara, Yusuf and Larbi, George. A. (eds). 2006. *Public Sector Reforms in Developing Countries: Capacity Challenges to Improve Services*. New York: Palgrave Macmillan and UNRISD Publications

Barber, Benjamin. R. 2001. 'The Uncertainty of Digital Politics: Democracy's Uneasy Relationship with Information Technology'. *Harvard International Review* Spring: 42–47

Barnett, Michael. 2005. 'Social Constructivism' in *The Globalization of World Politics: An Introduction to International Relation*. Third Edition edited by John Baylis and Steve Smith. Oxford; New York: Oxford University Press: 251–270

Bauchspies, Wenda K., Jennifer Croissant and Sal Restivo. 2006. *Science, Technology, and Society: A Sociological Approach*. London: Willey Blackwell

Bekkers, Victor and Vincent Homburg. 2007. 'The Myths of E-Government: Looking Beyond the Assumptions of a new and Better Government'. *The Information Society* 23(5): 373–382

Belle, C. and J. Trusler. 2005. 'An Interpretivist Case Study of a South African Rural Multipurpose Community Centre'. *The Journal of Community Informatics* 1(2): 140–157

Bevir, Mark. 2009. *Key Concepts in Governance*. London: Sage Publications

Bevir, Mark. 2010. *Democratic Governance*. Princeton, NJ: Princeton University Press

Bevir, Mark and R. A. W. Rhodes. 2010. *The State as Cultural Practice*. Oxford: Oxford University Press

Bhabha, Homi. 1994. *The Location of Culture*. London: Routledge

Bhatnagar, Subhash. C. 2009. *Unlocking E-Government Potential: Concepts, Cases and Practical Insights*. New Delhi: Sage Publications

Bhatnagar, Subhash. C. and Mayuri Odedra (eds). 1992. *Social Implications of Information Technology in Developing Countries*. New Delhi: Tata McGraw Hill

Bhatnagar, Subhash. C. and Robert Schware (eds). 2000. *Information and Communication Technology in Development: Cases from India*. New Delhi: Sage Publications

Bhattacharya, Jaijit (ed.). 2006. *Technology in Government*. Delhi: GIFT Publishing.

Bijker, W. E. and John Law (ed.). 1992. *Shaping Technology/Building Society: Studies in Sociotechnical Change*. Cambridge, MA: MIT Press

Bijker, W. E., Thomas P. Hughes, Trevor Pinch and Deborah G. Douglas (eds). 1987. *The Social Construction of Technology: New Directions in the Sociology and History of Technology*. Cambridge, MA: MIT Press

Bijker, W. E., Roland Bal and Ruud Hendriks. 2009. *The Paradox of Scientific Authority: The Role of Scientific Advice in Democracies*. Cambridge, MA: MIT Press

Bolgherini, Silvia. 2007. 'The Technology Trap and the Role of Political and Cultural Variables: A Critical Analysis of E-Government Policies'. *Review of Policy Research* 24(3): 259–275

Bose, Jayshree (ed.). 2006. *E-Governance in India: Issues and Cases*. Hyderabad: ICFAI University Press

Brah, Avtar and Annie E. Coombes (eds). 2000. *Hybridity and its Discontents Politics, Science, Culture*. London, New York: Routledge

Bruke, Peter. 2009. *Cultural Hybridity*. Cambridge: Polity Press

Canclini, Nestor Garcia. 1995. *Hybrid Cultures: Strategies for Entering and Leaving Modernity*. Minneapolis: University of Minnesota Press

Castells, Manuel. 2000. *The Rise of the Network Society. The Information Age: Economy, Society and Culture*. Vol. I, Second Edition. Cambridge, MA; Oxford, UK: Blackwell

Chakrabarty, Bidyut and Mohit Bhattacharya (eds). 2008. *The Governance Discourse: A Reader*. Delhi; Oxford: Oxford University Press

Chand, Vikram (ed.). 2010. *Public Service Delivery in India: Understanding the Reform Process*. New Delhi: Oxford University Press

Chatterjee, Partha. 2004. *The Politics of the Governed: Reflections on Popular Politics in Most of the World*. New York: Columbia University Press

Chaturvedi, H. R. and Subrata Kumar Mitra. 1982. *Citizen Participation in Rural Development*. Delhi: Oxford and IBH Publishing

Bibliography

Choudhary, Kameshwar (ed.). 2007. *Globalisation, Governance Reforms and Development in India*. New Delhi: Sage Publications

Cluster Asia and Europe in a Global Context Website, accessed 29 March 2012, http://www.asia-europe.uni-heidelberg.de/en/research/a-governnce-administration/more-about-a-governance-administration.html

Common Services Centres (CSCs), accessed 15 June 2011, http://www.mit.gov.in/content/common-services-centers

Corbridge, Stuart and John Harriss. 2000. *Reinventing India: Liberalization, Hindu Nationalism and Popular Democracy*. Polity Press: Cambridge, UK

Corbridge, Stuart, Glyn Williams, Manoj Srivastava and René Véron (eds). 2005. *Seeing the State: Governance and Governmentality in India*. New York: Cambridge University Press

Craig, David and Doug Porter (ed.). 2006. *Development Beyond Neoliberalism: Governance, Poverty Reduction and Political Economy*. London: Routledge

Dasgupta, Chandan and Stuart Corbridge (ed.). 2010. *Democracy, Development and Decentralisation in India: Continuing Debates*. New Delhi: Routledge

Deacon, Bob. 2007. *Global Social Policy and Governance*. London: Sage Publications

Deva, Vasu. 2005. *E-Governance in India: A Reality*. New Delhi: Commonwealth Publishers

Dreze, Jean and Amartya Sen. 1996. *India: Economic Development and Social Opportunity*. New Delhi: Oxford University Press

Eisenstadt, S. N. 1964. 'Social Change, Differentiation and Evolution'. *American Sociological Review* 29(3): 375–386

Eisenstadt, S. N. 2000. 'Multiple Modernities'. *Daedalus* 129(1): 1–29

Farrington, John, Priya Deshingkar, Craig Johnson and Daniel Start (eds). 2009. *Policy Windows and Livelihood Futures: Prospect for Poverty Reduction in Rural India*. New Delhi: Oxford University Press

Feenberg, Andrew. 1992. 'Subversion Rationalization: Technology, Power and Democracy'. *Inquiry* 35(3–4): 301–322

Feenberg, Andrew. 1999. *Questioning Technology*. London: Routledge

Foucault, Michel. 1980. *Power and Knowledge: Selected Interviews and Other Writings 1972–77*. Brighton: Harvester Press

Frissen, P. H. A. 1999. *Politics, Governance and Technology: A Postmodern Narrative on the Virtual State*. Cheltenham, UK: Edward Elgar

Gerring, John and Strom C. Thacker. 2008. *A Centripetal Theory of Democratic Governance*. New York: Cambridge University Press

Government of India (GOI):

2000, 2008. *Information Technology Act 2000 and IT (Amendment) Act 2008*, accessed 21 April 2012, http://www.mit.gov.in/content/information-technology-act

2002. *Tenth Five Year Plan (2002–2007)*, accessed 21 April 2012, http://planningcommission.nic.in/plans/planrel/fiveyr/welcome.html

2006a. *E-Readiness Report*, accessed 21 April 2012, http://mit.gov.in/sites/upload_files/dit/files/downloads/eready2006/Forewardcontents.pdf

2006b. *National e-Governance Plan*, accessed 21 April 2012, http://www.negp.gov.in/

2007. *Eleventh Five Year Plan (2007–2009)*, accessed 21 April 2012, http://planningcommission.nic.in/plans/planrel/fiveyr/welcome.html

2008a. *E-Readiness Report 2*, accessed 15 May 2012, http://www.scribd.com/doc/44296404/E-Readiness-Report-202008

2008b. *11th Report of The 2nd Administrative Reforms Commission: Promoting E-Governance: the Smart Way Forward*, accessed 21 April 2012, http://arc.gov.in/11threp/ARC_11th_report.htm

2010a. *Mid Term Assessment of CSC Initiative*. Prepared for CSCs, Department of Information and Technology Government of India by IMRB International, New Delhi April, accessed 23 September 2013, http://apna.csc.gov.in/attachments/article/174/IMRB_DIT_Mid_Term_CSC_Assessment_Detailed_Report_Oct_2010.pdf

2010b. *National e-Governance Plan: Meeting of the National e-Governance Advisory Group, Background Papers*, Department of Information Technology, Ministry of Communication and Information Technology, 12th November, accessed 15 May 2012, http://www.mit.gov.in/sites/upload_files/dit/files/documents/12th_Nov_NAG_261110.pdf

2011a. *The Draft Electronic Delivery of Services Bill 2011*, Department of Electronics and Information Technology, accessed 23 September 2013, http://deity.gov.in/sites/upload_files/dit/files/Electronic_Delivery_of_Services_Bill_2011_16thNov_Legal_17112011.pdf

2011b. *Saaransh: A Compendium of Mission Mode Projects under NeGP 2011*, accessed 21 April 2012, http://mit.gov.in/sites/upload_files/dit/files/Compendium_FINAL_Version_220211.pdf

2012. *Framework for Mobile Governance*, Department of Electronics and Information Technology, accessed 21 April 2012, http://mit.gov.in/content/framework-mobile-governance

Graham, John, Bruce Amos and Tim Plumptre. 2003. 'Principles of Good Governance in the 21st Century'. *Institute on Governance Policy Brief* No.15, Ottawa, Ontario: IOG, August

Grindle, Merliee S. 2007. *Going Local: Decentralization, Democratization and the Promise of Good Governance*. Princeton, NJ: Princeton University Press

Gupta, M. P. 2010. 'Tracking the Evolution of E-Governance in India'. *IJEGR* 6(1), January–March: 46–58

Hasan, Zoya (ed.). 2000. *Politics and State in India: Readings in Indian Government and Politics – 3*. New Delhi: Sage Publications

Hawley, John C. (ed.). 2001. *The Encyclopedia of Postcolonial Studies*. Westport, CT: Greenwood Press.

Heeks, Richard (ed.). 2001. *Reinventing Government in the Information Age: International Practice in IT-enabled Public Sector Reform*. London: Routledge

Heeks, Richard. 2003. 'Most e-Government-for-Development Projects Fail: How Can Risks be Reduced?' *Institute of Development Policy and Management, Working Paper* No. 14, University of Manchester

Heeks, Richard. 2004 'eGovernment as a Carrier of Context'. *Institute of Development Policy and Management, Working Paper* No. 15, University of Manchester

Hertz, Rosanna and Jonathan B. Imber (ed.). 1995. *Studying Elites Using Qualitative Methods*. Thousand Oaks, CA: A Sage Publications

Hout, Wil. 2007. *The Politics of Aid Selectivity: Good Governance Criteria in World Bank, US and Dutch Development Assistance*. London; New York: Routledge

Howes, Stephen, Ashok K. Lahiri, Nicholas Herbert Stern (eds). 2003. *State-Level Reforms in India: Towards More Effective Government*. New Delhi: Macmillan India

Huntington, Samuel P. 1968. *Political Order in Changing Societies*. New Heaven: Yale University Press

Hyden, Goran, Julius Court and Kenneth Mease. 2005. *Making Sense of Governance: Empirical Evidence from 16 Developing Countries*. New Delhi: Viva Books

Indian Institute of Management, Ahmedabad. *Information Technology in Developing Countries: A Newsletter from Indian Institute of Management Ahmedabad*, accessed 23 September 2011, http://www.iimahd.ernet.in/egov/ifip/wg.htm

144 Bibliography

Jayal, Niraja Gopal. 2001. 'Reinventing the State: The Emergence of Alternative Models of Governance in India in the 1990s' in *Democratic Governance in India: Challenges of Poverty, Development and Identity*. Edited by Niraja Gopal Jayal and Sudhir Pai. New Delhi: Sage Publications

Jayal, Niraja Gopal and Sudhir Pai (eds). 2001. *Democratic Governance in India: Challenges of Poverty, Development and Identity*. New Delhi: Sage Publications

Jenkins, Robert. S. 1995. 'Liberal Democracy and the Political Management of Structural Adjustment in India: Conceptual Tensions in the Good Government Agenda'. *IDS Bulletin* 26(2), April: 37–48

Jessop, Bob. 1998. 'The Rise of Governance and the Risks of Failure: The Case of Economic Development'. *International Social Science Journal* 50(155), March: 29–45

Joseph, Sarah. 2001. 'Democratic Good Governance: New Agenda for Change'. *Economic and Political Weekly* 36 (12), March 24–30:1011–1014

Joseph, T. M. (ed.). 2009. *Governance Reform: Challenges Ahead*. New Delhi: Kanishka Publishers

Kaufmann, Daniel, Aart Kraay and Massimo Mastruzzi. 2008. *Governance Matters VII: Aggregate and Individual Governance Indicators 1996–2007*. World Bank, accessed 23 September 2011, http://info.worldbank.org/governance/wgi/pdf/GovernanceMatters VII.pdf

Kaviraj, Sudipta. 2010. *The Trajectories of the Indian State: Politics and Ideas*. Ranikhet: Permanent Black

Kjaer, Anne Mette. 2004. *Governance: Key Concepts*. Cambridge: Polity Press

Knack, Stephen. 2008. 'Governance and Growth' in *Good Governance in Developing Countries: Interdisciplinary Perspectives*. Edited by Kerstin Koetschau and Thilo Marauhn. Frankfurt am Main: Peter Lang

Kohli, Atul. 1989. 'The Politics of Economic Liberalization'. *World Development* 17(3): 305–328

Kohli, Atul. 1990. *Democracy and Discontent: India's Growing Crisis of Governability*. New York: Cambridge University of Press

Kohli, Atul (ed.). 2001. *The Success of India's Democracy*. Cambridge: Cambridge University Press

Kohli, Atul. 2009. *Democracy and Development in India: From Socialism to Pro-Business*. New Delhi: Oxford University Press

Kooiman, Jan. 1993. *Modern Governance*. London: Sage Publications

Kooiman, Jan. 2003. *Governing as Governance*. London: Sage Publications

Loader, Brian D. (ed.). 1998. *Cyberspace Divide: Equality, Agency and Policy in the Information Society*. London; New York: Routledge

Lock, Andy and Tom Strong. 2010. *Social Constructionism: Sources and Stirring in Theory and Practice*. Cambridge: Cambridge University Press

McLeod, John (ed.). 2007. *The Routledge Companion to Postcolonial Studies*. London, New York: Routledge

Madon, Shirin. 2009. *E-Governance for Development: A Focus on Rural India*. New York: Palgrave Macmillan

Mahadevia, Darshini. 2005. 'From Stealth to Aggression: Economic Reform and Communal Politics in Gujarat' in *The Politics of Economic Reforms in India*. Edited by Jos Mooij. New Delhi: Sage Publications: 291–321

March, James G. and Johan P. Olsen. 1989. *Rediscovering Institutions*. New York: Free Press

March, James G. and Johan P. Olsen. 1995. *Democratic Governance*. New York: Free Press

Mathur, Dhrupad, Piyush Gupta and A. Sridevi. 2009. 'E-Governance Approach in India-The National e-Governance Plan (NeGP)' in *Transforming Government: eGovernment Initiatives in India*. Edited by R. K. Bagga and Piyush Gupta. Hyderabad: ICFAI University Press: 3–50

Meijer Albert, Keer Boersma and Pieter Wagenaar (eds). 2009. *ICTs, Citizens and Governance: After the Hype!* Amsterdam: IOS Press

Mishra, Harekrishna (ed.). 2009. *Governance of Rural Information Communication Technologies: Opportunities and Challenges*. Delhi: Academic Foundation

Mitra, Subrata K. 1991. 'Room to Manoeuvre in the Middle: Local Elites and the Politics of Development in India'. *World Politics* 43(3): 390–413

Mitra, Subrata K. 1999a. *Culture and Rationality: Politics of Social Change in Post-colonial India*. New Delhi: Sage

Mitra, Subrata K. 1999b. 'Flawed Paradigms: Some "Western" Models of Indian Politics' in *Culture and Rationality: Politics of Social Change in Post-colonial India*. By Subrata K. Mitra. New Delhi: Sage: 39–63.

Mitra, Subrata K. 2006. *The Puzzle of India's Governance: Culture, Context and Comparative Theory*. Oxon; New York: Routledge

Mitra, Subrata K. 2012. 'From Comparative Politics to Cultural Flow: The Hybrid State, and Resilience of the Political System in India' in *Conceptualising Cultural Hybridisation: Transcultural Research – Heidelberg Studies on Asia and Europe in a Global Context*. Edited by P. W. Stockhammer. Berlin; Heidelberg: Springer: 107–132

Mitra, Subrata K., Malte Pehl and Clemens Spiess (eds). 2010. *Political Sociology: The State of the Art*. Frankfurt: Barbara Budrich Publishers

Mooij, Jos (ed.). 2005. *The Politics of Economic Reforms in India*. New Delhi: Sage Publications

Munshi, Surendra and Biju Paul Abraham (eds). 2004. *Good Governance, Democratic Societies and Globalization*. New Delhi: Sage

Naavi.org. *IT ACT Articles*, accessed 21 April 2012, http://www.naavi.org/views_2008.htm

Nagy, Hanna, Ken Guy and Erik Arnold (eds). 1995. *Diffusion of IT: Experience of Industrial Countries and Lessons for Developing Countries*. World Bank Discussion Papers, Washington, DC: World Bank

Nash, Kate and Alan Scott (ed.). 2001, 2004. *The Blackwell Companion to Political Sociology*. MA: Blackwell Publishing

NASSCOM. 2010. *E-Governance and IT services Procurement: Issues, Challenges, Recommendations: A NASSCOM Study*. New Delhi: NASSCOM

National Social Watch India. 2007. *Citizen's Report on Governance and Development*. New Delhi: Sage Publications

Nayak, Bhabani Shankar. 2007. *Nationalising Crises: The Political Economy of Public Policy in Contemporary India*. New Delhi: Atlantic

Neumayer, Eric. 2003. *The Pattern of Aid Giving: The Impact of Good Governance on Developing Assistance*. London; New York: Routledge

Olsen J. K. B., S. A. Pedersen and V. F. Hendricks (eds). 2009. *A Companion to the Philosophy of Technology*. London: Wiley-Blackwell

Oxford Dictionaries Online, 'Governance', accessed 15 June 2011, http://oxforddictionaries.com/page/askoxfordredirect

Bibliography

Panda, Santosh. 2007. 'Globalisation, Culture and Information Communication Technology in India' in *Globalisation, Governance Reform and Development in India*. Edited by Kameshwar Choudhary. New Delhi: Sage: 443–461

Pierre, Jon (ed.). 2000. *Debating Governance: Authority, Steering and Democracy*. Oxford: Oxford University Press

Plumptre, Tim and John Graham. 1999. 'Governance and Good Governance: International and Aboriginal Perspective'. Canberra, *Institute of Governance*: 1–27, accessed 21 February 2011, http://dspace.cigilibrary.org/jspui/bitstream/123456789/11075/1/Governance%20 and%20Good%20Governance.pdf?1

Prabhu, Anjali. 2007. *Hybridity: Limits, Transformation, Prospects*. New York: State University of New York Press

Prabhu, C. S. R. 2000. *E-Governance: Concepts and Case Studies*. New Delhi: Prentice Hall of India

Proceedings of 3rd International Conference on Information Communication Technologies and Development. 2009. New Jersey: IEEE Press, Piscataway, accessed 23 April 2012, http://dl.acm.org/citation.cfm?id=1812530&picked=prox

Raghavan, V. R. (ed.). 2007. *Civil Society and Governance in Modern India*. Chennai: East West Books

Ramesh, G., Vishnu Prasad Nagadevara, Gopal Naik, Anil B. Suraj (eds). 2010. *Public–Private Partnerships*. New Delhi: Routledge Chapman and Hall

Ramesh, M. and Scott Fritzen (eds). 2009. *Transforming Asian Governance: Rethinking Assumptions, Challenging Practices*. London: Routledge

Rammert, Werner. 1997. 'New Rules of Sociological Method: Rethinking Technology Studies'. *The British Journal of Sociology* 48(2): 171–191

Ray, Jayanta Kumar and Muntassir Mamoon. 2007. *Essays on Politics and Governance in Bangladesh, India, Pakistan and Thailand*. Kolkata: Towards Freedom

Reddick, Christopher G. (ed.). 2010. *Comparative E-government*. Integrated Series in Information Systems Vol. 25. New York; London: Springer

Riggirozzi, Pia. 2009. *Advancing Governance in the South: What Roles for International Financial Institutions in Developing States?* Hampshire: Palgrave, Macmillan

Rosenau, James N. 1995. 'Governance in 21st Century'. *Global Governance* 1, Winter: 13–44

Rostow W. W. 1960. *The Stages of Economic Growth: A Non-Communist Manifesto*. Cambridge: Cambridge University Press

Ruparelia, Sanjay, Sanjay Reddy, John Harriss and Stuart Corbridge. (eds). 2011. *Understanding India's New Political Economy: A Great Transformation?* Oxon: Routledge

Sachdeva, Sameer. 2009. 'Change Management for E-Governance'. *I-Ways Journal of E-Government Policy and Regulation* 32: 109–117

Saith, Ashwani, M. Vijayabaskar and V. Gayatri (ed.). 2008. *ICT and Indian Social Change: Diffusion, Poverty and Governance*. New Delhi: Sage

Santiso, Carlos. 2001. 'International Co-operation for Democracy and Good Governance: Moving Toward A Second Generation?' *European Journal of Development Research* 13(1), June: 154–180

Saraswati, Jyothi. 2008. 'The Indian IT Industry and Neo-liberalism: The Irony of Mythology'. *Third World Quarterly* 29(6): 1139–1152

Sayo, Phet, James George Chacko and Gopi Pradhan (eds). 2004. *ICT Policies and e-Strategies in the Asia-Pacific: A Critical Assessment of the Way Forward*. United Nations Development Programme – Asia-Pacific Development Information Programme. New Delhi: Elsevier

Bibliography 147

Schwarz, Henry and Sangeeta Ray (eds). 2000. *A Companion to Postcolonial Studies*. Malden, MA: Blackwell Publishing

Scott, James. C. 1985. *Weapon of the Weak: Everyday Forms of Peasant Resistance*. New Heaven: Yale University Press

Senarclens, Pierre de. 1998. 'Governance and the Crisis in International Mechanism of Regulation'. *International Social Science Journal* 50(155), March: 91–104

Seshagiri, N. 1999. 'The Informatics Policy in India'. *Information Systems Frontiers* 1(1): 107–116

Silverman, David (ed.). 2004/2011. *Qualitative Research: Issues of Theory, Method and Practice*. Los Angeles: Sage Inc

Silverman, David and Amir Marvasti. 2008. *Doing Qualitative Research: A Comprehensive Guide*. Los Angeles: Sage Inc

Sinha, R. P. 2006. *E-Governance in India: Initiatives and Issues*. New Delhi: Concept Publishing

Sismondo, Sergio. 2010. *An Introduction to Science and Technology Studies*. London: Blackwell

Sivaramkrishnan, Arvind. 2012. *Public Policy and Citizenship: Battling Managerialism in India*. New Delhi: Sage Publications

Sreekumar, T. T. 2008. 'Decrypting E-Governance: Narratives, Power Play and Participation in the Gyandoot Intranet' in *ICTs and Indian Social Change: Diffusion, Poverty, Governance*. Edited by Ashwani Saith, M. Vijayabaskar and V. Gayathri. New Delhi: Sage Publications: 160–191

Subramanian, Ramesh. 2006. 'India and Information Technology: A Historical and Critical Perspective'. *Journal of Global Information Technology Management* 9(4), October: 28–46

Traunmueller, Roland (ed.). 2003. *Electronic Government*. Second International Conference, EGOV 2003 Prague, Czech Republic, 1–5 September, 2003 Proceedings. Berlin; Heidelberg: Springer

UNDP Report. 1997. *Governance and Sustainable Human Development: A UNDP Policy Document*. New York: The United Nations Development Programme, accessed 14 March 2010, http://mirror.undp.org/magnet/policy/summary.htm

UNESCAP. 'What is Good Governance?', accessed 12 May 2009, http://www.unescap.org/pdd/prs/ProjectActivities/Ongoing/gg/governance.asp

UNESCO and Government of India. 2005. *E-Government Tool Kit for Developing Countries*. UNESCO, Asia-Pacific Bureau for Communications and Information and National Informatics Centre, Government of India. UNESCO: New Delhi, accessed 14 March 2010, http://unesdoc.unesco.org/images/0013/001394/139418e.pdf

Vanaik, Achin and Rajeev Bhargava. 2010. *Understanding Contemporary India: Critical Perspectives*. Hyderabad: Orient Blackswan

Webster, Frank. 2006. *Theories of the Information Society*. Third Edition. London: Routledge

Werner, Michael and Benedicte Zimmermann. 2006. 'Beyond Comparison: Histoire Croisee and the Challenge of Reflexivity'. *History and Theory* 45(1), February: 30–50

Woods, Ngaire. 1999. 'Good Governance in International Organizations'. *Global Governance*, 5 (1), Jan–March, accessed 25 August 2009, http://www.globaleconomicgovernance.org/wp-content/uploads/Good%20Governance%20in%20International%20Organizations.pdf

World Bank Report. 1989. *Sub-Saharan Africa: From Crisis to Sustainable Growth – A Long Term Perspective Study*. Vo.1, World Bank, accessed 12 September 2009, http://www-wds.worldbank.org/external/default/WDSContentServer/IW3P/IB/1999/12/02/000178830_98101901364149/Rendered/PDF/multi0page.pdf

Wyatt, Sally, Flis Henwood, Nod Miller and Peter Senker (eds). 2000. *Technology and In/Equality: Questioning the Information Society*. London; New York: Routledge

Index

Aadhaar. See UID, UIDAI
accountability 1–2, 5, 9, 14, 18, 22–4, 28, 31, 38, 40–1, 48, 54, 57–8, 60–1, 63, 73, 75–6, 79, 98, 110, 113–15, 118–34, 135
agencification 6
Andhra Pradesh 41–2, 44, 67, 81–5, 95–6, 98–100, 105, 109, 111–12, 131–2
asymmetry. See transcultural, transculturality

Bhabha Committee 51
Bhabha, Homi 21, 34–5, 137
Bhatnagar, Subhash 4, 126, 141
Bhoomi, 65
Bijker, W.E. 32, 141
Block Development Officer (BDO) 92–3, 96, 100
business process re-engineering (BPR) 4, 23
bureaucracy 42, 48, 88, 91, 94, 98–9, 101–2, 104–6, 109, 112, 114, 127, 139

case study 4, 24, 26–7, 40–1, 44–6, 71, 77–105, 126, 131–2, 138, 141
change management 4, 23, 64, 67, 105–6, 146
changing societies. See Mitra, Subrata K.
Chatterjee, Partha 36, 141
civil service reform 2, 13–15, 28, 60–1
CMS Computers Ltd 83–4, 89
code governance 61
Cold War 5–6, 13, 28, 106–7, 117, 125
Common Services Centres (CSCs) Scheme 24, 40–6, 62, 64, 68, 70–1, 77–86, 88–95, 97–106, 111–12, 114–15, 126–7, 131–3, 138–9, 142–3
comparative politics 7, 15, 25, 35, 117, 145
Course on Computer Concept (CCC) 104

decentralization 2, 6, 13, 15, 16, 18, 33, 60–1, 76, 91, 104, 123, 140, 142, 143
democracy 3, 5, 6, 13–14, 29, 42, 48, 110, 113–14, 118, 125, 139–40, 142, 144, 146; democratic governance 9, 29, 36, 118, 141–2, 144–5
Department of Electronics (DOE) 51; 52–3
Department of Electronics and Accreditation of Computer Courses (DOEACC) 104
Department of Information Technology (DIT) 64; DIT 104, 129
Department of Information Technology and Communication 89–90
Department of Panchayat and Rural Development 92
Department of Telecommunications (DOT) 53
deregulation, corporatization. See economic liberalization
digital divide 36, 74, 104–5, 111, 129, 135
digital society 58, 138
District e-Governance Society 89, 91
District Rural Development Agency 67
District Rural Development Authority 66

economic development. See democracy
economic liberalization 4, 16, 17–18, 20, 25, 106–7
economy of power. See Foucault
e-Courts 69
e-District 71, 81
efficiency 1–5, 9, 14, 28, 59–61, 63–5, 73, 75–6, 85, 88, 107, 110, 113–15, 118, 135

e-Gram 85, 94, 99
Electronic Commission 51
Eleventh Five Year Plan 24, 62, 142. See Five Year Plans
elite strategy 20, 33, 38, 47, 112, 121; elite strategies 37, 110
e-Mitra 42, 89
E-Service Delivery Bill 75–6
Eurocentric 20–1, 49, 121, 137; Eurocentrism 137

Feenberg, Andrew 33, 128, 142
Five Year Plans 24, 58, 62, 104, 142
flows. See transculturality
focused group discussion (FGD) 43, 132, 138
Foucault, Michel 8–9, 46, 47, 119, 122, 142
Framework for Mobile Governance 129
FRIENDS 66–7

G2C, G2B, G2G 61–2, 64, 68, 80–1, 83–93, 95–7, 103, 133, 138; B2C 80–1, 83–4, 86–7, 89, 92–3, 95–6, 103, 133, 138
good governance 1–2, 4, 12–16, 19, 23, 28–9, 33, 37, 58–62, 76, 103, 106–10, 116–18, 124–6, 129, 140, 143–7
governance reform. See 'good governance'
gram panchayat 83–4, 86–7, 92
Greater Visakhapatnam Municipal Corporation (GVMC) 83
Gujarat 41–2, 81, 85–8, 94–6, 98–9, 101, 106, 109–11, 115, 131, 132, 144
Gujarat Industrial Development Corporation (GIDC) 87
Gyandoot 66, 147

Heeks, Richard 108, 126–7, 143
hybridity 10, 21, 25, 33–5, 49, 111–13, 116, 119, 122, 129, 137, 139, 141, 146
hybridization. See hybridity

ideal type. See Weber, Max
International Monetary Fund (IMF)16
Information Technology (IT) Act 2000; Amendment to the IT Act 2008 55–8, 142
institutional reform 2, 15, 33, 100
institutionalism 7–8, 19–20, 30–1, 113, 118, 121, 128 neo-institutionalism 19–20, 30, 121, 128; historical institutionalism 30; sociological institutionalism 30, 31; rational choice 7, 30, 48
International Organizations. See good governance
international relations 7, 25, 117, 138
interpretive flexibility 32

Jayal and Pai 11–14, 16–17, 28, 32, 35

Kjaer, Anne Matte 6–8, 14–15, 19, 28, 30, 123, 144

legitimacy 7, 9–10, 14, 16, 21–3, 25, 29, 33, 35, 38, 46, 109, 112–15, 118–19, 122, 137
legitimacy deficit 10, 21, 23, 25, 33, 35, 109, 112
local contextual dynamics 99
Lokvani 66, 81

Madon, Shirin 4, 19, 50, 55, 66–7, 126–7, 144
Mahatma Gandhi National Rural Employment Guarantee Act 87; MGNREGA 92–3
Minicomputer Policy 51–2
Mission Mode Projects 5, 143; (MMPs) 5, 41, 62–4, 68, 71, 102, 115, 138, 143
modernization 12, 73; modernizing 17, 29, 108, 122
Modi, Narendra 42, 99; Modi government 109

Naidu, Chandra Babu 42, 94, 99; Naidu government 109
National Association of Software and Service Companies (NASSCOM) 53, 54, 145
National e-Governance Plan (NeGP) 4, 5, 24, 37, 41, 62–5, 67–8, 70–2, 76–9, 81, 102–5, 134, 138, 142–3, 145
National Informatics Centre (NIC) 53, 54, 67; NICNET 53–4
National Task Force on IT and Software Development 1998 55
networks of power relations. See Foucault
New Public Management (NPM) 12, 117, 123; new public administration management strategies 13

online monitoring tool 83–4, 89, 92–3, 133, 138

Panchayati Raj Institutions (PRIs) 16; PRIs 60–1
participation 2–3, 5, 11, 13–15, 17, 22–3, 38, 40–1, 45, 60–1, 64, 70–1, 73, 76, 79, 97, 105, 114, 125–6, 135, 139, 141, 147
policy drive 50, 90, 94, 111
policy network 6, 9, 22, 35, 38–40, 103, 110, 117, 121, 123
political reform. See good governance
political skill. See elite strategy
political society. See Chatterjee, Partha
political strategy. See hybridity
political will 63, 65, 94, 98, 100, 102, 112
Postcolonial, 5–6, 10, 15, 20, 21, 25, 26, 29, 33, 34–6, 48–9, 106, 115–16, 121–3, 126, 128–9, 137, 145
predictability 22–4, 40–1, 45, 59, 107, 114
privatization 2, 4, 6, 12–15, 28, 57, 123
public administration 4, 6, 12, 24, 30, 33, 60, 72, 76, 105, 114–15, 117, 124 5; public administration reform 6, 14, 23, 33; public sector reform 6, 105, 123, 140, 143
public–private partnership, (PPP) 23, 31, 39–41, 46, 47, 55, 57, 58, 66–7, 73, 75, 79, 81, 85, 88, 94, 97, 103, 107, 111, 114, 121, 134

Rajasthan 41–3, 71, 81, 88–91, 94–6, 98–100, 105, 112, 131–2, 139
Rajiv Internet Village (RIV) 82, 85
Rapid Assessment Round (RAR) 81, 82
Record of Rights (RoRs) 65, 89, 95
relevant social groups 32
Reliance Communications Limited 91
Right to Information Act, 2005 60; right to information (RTI) 2, 14, 28, 60, 70–1, 78, 81
room to manoeuvre 31, 38, 110, 145
Rural e-Seva 67
Rural Service Delivery Points (RSDPs) 82, 85

state, market, civil society 16, 22, 59, 104, 124 5
Structural Adjustment Programmes (SAPs) 13, 16
Saraswati, Jyothi 51–3, 146
SCA. See Common Sevices Centres

Science and Technology Studies (STS) 121, 147; sociology of science 121
Scott, James 47–8, 137, 147
SDA. See Common Sevices Centres
SMART 61
social construction of technology. See social constructivism
Software Technology Parks (STPs) 53
Soochaks 66, 136. See also Gyandoot
Soochanalayas 66, 136. See also Gyandoot
Sreekumar, T.T. 4, 19–20, 32, 50, 54, 66–7, 99, 107–8, 128, 147
Sreeven Infocom 83
SREI Sahaj e-Village Limited 91
State Data Centres (SDCs) 41, 62, 64, 68, 71
State-Wide Area Networks (SWANs) 41, 62, 64, 68, 71
strategic reform 5, 9–10, 18–22, 24, 26, 30, 35, 38, 50, 58, 61, 76, 101–3, 105–9, 113–16, 118–23, 126–30, 137
structure and agency 8, 19, 101, 111, 129
subversion 25, 127–8

talati 86–8, 136
taluk 65, 69, 86–7, 136; *taluka* 88
Tathya Mitra 91
TAXNET 68
technological determinism 20, 32, 101, 108, 119, 128
tehsil 65, 71, 83, 90, 136
Tenth Five Year Plan 104, 142. See also Five Year Plans
The 11th Report of the Second Administrative Reform Commission (2008) 72
third space. See Bhaba, Homi
transcultural 10, 19, 21, 33–4, 36, 49, 116, 121–2, 129, 137–9, 145; transculturality 34, 138
transparency 1–3, 5, 13–14, 18, 22–4, 28, 40–1, 45, 49, 54, 57–8, 60–1, 63–5, 71, 73, 75, 76, 98, 107, 109–10, 115, 117, 135

United Nations Development Programme 14; UNDP 28, 50, 53–4, 103, 116, 140, 147
United Nations Economic and Social Commission for Asia and the Pacific (UNESCAP) 14, 28, 147
unique ID (UID) 62, 64, 68–69; Unique Identification Authority of India (UIDAI) 64, 69

value rationality 30, 138. See also Weber, Max
village level entrepreneurs (VLEs) 40, 43, 44–5, 79, 81–5, 89–91, 93–4, 96–8, 100–1, 103–5, 112, 115, 127, 132–3
Voluntary Organizations (VOs) 60, 61

weapon of the weak. See Scott, James
Weber, Max 14, 30, 137, 138, 139
West Bengal 41–3, 71, 81, 91–3, 95–6, 98–100, 105, 109, 131–2
World Bank 3, 12–15, 23, 28, 37, 43, 50, 54, 103, 116, 143–5, 148

Zoom 89